D1486778

The U.S. Army Stability Operations Field Manual

THE UNITED STATES ARMY

The U.S. Army Stability Operations Field Manual

U.S. Army Field Manual No. 3-07

The University of Michigan Press Edition

FOREWORD BY Lieutenant General William B. Caldwell, IV

WITH A NEW FOREWORD BY Michèle Flournoy and Shawn Brimley
and a
NEW INTRODUCTION BY Janine Davidson

THE UNIVERSITY OF MICHIGAN PRESS • ANN ARBOR

Foreword and Introduction to the University of Michigan Press Edition
Copyright © 2009 by the University of Michigan
All rights reserved
Published in the United States of America by
The University of Michigan Press
Manufactured in the United States of America
♾ Printed on acid-free paper

No copyright is claimed for the original text of U.S. Army Field Manual No. 3-07
Stability Operations, first issued on 6 October 2008.

2012   2011   2010   2009   4   3   2   1

U.S. CIP data applied for.

ISBN-13: 978-0-472-03390-4
ISBN-10: 0-472-03390-5

Foreword to the University of Michigan Press Edition

Stability Operations in a Changing Strategic Context

Michèle Flournoy and Shawn Brimley

Approximately six years ago, during a brief respite from battle as the 101st Airborne fought north into the outskirts of Baghdad, the Division's commander, Major General David Petraeus, posed a question to embedded *Washington Post* reporter Rick Atkinson: "How does this end, eight years and eight divisions?"[1] Indeed, looking back, this question has become one of the most prescient and disturbing of America's post-9/11 experience. In Iraq and Afghanistan, we initiated offensive military operations at a time and place of our choosing, but, as has become all too clear, the United States has comparatively little agency in determining how and when its military operations come to an end.

Readers may be familiar with the term *fog of war*. Most in America's defense community will associate that term with Carl von Clausewitz, a Prussian military officer who wrote in his 1848 tome *On War* that war tends to be "wrapped in a fog of greater or lesser uncertainty."[2] That the act of warfare is an immutably human affair, and is thus almost completely unpredictable and non-linear, is a lesson America has learned and *re*learned at great cost. Clausewitz, who experienced warfare at a very young age, also wrote: "Everything in war is very simple, but the simplest thing is difficult."[3] This difficulty, this *friction* as Clausewitz called it, "is the force that makes the apparently easy so difficult." These simple truths—that war is by nature uncertain, and that during war even simple tasks are tremendously difficult—are deeply relevant to the question of how best to prepare America's military for the challenges of today and tomorrow. The humility in accepting that U.S. combat power alone cannot, in the end, produce lasting political change and enduring stability is the basic proposition at the core of FM 3-07 *Stability Operations*. Such a proposition is as simple as it is revolutionary.

America today is struggling to bring two major conflicts to satisfactory conclusions. Security gains in Iraq are encouraging, but the process of translating lower levels of violence into enduring stability and governance continues. America is not winning in Afghanistan today, and the effort there is greatly

---

1. Rick Atkinson, *In the Company of Soldiers* (New York: Henry Holt, 2004), 167.
2. Carl von Clausewitz, *On War* (New Jersey: Princeton University Press, 1976), 101.
3. Ibid., 119.

complicated by the safe haven Al Qaeda and the Taliban enjoy in the ungoverned tribal areas of Pakistan's Northwest Frontier Province. In both these conflicts, and indeed in most of America's military operations since the end of the Cold War, the struggle to either prevent conflict from arising or to foster lasting stability once the shooting subsides has been—in both frequency and difficulty—the main challenge.

A Changing World

The urgency with which the Army produced FM 3-07 *Stability Operations,* and FM 3-24 *Counterinsurgency,* reflects not only the exegesis of wartime but also the recognition that the changing nature of the international system will require the U.S. military to be prepared for a wide spectrum of threats and conflicts. To appreciate how important FM 3-07 will likely become, it is worth stepping back to examine the broader international security environment and America's place in a changing world.

The type of fog and friction that makes warfare at the operational level so unpredictable and difficult also applies at the level of national strategy. After shocks that produce or punctuate major shifts in the international system—such as the Soviet Union's first nuclear tests in 1949, the fall of the Berlin Wall in 1989, and the terrorist attacks of September 11, 2001—the strategic vision necessary to plan and prioritize anything beyond current imperatives tends to be obscured. The thick conceptual fog produced by strategic shocks is part of the reason why it often takes time for policymakers to perceive and then to react adequately to system-level changes.[4] In the contemporary era, the attacks of 9/11 arguably obscure as much as they reveal about future threats to American power. Nearly eight years after that horrible day, some of the fog associated with those attacks has lifted, and the contours of the security environment can be perceived with some degree of clarity.

For example, the National Intelligence Council's 2008 report, *Global Trends 2025: A Transformed World,* concluded that the foundations of power in the 21st century are shifting in profound ways. "The international system—as constructed following the Second World War—will be almost unrecognizable by 2025," the NIC concluded, "owing to the rise of emerging powers, a globalizing economy, an historic transfer of relative wealth and economic power from West to East, and the growing influence of nonstate actors."[5] Fareed Zakaria, editor of *Newsweek International,* has boiled down this complex shift to one

---

4. For example, while the emergence of the Soviet Union as a profound threat to Western powers was obvious to most by the end of the Second World War, it was not until the completion of NSC-68 in 1950 that the contours of what would become America's four decade–long Cold War strategy of containment fully materialized.

5. National Intelligence Council, *Global Trends 2025: A Transformed World* (Washington, DC: U.S. Government Printing Office, November 2008), vi.

memorable phrase: "the rise of the rest."[6] Richard Haass of the Council on Foreign Relations has written that this shift heralds the emergence of a nonpolar world, one in which power is far more distributed among a variety of state and nonstate actors than it is concentrated among a handful of great state powers.[7] This shift to a more complex world will place immense burdens on American statecraft, as changes of this magnitude will have follow-on consequences that are impossible to predict today. Furthermore, the demands associated with this shift in the international system will be exacerbated by the ongoing process of climate change, increasing resource scarcity, demographic change in critical regions, and economic pressures created by the current financial crisis and globalization more broadly. It is imperative that America maintain its balance while the world undergoes this profound and lasting shift in international affairs.

The Emerging Operational Environment

As rising powers and increasingly powerful nonstate actors alter the very architecture of the international system, the U.S. military must prepare for a difficult operating environment.[8] America's recent wartime experience and insights derived from other contemporary conflicts suggest that the U.S. military will face three core challenges: rising tensions in the global commons, hybrid forms of warfare, and threats posed by weak and failing states.

First, as other powers rise and as nonstate actors become more powerful, the United States will need to pay more attention to emerging risks associated with the global commons, those areas of the world—sea, space, air, and cyberspace—that no one state controls but that constitute the fabric or connective tissue of the international system. A series of recent trends—from anti-satellite missile tests and increased cyberattacks from state and nonstate actors, to rising tensions in the far north, the emergence of more capable naval forces, and the scourge of piracy—highlight the need for the United States to work with its allies and partners to maintain relative peace and stability throughout the global commons.[9]

Second, there is an emerging consensus in America's defense community that future adversaries are likely to challenge U.S. interests by employing perceived asymmetric advantages at both ends of the conflict spectrum. America's continued advantages in conventional conflicts are likely to incentivize future adversaries toward the types of insurgent tactics seen in Iraq and Afghanistan, the highly kinetic and distributed forms of attacks utilizing advanced anti-armor

---

6. Fareed Zakaria, *The Post-American World* (New York: Norton, 2008).

7. See Richard Haass, "The Age of Nonpolarity," *Foreign Affairs* (May/June 2008).

8. See U.S. Joint Forces Command, *The Joint Operating Environment* (Washington, DC: U.S. Joint Forces Command, 2008).

9. See Department of Defense, *National Defense Strategy* (Department of Defense, June 2008).

and anti-ship munitions of the type seen in the 2006 Lebanon War, or both. Naval and air forces are unlikely to face near-peer challengers in the medium term but are likely to face adversaries with sophisticated anti-access capabilities. The 2007 maritime strategy, *A Cooperative Strategy for 21st Century Seapower,* correctly states that modern wars are "increasingly characterized by a hybrid blend of traditional and irregular tactics, decentralized planning and execution, and non-state actors using both simple and sophisticated technologies in innovative ways."[10]

Third, the changing international environment will continue to put pressure on the modern state system, and this will likely increase the frequency and severity of the challenges associated with chronically weak or outright failing states. Indeed, there may be a paradox emerging in the 21st century international system: as the world becomes increasingly multipolar or nonpolar, defined in part by the rise of newly powerful states, this process will accelerate the decline of other states that—by virtue of poor leadership, economics, or geography—are unable to adapt to a new era. The challenges of weak and failing states to American interests are legion, but two are most acute: these undergoverned states are often catalysts for the growth of radicalism and extremism; and some states at risk are critically important to enduring American interests. Conflict in the 21st century is at least as likely to result from the problem of state weakness as from state strength. It is here that capabilities optimized for stability operations are most relevant.

Grand Strategy in an Era of Transition

Given the gradual but fundamental evolution of the international system and the related changes to the operating environment U.S. military forces are likely to encounter for the foreseeable future, it is worth thinking about how America can best conceptualize a grand strategy during this time of transition. For example, the genius of America's Cold War strategy lay in the two-pronged approach outlined in NSC-68: "One is a policy which we would probably pursue even if there were no Soviet threat. It is a policy of attempting to develop a healthy international community. The other is the policy of 'containing' the Soviet system."[11] By recognizing that constructing and then sustaining a functioning international system were inherently advantageous to America's long-term interests, Cold War strategists such as George Kennan and Paul Nitze laid the conceptual groundwork that ultimately enabled U.S. victory almost forty years later.

While the challenges facing America today appear entirely different than

---

10. Gary Roughead, James Conway, and Thad Allen, *A Cooperative Strategy for 21st Century Seapower* (October 2007), 6.

11. NSC 68, reproduced in Ernest May, *American Cold War Strategy: Interpreting NSC 68* (New York: Bedford/St. Martin's, 1993).

the unitary threat of the Soviet Union, some important characteristics are actually quite similar. The foundations of the international system are changing, America faces challenges from transnational ideologies and alternative economic models utilized by rising powers, and emerging technologies are enabling the spread of destructive and disruptive power. Moreover, American policymakers today—like their Cold War–era predecessors—are coming to grips with the imperative to deal with modern threats while ensuring that the fundamentals of America's economy remain sound.

If America is to employ a truly grand strategy in this era of transition, it must stem from the recognition that our core interests as a nation are very much commensurate with the stable functioning of the international system that Americans helped design and build in the aftermath of the Second World War.[12] If our Cold War predecessors understood that *creating* an international system based on American principles was critical, contemporary strategists must recognize that *sustaining* this system in the context of today's myriad challenges must remain at the core of a 21st century American grand strategy.

Such a strategy would rest on two core pillars. First, that the modern international system remains rooted in the power and efficacy of individual states. While powerful nonstate actors are sure to be a key feature of the international environment, conserving the state as the basic actor most responsible for those who live within its boundaries will remain fundamental.[13] Second, that American power is best deployed in the pursuit of that which strengthens the international system. For example, utilizing American power to provide global public goods such as open and safe sea lanes, effective orbital communications, relative security for commerce in cyberspace, and healthy international organizations to mediate disputes and convene dialogue would go a long way toward meeting America's basic interests while legitimizing our role in the world.[14]

21st Century Military Strategy

If policymakers were to conceptualize a grand strategy around the imperative to sustain an international system that is inherently advantageous to our core

---

12. James Steinberg had argued: "Far from justifying a radical change in policy, the evolution of the international system since the collapse of the Soviet Union actually reinforced the validity of the liberal internationalist approach." See James Steinberg, "Real Leaders Do Soft Power: Learning the Lessons of Iraq," *Washington Quarterly* (Spring 2008): 159.

13. See Sarah Sewall, "America after the Elections: A Strategy of Conservation," *Survival* (November–December 2008): 79–98.

14. Joseph Nye has argued that America would gain doubly from such a strategy: "from the public goods themselves and from the way they legitimize power in the eyes of others. This means giving top priority to those aspects of the international system that, if not attended to properly, would have profound effects on the basic international order and therefore on the lives of large numbers of Americans, as well as others." See Joseph Nye, "Recovering American Leadership," *Survival* (February–March 2008): 64.

interests, it would not only signal America's intent to the rest of the world, it would also allow the U.S. military to better prepare and prioritize for a challenging future.

Ensuring that the world's oceans, cyberspace, common airspace, and orbital space remain relatively free and open for travel, commerce, and communication should constitute core missions for America's military, and those missions are fundamental to the maintenance of U.S. interests. America's military forces are likely to be utilized for two other core missions: directly countering those state or nonstate actors who attack U.S. interests at home or abroad; and engaging in pre- or postconflict stability operations to prevent or redress state failure and the resulting adverse regional and global consequences. Most of these tasks will be cross cutting and joint by nature, and all agencies of government need to be prepared to act in support of national objectives.

Placed within America's broader strategic context, stability operations clearly constitute an extremely important pillar of a likely 21st century national security agenda, and ensuring that the U.S. military is able to perform these operations effectively will remain a central task of uniformed and civilian defense leaders.

And while it is extremely unlikely that America will decide to preemptively invade and occupy a foreign nation any time in the foreseeable future, the task of working by, with, and through partners and allies in order to help important states remain able to function in a changing international environment will remain central to America's strategic posture. Secretary of Defense Robert Gates has written that the kind of capabilities needed to deal with the problem of state weakness or failure "cannot be considered temporary diversions. The United States does not have the luxury of opting out because these scenarios do not conform to preferred notions of the American way of war."[15]

FM 3-07 *Stability Operations* is a small but very significant part of the answer to the vexing question of how America's military and interagency partners can best deal with the complex task of maintaining or reestablishing a safe and secure environment in an area at risk. It is part of a much larger doctrinal and policy framework. And while aspects of strategic guidance are sure to change, the emphasis on ensuring that America's tools of statecraft are prepared for stability operations will, if anything, only increase over time.

However, it is important to emphasize what FM 3-07 is *not*. This doctrinal manual is not a proxy for American grand strategy, and it is by no means an advocacy document or an argument about what U.S. national security strategy should be. What you will read in these pages is the Army's attempt to grapple with how these missions fit into the wider spectrum of military operations and

---

15. Robert Gates, "A Balanced Strategy: Reprogramming the Pentagon for a New Age," *Foreign Affairs* (January–February 2009).

how best to conceptualize and execute stability operations in a joint, interagency, and intergovernmental context.

FM 3-07 is also not an argument concerning overseas force posture, nor is it an argument to alter the Army's force structure or make major shifts in budget priorities. This manual was designed and written with a specific audience in mind: those U.S. field commanders and interagency partners who will be asked to do what America's military has been required to do throughout its history—help nations at risk of collapse or emerging from war to regain their footing and provide safety and security for their populations.

Finally, the question David Petraeus asked in 2003—"How does this end?"—is a question that should continue to haunt policymakers, particularly those civilians tasked with deciding where and how America's men and women might be placed at risk in order to defend U.S. national interests. In the context of 2009 and beyond, however, Petraeus's question becomes a challenge as much as it is an inquiry. Senior military and civilian leaders have an obligation to attempt to provide a better response than was provided to our troops in 2003. FM 3-07 *Stability Operations* goes a long way toward doing just that.

Introduction to the University of Michigan Press Edition

Next Generation Doctrine

Janine Davidson

In October 2004 I spent a week interviewing and observing soldiers from the 1st Brigade Combat Team (BASTOGNE) of the 101st Airborne Division at Fort Campbell, Kentucky. The Division had spent the past year in Iraq, where it fought in the initial invasion and then conducted postcombat stability and reconstruction operations in the northern city of Mosul. By the time I visited that fall, they had been home less than six months and were already beginning predeployment training for their second rotation. This time they would spend a year in Kirkuk, where they would try to stabilize one of the most dangerous and politically volatile regions in the country.

Before redeploying to Iraq, the commanders at every level from brigade to platoon would swap, giving new officers a chance to lead. One afternoon, I attended a change of command ceremony for one of the companies. As I listened to the outgoing captain address his soldiers for the last time, I was struck by the list of accomplishments he recounted from their shared year in Iraq. It was not the numbers of enemy captured or killed or other traditional acts of military bravery that this young officer seemed most proud of—although there were those stories to tell too. Rather, his list was about the schools his soldiers had built, the markets and health clinics they had opened, and the relationships they had built with local Iraqis. These were the things he had learned that would win the peace. They were not, however, the tasks for which he or his soldiers had trained before the invasion in 2003.

The soldiers I met that week were eager to share their experiences. Some admitted to having been dismayed and frustrated following the major combat phase, when they were required to stay in theater to reconstruct the country. Wasn't that someone else's job, they asked, perhaps a task for the Department of State or the United Nations? Others—many of whom had served in the Balkans in the 1990s—quickly began to apply some of the lessons they had learned there in working with the civilian population. All were proud of the way they had adapted on the fly—and all were determined to deploy better prepared this next time around.

Former chief of staff of the Army General Gordon Sullivan used to say, "Soldiers only eat when they are hungry, and then they eat everything in sight."

The soldiers I met were hungry for knowledge as they prepared to redeploy. Where they found formal doctrine wanting, junior officers started an online community of practice, called "companycommand.com," where they shared their experiences from the field and on the training grounds. They downloaded training materials from the Center for Army Lessons Learned and from each other to update their predeployment programs. They shared reading lists about everything from Iraqi history and culture to economic development, military governance, peacekeeping, and counterinsurgency. Their experience would inform the next generation of military doctrine and reflect their realization, hard earned in the field, that in the complex 21st century conflict environment, American soldiers needed to be prepared for a full spectrum of tasks, not just major combat.

The real life experience of these soldiers informs this field manual, and it was with soldiers' needs in mind that the writing team, composed of practitioners with deep field experience as well as a formidable grasp of current best practice, produced the handbook that follows.

Next Generation Doctrine

It is no coincidence that this field manual was written by a member of this new post–Cold War generation with the help of a large community of practitioners and experts, both civilian and military. The career of the lead author, Lieutenant Colonel Steve Leonard, included deployments with the 101st Airborne Division in the first Gulf War and later during the invasion and aftermath in Iraq. He also was a graduate of the Army's elite School of Advanced Military Studies and was involved in the Balkans, the domestic response to the 9/11 attacks, and operations in Afghanistan. This long experience prepared him well for his new task as doctrine writer. Steve understood firsthand that the Army's ability to adapt on the fly would only take them so far: he had been there. For true success in stability operations, there needed to be a whole-of-government effort in which civilians and military had a common frame of reference. Steve's unique talent was his ability to know what he did not know and to reach beyond his own military community for answers. His good fortune was that he had the support of Lieutenant General William B. Caldwell, commanding general of the Army's Combined Arms Center at Fort Leavenworth and the manual's chief sponsor, who understood the importance of reaching beyond the Army. The team of experts he built to discuss, review, and write parts of this manual came from U.S. government agencies, including the Departments of State, Commerce, Agriculture, Justice, and Treasury, as well as myriad nongovernmental organizations, experts, and allies.

The United States Institute of Peace team, under the leadership of Beth Cole, also played a critical role in bringing these communities together by facilitating numerous writing workshops and hosting the civil-military working group. Because the process of writing this manual led to the building of new relationships within and outside government, and collaborative debate about how best to conduct stability operations, the process might prove to be almost as important as the final product. This team, under the leadership of LTC Leonard and LTG Caldwell, recognized the importance of generating a vibrant interagency dialogue and has thus set an extremely high bar for future whole-of-government efforts in doctrine and strategy.

FM 3-07 *Stability Operations* reflects a long journey by the American military and a series of hard operational lessons learned by the post–Cold War generation. It underscores recognition that in addition to fighting and winning our nation's battles, the military will continue to be called on to bring peace and order to societies under stress. As doctrine, FM 3-07 fills a profound intellectual void by describing the complex 21st century landscape and articulating the military's unique role in bringing order to chaos.

The manual's emphasis on the "comprehensive approach," and the very process by which the manual was written, highlights the understanding that the military cannot succeed in these environments on its own. In stability operations, military units have to coordinate their efforts with civilian partners and other independent organizations who work together, ideally (but not always) toward a common objective. This manual, published at a time when the U.S. military is stretched thin in Iraq, Afghanistan, and beyond, has generated heated debate and raised almost as many questions as it answers.

The Debate

On one side of the debate are those who see this new manual as a great step forward in helping the military make sense of the complex, violent, and population-focused environments in which it increasingly finds itself. To the extent that, as Secretary of Defense Robert Gates has argued, our future conflicts are likely to look like our current ones, it is high time we stopped muddling through and got serious about learning how to operate in environments other than conventional high tech peer-to-peer combat. On the other side, however, are those who see the new doctrine as another dangerous step on the slippery slope toward U.S. imperialism.[1] The better we become at nation-building, the critics claim, the more likely we are to try to do more of it. Moreover, teaching soldiers how to do stability operations not only erodes their war-fighting skills (i.e., their "real" mission), but it lets the civilian agencies who are supposed to conduct these noncombat tasks off the hook in building their own capabilities.

---

1. Jason Brownlee, "Imagining the Next Occupation," *Middle East Report* 249 (Winter 2008), http://www.merip.org/mer/mer249/mer249.html.

The ability to hold such robust and honest debates over the appropriate use of force and the design of our military and civilian agencies is an important strength of our democracy. Our civilian leaders should think deeply about these issues well before crises arise. They should understand the use of force as a core instrument of American power but should also understand its limitations. As today's doctrine makes clear, the military is capable of operating across a wide spectrum of conflict, from war to peace.[2] Whereas traditional military doctrine clearly articulates the ways and means for fighting enemy armed forces, FM 3-07 outlines what the military, along with civilian partners, can do before, during, and after such fights in order to protect noncombatant civilians and set a trajectory for peace. Thus, the new doctrine adds options other than waging high-intensity warfare to our national security tool kit. It does not, however, dictate to civilian leaders in the White House or Congress whether or where to deploy these tools or which of them should be used.

Readers who see this manual as a mandate for imperialism, or a tool for invading and occupying other countries, seriously misunderstand the purpose and role of military doctrine. It is not the military's job to determine *when, where,* or *why* it will be asked to fight wars, enforce peace, or save lives around the world. Such decisions are the prerogative, rightly and jealously guarded, of elected civilian leaders. Rather, it is the military's job to determine *how* best to accomplish the tasks it is most likely to be called on to conduct. History has shown that where military leaders have attempted to dictate to civilian leaders, or otherwise limit America's options for the use of force, they have only set themselves—and the nation—up for frustration or, worse, failure.

Those who see this manual as an attempted takeover by the military of core civilian functions should read the manual very carefully and then look more closely at the actual capability and capacity of America's civilian agencies. For the majority of the "essential stability tasks" outlined in this doctrine, FM 3-07 clearly articulates the military's role as a "supporting" one. The *comprehensive approach,* on which FM 3-07 is based, recognizes that there are many nonmilitary actors with more appropriate skill sets than the military possesses who are involved in stability missions. Thus the doctrine calls for a division of labor in which military and civilians work together in the field toward a common objective and do not displace or compete with each other.

Unfortunately, the capacity of the civilian elements of U.S. power as described in FM 3-07 is in most cases extremely limited or simply unavailable. It has become clichéd to note that there are more lawyers, more civil engineers, and even more musicians in the Department of Defense than there are foreign service officers at the Department of State. Likewise, the United States Agency for International Development (USAID), which some might expect would provide most expeditionary civilian reconstruction expertise, has suffered a 75

---

2. United States Army Field Manual 3-0 *Operations* (2008).

percent reduction in numbers since the 1970s.[3] Many military officers might be shocked to learn that there are fewer than two thousand USAID officials on the payroll (less than the size of one Army brigade combat team).[4]

Having lived it in the field, the writers of FM 3-07 understand this dilemma. The manual reflects the delicate truth that expeditionary civilians exist neither in the numbers, nor with the skill sets, required for today's operations. This manual is therefore a call to policymakers and legislators to either rebalance the national security portfolio by adequately resourcing these critical civilian agencies or to accept that soldiers and marines will continue to fill the gap—and therefore will need to know how to do so. Although the entire civilian and military community of practice holds out hope that U.S. civilian agencies will eventually be adequately resourced, the manual reminds the reader that "in the event civilians are not prepared to perform those tasks, military forces will assume that responsibility."[5] This is a clear acknowledgment by military leaders that they will no longer be content to muddle through but will actively prepare to conduct the missions they are increasingly called on to perform.

The other controversial truth reflected in FM 3-07 is that even if or when the numbers of expeditionary civilians are increased across the U.S. government, there will still be many instances in which it is too dangerous for these civilians to deploy. This means the military must understand the environment and must be prepared to respond appropriately no matter what. They should know how to get started on the right path so they can hand off tasks to the host country or to the civilian experts once it is safe enough for them to arrive. At a minimum, the military must know how to "first do no harm" to long-term strategic and development objectives. By providing the broad framework for determining what needs to be done, FM 3-07 is an excellent resource for both military and civilians.

As obvious these last points may seem, they are actually a radical departure for U.S. military doctrine. In writing doctrine or developing education and training programs, the traditional military response was been to ignore stabilization and reconstruction requirements, claiming these were not military jobs. Militarily unappealing stability tasks, when they did appear in formal doctrine, were often simply assigned to other agencies.[6] Having been stuck with these missions throughout history, troops have had to learn these tasks "on the job" and have coped as best they could. From the American frontier to Vietnam,

---

3. J. Anthony Holmes, "Where Are the Civilians? How to Rebuild the U.S. Foreign Service," *Foreign Affairs* 88, no. 1 (January–February 2009).

4. A brigade combat team, the basic Army unit, ranges in size from 2,500 to 3,500 soldiers.

5. This reflects the policy of the Department of Defense, as stated in DoD Directive 3000.05 *Stability, Security, Transition, and Reconstruction (SSTR) Operations,* signed by the Deputy Secretary of Defense on November 28, 2005.

6. Department of Defense, Joint Publication 3-08 *Joint Doctrine for Interagency Coordination,* 2 vols. (Washington, DC: U.S. Government Printing Office, 1996).

Somalia, the Balkans, and beyond, that approach has led to frustration and in some cases failure in the field.[7]

The fact that civilian agencies lacked the capabilities assigned to them in the military's doctrine and planning processes became undeniably apparent following the fall of Baghdad in 2003.[8] Once again the military found itself conducting tasks for which it was inadequately prepared. This time, however, its on-the-job learning was rapidly disseminated and eventually translated into new doctrine, education, and training. This enhanced ability to adapt was the result of post-Vietnam organizational learning processes implemented across the U.S. Army that promoted a culture of learning among this generation of leaders. FM 3-07 is the latest in the line of transformational doctrine intended to institutionalize, rather than ignore or purge, the experience of the last three decades.

The Journey to FM 3-07

The learning culture that provided the foundation for FM 3-07 evolved in the years following the Vietnam War. Ironically, the processes that were put in place were designed to accelerate the institutionalization of a new way of war fighting, with very little reference to stability operations. In turning away from Vietnam and toward the Soviet Cold War threat, most of the U.S. military refocused on its perennial preference for big battle warfare. The U.S. Army would not organize, train, or equip its forces to fight insurgencies, stabilize countries, or rebuild nations but rather would focus on armored, possibly nuclear, combat on the European central front against the Warsaw Pact. At the highest level of the Army, the leadership outlined a new theory of war fighting, "AirLand Battle doctrine," and directed that the Army's capstone doctrinal manual, FM 100-5 *Operations,* be updated accordingly.[9] Most military historians view this era as a time of intellectual renaissance leading to a transformation of the "hollow Army" that had been "broken" by the Vietnam War.[10] Two key factors enabled this transformation: new doctrine and an emphasis on organizational learning.

AirLand Battle doctrine would support the military's core mission to "fight and win the nation's wars" by articulating how ground and air forces would

---

7. Andrew Krepinevich, *The Army in Vietnam* (Baltimore: Johns Hopkins University Press, 1988); James Fallows, *Blind into Baghdad: America's War in Iraq* (New York: Vintage, 2006).

8. Thomas Ricks, *Fiasco: The American Military Adventure in Iraq* (New York: Penguin, 2006); L. Paul Bremer, *My Year in Iraq: The Struggle to Build a Future of Hope* (New York: Simon and Schuster, 2006); Michael Gordon and Bernard Trainor, *Cobra II: The Inside Story of the Invasion and Occupation of Iraq* (New York: Pantheon, 2006).

9. AirLand Battle doctrine was the second, and more enduring, post-Vietnam revision. It followed *Active Defense,* which was the focus of FM 100-5 in 1976.

10. James Kitfield, *Prodigal Soldiers: How the Generation of Officers Born of Vietnam Revolutionized the American Style of War* (New York: Brassey's, 1997).

coordinate operations to defeat the Soviet military. In reality, however, the new doctrine as published in 1986 would emphasize the "fighting" part, and the "winning," or stabilizing, part would be left to others. The Army's AirLand Battle, like the Marine Corps' "Maneuver Warfare," was entirely focused on combating enemy forces, with an inherent assumption that winning battles and campaigns, if done correctly through the application of sound tactics and "operational art," could be the same as winning wars. The other assumption inherent in the choice to ignore the importance of stability operations was that an Army organized, trained, and equipped for AirLand Battle could easily conduct other "lesser" missions if absolutely necessary.

To ensure that the organization learned this new doctrine, the services infused its themes into education and, more important for the learning culture, training. The Army built enormous new training centers in California, Germany, and Louisiana to rehearse this new doctrine in as realistic an environment as possible. The training center exercises were designed for the military to "learn by doing" and involved an extensive "get to the ground truth" After Action Review process in which every movement, including every mistake made, was taken apart and analyzed during the unit debrief in a nonattribution environment. This process became the backbone of the Center for Army Lessons Learned (CALL) process that today collects observations from the real life battlefield as well as the training centers and feeds the lessons directly back into the training scenarios.

As a generation of troops cycled through these centers, the After Action Review became ingrained in the organizational culture. The idea that one was expected to make mistakes in order to learn from them was revolutionary for such a traditional organization. Observation, assessment, and frank discussions became "standard operating procedure" for every service member. A penchant for bottom-up information also developed that was clearly evident throughout the 1990s as the Army deployed for peacekeeping operations at a steady pace. Because there was a paucity of doctrine for such missions, the CALL pamphlets and the national training center training materials became valuable resources for units preparing to deploy.

Lessons from Somalia, Haiti, and the Balkans fed the scenario development of the Joint Readiness Training Center (JRTC) in Louisiana and the Combat Maneuver Training Center (CMTC) in Hohenfels, Germany, where many units prepared for peacekeeping throughout the 1990s. This dynamic learning loop, designed to institutionalize AirLand Battle doctrine in the 1980s, thus served a new generation learning stability operations on the job. Many veterans of these peace operations will recognize similar themes from these missions throughout FM 3-07. This is not an accident.

Doctrine throughout the 1990s was updated to reflect current experience. Some of the more significant manuals included FM 100-23 *Peace Operations* in 1994, JP 3-07 *Military Operations Other than War* (*MOOTW*) in 1995, and the two-volume manual *Interagency Coordination during Joint Operations* (JP 3-08) in 1996. By the end of the decade, new manuals on stability operations were being written, but they would not quite be ready and in the system prior to the invasions of Afghanistan and Iraq.[11] Still, many of the concepts and techniques were already being practiced in the field.

The existence of doctrine is not always an indication of how a military will operate. The material must be integrated throughout the education and training system and then demonstrated in the field. This can be a top-down or a bottom-up process. As discussed above, AirLand Battle doctrine, like the "Active Defense" doctrine that preceded it, went from theory to practice in a top-down process led by leadership who actively sought to integrate it into the learning system of the Army. By contrast, *Peace Operations* and *MOOTW* doctrine in the 1990s was based less on theory but rather reflected the bottom-up experiences of a significant portion of the U.S. Army. It was still not widely taught or discussed, except by units about to deploy to the Balkans. Thus, while the institutionalization of the experience did not permeate the entire organization, the part of the military that was engaged in these missions did learn and adapt. This was a noteworthy achievement as it provided an intellectual "handrail" for many in the Army who found themselves conducting postwar reconstruction and stabilization operations following the fall of Baghdad in 2003.

A significant population of military officers, especially in the Army, had served in Somalia, Haiti, and the Balkans and were able to leverage their personal experience on the ground in Iraq where formal predeployment preparation and planning for such tasks had been lacking.[12] Many of the more progressive initiatives implemented by commanders, such as 1st Cavalry Division commander Major General Peter Chiarelli's use of SWETI (sewage, water, education, trash, and information) "lines of operation" in Baghdad and similar techniques implemented by Major General David Petraeus of the 101st Airborne Division in Mosul, had been developed on the ground in the Balkans. Although such techniques had yet to make their way into formal doctrinal manuals, they had been published by the Center for Army Lessons Learned in widely disseminated pamphlets and articles and had been written into training scenarios at the Joint Readiness Training Center in Louisiana well before the invasion of Iraq. Those who had not experienced this training or had not deployed on peacekeeping missions in the 1990s quickly learned from those who had and began to file their own reports back from the field. FM 3-07 thus reflects bottom-up collective experiential learning by the post–Cold War generation of military leaders

---

11. See, for instance, FM 3-0 *Operations,* which introduced the idea of "Full Spectrum Operations" and replaced FM 100-5 (2001); FM 3-07.31 *Tactics, Techniques, and Procedures for Peace Ops* (2003); and FM 3-07 *Stability and Support Ops* (2003).

12. On prewar planning, see Joseph J. Collins, "Choosing War: The Decision to Invade Iraq and Its Aftermath," National Defense University Occasional Paper, April 2008.

and demonstrates how far the military has come in developing a learning culture since the end of the Vietnam War.

That the military adapted as well as it did might have come as a surprise to many observers. Due to the publication of an influential book on counterinsurgency by one of the Army's own thought leaders, many assumed that the U.S. Army lacked a "learning culture" and would thus be incapable of adapting on the ground in Iraq.[13] On the contrary, the U.S. Army that crossed the line into Iraq in 2003 was not the inflexible organization caricatured in the popular narrative about Vietnam. In the attempt to remake the Army after Vietnam, the leadership had developed new "lessons learned" systems designed to capture bottom-up experience from the field and filter it back into doctrine and training. Through the development of this after-action process and the training-oriented lessons learned system, the military developed a "get me the answers" culture, one that is more predisposed to question, evaluate, and share information and new ideas than ever before. The new culture was reflected in the ability of soldiers like the BASTOGNE brigade to adapt in the field and in the innovative process by which FM 3-07 was developed.

A "Comprehensive Approach" to Writing Doctrine

Dwight D. Eisenhower rightly observed that "planning is everything; the plan is nothing." The same might be said for doctrine. Ultimately, the role of doctrine is to provide a baseline of understanding for those who will be required to operate together. Thus, the doctrine-writing process is an opportunity to debate ideas, iron out differences, and compare experiences *before* they are tested in the field again. This process is easier when those involved are part of the same organizational culture or if they have shared operational experiences. In the comprehensive approach to stability operations, where success relies on the participation of numerous actors from different agencies and backgrounds, organizational cultures often clash, and one cannot assume a common framework for action.

Traditionally, military doctrine has been limited to "military" tasks, and the assumption has been that partner agencies and allies will carry out the nonmilitary tasks. In the 1990s, the U.S. military wrote doctrine *about* other agencies but not necessarily *with* those other agencies. In doing so, doctrine writers were often overly optimistic about what other actors might bring to the game. The two-volume JP 3-08 *Interagency Coordination during Joint Operations,* written in the 1990s, outlined the expertise of civilian government and nongovernmental agencies but failed to note how limited their actual *capacity* was. This was exacerbated by the Army's organizational culture. For instance, a soldier reading in a field manual that another agency "has the lead" for a certain task is

---

13. John A. Nagl, *Learning to Eat Soup with a Knife: Counterinsurgency Lessons from Malaya and Vietnam* (Chicago: University of Chicago Press, 2005).

extremely likely to expect that civilian agency to take on its responsibility as a military unit might: in a relatively self-sufficient manner, logistically and otherwise. Meanwhile, reading the same passage in the same field manual, a member of that civilian agency—which, like most civilian agencies of the federal government, may be primarily responsible for setting policy rather than field execution—is highly likely to read its responsibility as one in which it directs the strategy and the actions of others but does not necessarily conduct all the tasks by itself. More often, members of the civilian agencies might simply be unaware of the tasks the military has "allocated" to their agency, often without consultation or consideration of actual capacity. The result of this mismatch in perception was a series of unrealistic expectations and frustration over the inability of other agencies to do "their part"—that is, what the military had assumed was their part, often without consulting them.

FM 3-07 took a different tack. The writers actively sought the perspective of other agencies as well as nongovernmental organizations. They wanted to know what their actual capabilities were as well as how they viewed themselves operating as part of the comprehensive approach in the field. Through a series of conferences, roundtables, and workshops with thought leaders and representatives from various agencies throughout the government, in the NGO community, and among allies, LTC Leonard was able to glean the latest thought, theory, lessons, and controversies from the widest possible group of experts. Detailed debates over language, connotations, and social science theory and recent lessons learned from the field took place over a ten-month period, with some of these nonmilitary participants contributing actual text to the finished product.

In the end, FM 3-07 was written *for* and *by* the civilian-military community of practice, which extends well beyond the U.S. Army. Although the book is officially a military manual, paid for and sponsored by the U.S. Army, it is in every other way, shape, and form a true interagency, whole-of-government product.

If there is one thing this manual makes very clear, it is that stability operations are not rocket science—they are actually much more complex and uncertain. The soldiers I met in the fall of 2004 knew this firsthand. Now, because of FM 3-07, the next generation of soldiers—as well as their civilian counterparts and the policymakers above them—will have a better understanding of the complexity and cost of these missions. For that, as well as for the dialogue it has sparked over why the United States conducts these missions and how best to resource them, FM 3-07 is a great accomplishment.

FM 3-07

STABILITY OPERATIONS

OCTOBER 2008

DISTRIBUTION RESTRICTION:
Approved for public release; distribution is unlimited.

HEADQUARTERS
DEPARTMENT OF THE ARMY

This page intentionally left blank.

Foreword

Since the terrorist attacks on the American people seven years ago, we have been engaged in an epic struggle unlike any other in our history. This struggle, what may be the defining ideological conflict of the 21st century, is marked by the rising threat of a violent extremist movement that seeks to create anarchy and instability throughout the international system. Within this system, we also face emerging nations discontented with the status quo, flush with wealth and ambition, and seeking a new global balance of power. Yet the greatest threat to our national security comes not in the form of terrorism or ambitious powers, but from fragile states either unable or unwilling to provide for the most basic needs of their people.

As the Nation continues into this era of uncertainty and persistent conflict, the lines separating war and peace, enemy and friend, have blurred and no longer conform to the clear delineations we once knew. At the same time, emerging drivers of conflict and instability are combining with rapid cultural, social, and technological change to further complicate our understanding of the global security environment. Military success alone will not be sufficient to prevail in this environment. To confront the challenges before us, we must strengthen the capacity of the other elements of national power, leveraging the full potential of our interagency partners.

America's future abroad is unlikely to resemble Afghanistan or Iraq, where we grapple with the burden of nation-building under fire. Instead, we will work through and with the community of nations to defeat insurgency, assist fragile states, and provide vital humanitarian aid to the suffering. Achieving victory will assume new dimensions as we strengthen our ability to generate "soft" power to promote participation in government, spur economic development, and address the root causes of conflict among the disenfranchised populations of the world. At the heart of this effort is a comprehensive approach to stability operations that integrates the tools of statecraft with our military forces, international partners, humanitarian organizations, and the private sector.

The comprehensive approach ensures unity of effort among a very rich and diverse group of actors while fostering the development of new capabilities to shape the operational environment in ways that preclude the requirement for future military intervention. It postures the military to perform a role common throughout history—ensuring the safety and security of the local populace, assisting with reconstruction, and providing basic sustenance and public services. Equally important, it defines the role of military forces in support of the civilian agencies charged with leading these complex endeavors.

Field Manual 3-07, *Stability Operations*, represents a milestone in Army doctrine. It is a roadmap from conflict to peace, a practical guidebook for adaptive, creative leadership at a critical time in our history. It institutionalizes the hard-won lessons of the past while charting a path for tomorrow. This manual postures our military forces for the challenges of an uncertain future, an era of persistent conflict where the unflagging bravery of our Soldiers will continue to carry the banner of freedom, hope, and opportunity to the people of the world.

WILLIAM B. CALDWELL, IV
Lieutenant General, U.S. Army
Commander
U.S. Army Combined Arms Center

This publication is available at
Army Knowledge Online (www.us.army.mil) and
General Dennis J. Reimer Training and Doctrine
Digital Library at (www.train.army.mil).

Field Manual
No. 3-07

Headquarters
Department of the Army
Washington, DC, 6 October 2008

Stability Operations

Contents

*This publication supersedes FM 3-07, 20 February 2003.

Figures

Tables

Preface

Field Manual (FM) 3-07 is the Army's keystone doctrinal publication for stability operations. FM 3-07 presents overarching doctrinal guidance and direction for conducting stability operations, setting the foundation for developing other fundamentals and tactics, techniques, and procedures detailed in subordinate field manuals. It also provides operational guidance for commanders and trainers at all echelons and forms the foundation for Army Training System curricula.

The six chapters that make up this edition of *Stability Operations* constitute the Army's approach to the conduct of full spectrum operations in any environment across the spectrum of conflict. This doctrine focuses on achieving unity of effort through a comprehensive approach to stability operations, but remains consistent with, and supports the execution of, a broader "whole of government" approach as defined by the United States Government (USG). The core of this doctrine includes the following:

- Chapter 1 describes the strategic context that frames the Army's comprehensive approach to stability operations. It includes discussion of the strategic environment, USG strategy and policy, and interagency efforts to define an integrated approach to stability operations that leverages the collective efforts of a wide array of actors toward a commonly understood and recognized end state.

- Chapter 2 links full spectrum operations to broader efforts aiming to achieve stability, emphasizing the simultaneous nature of offensive, defensive, and stability tasks. It describes the phasing paradigm that defines stability operations activities conducted before, during, and after combat operations. Finally, the chapter links the primary stability tasks with broader interagency stability sectors to provide the foundation for civil-military integration at the tactical level.

- Chapter 3 addresses the essential stability tasks that comprise military stability operations. It provides a detailed discussion of each of the five primary stability tasks, and describes the subordinate tasks that constitute the range of activities in stability operations. It includes doctrine that describes the role of civil affairs forces in stability operations as the commander's conduit for civil-military integration. Finally, it describes development of mission-essential and directed task list development to support stability operations.

- Chapter 4 discusses the fundamental principles of the detailed component of planning, focused on the stability element of full spectrum operations. It builds on the precepts established in FMs 3-0 and 5-0, providing a systemic approach to planning and assessing stability operations.

- Chapter 5 addresses transitional military authority and provides doctrine concerning command responsibility, establishment, and organization of military government to support stability operations. It includes principles for establishing judicial structures to enable transitional military authority.

- Chapter 6 provides the doctrinal foundation for security sector reform, and introduces security force assistance as the capacity-building activity that encompasses organizing, training, equipping, rebuilding, and advising host-nation security forces. It also sets disarmament, demobilization, and reintegration as a fundamental element of security sector reform.

Seven appendixes complement the body of the manual.

Army doctrine is consistent and compatible with joint doctrine. FM 3-07 links stability operations doctrine to joint operations doctrine as expressed in joint doctrinal publications, specifically, Joint Publication (JP) 3-0 and JP 5-0. FM 3-07 expands on the fundamental principles of operations expressed in FM 3-0 and links those principles to a comprehensive approach to stability operations within the framework of full spectrum operations. FM 3-07 also uses text and concepts developed in conjunction with North Atlantic Treaty Organization partners.

The principal audience for FM 3-07 is the middle and senior leadership of the Army, officers in the rank of major and above, who command Army forces or serve on the staffs that support those commanders. It is just as applicable to the civilian leadership of the Army. This manual is also intended to serve as a resource for the other government agencies, intergovernmental organizations, agencies of other governments, international organizations, nongovernmental organizations, and private sector entities who seek to develop a better understanding of the role of the military in broader reconstruction and stabilization efforts.

FM 3-07 uses joint terms where applicable. Most terms with joint or Army definitions are in both the glossary and the text. *Text references*: Definitions for which FM 3-07 is the proponent publication are in boldfaced text. *Glossary references*: Terms for which FM 3-07 is the proponent (authority) publication include an asterisk in the glossary entry. These terms and their definitions will be included in the next revision of FM 1-02. For other definitions within the text, the term is italicized and the reference number of the proponent publication follows the definition.

The term "adversaries" includes both enemies and adversaries when used in the context of joint definitions.

FM 3-07 applies to the Active Army, the Army National Guard/Army National Guard of the United States, and U.S. Army Reserve unless otherwise stated.

This manual contains copyrighted material.

Headquarters, U.S. Army Training and Doctrine Command, is the proponent for this publication. The preparing agency is the Combined Arms Doctrine Directorate, U.S. Army Combined Arms Center. Send written comments and recommendations on a DA Form 2028 (Recommended Changes to Publications and Blank Forms) by mail to Commander, U.S. Army Combined Arms Center and Fort Leavenworth, ATTN: ATZL-CD (FM 3-07), 201 Reynolds Avenue, Fort Leavenworth, KS 66027-2337; by e-mail to leav-cadd-web-cadd@conus.army.mil; or submit an electronic DA Form 2028.

ACKNOWLEDGMENTS

The copyright owners listed here have granted permission to reproduce material from their works. When published, other sources of quotations will be listed in the source notes.

Losing the Golden Hour: An Insider's View of Iraq's Reconstruction, by James Stephenson. Reproduced with permission of Potomac Books, Incorporated. Copyright © 2007.

"The Nine Principles of Reconstruction and Development," by Andrew S. Natsios. Reproduced with permission of *Parameters*. Copyright © 2005.

State-Building: Governance and World Order in the 21st Century, by Francis Fukuyama. Reproduced with permission of Cornell University Press. Copyright © 2004.

Introduction

Today, the Nation remains engaged in an era of persistent conflict against enemies intent on limiting American access and influence throughout the world. This is a fundamental clash of ideologies and cultures, waged across societal abysses separating rich ethnic and religious traditions and profound differences in perspective. The Nation is embarking on a journey into an uncertain future where these precipitous divides threaten to expand as a result of increased global competition for natural resources, teeming urban populations with rising popular expectations, unrestrained technological diffusion, and a global economy struggling to meet the mounting demands from emerging markets and third world countries.

The character of this conflict is unlike any other in recent American history, where military forces operating among the people of world will decide the major battles and engagements. The greatest threats to our national security will not come from emerging ambitious states but from nations unable or unwilling to meet the basic needs and aspirations of their people. Here, the margin of victory will be measured in far different terms from the wars of our past. However, time may be the ultimate arbiter of success: time to bring safety and security to an embattled populace; time to provide for the essential, immediate humanitarian needs of the people; time to restore basic public order and a semblance of normalcy to life; and time to rebuild the institutions of government and market economy that provide the foundations for enduring peace and stability. This is the essence of stability operations.

Joint doctrine provides a definition for stability operations that captures the role of military forces to support broader governmental efforts:

> *[Stability operations encompass] various military missions, tasks, and activities conducted outside the United States in coordination with other instruments of national power to maintain or reestablish a safe and secure environment, provide essential governmental services, emergency infrastructure reconstruction, and humanitarian relief* (JP 3-0).

This manual proceeds from that definition to establish the broad context in which military forces assume that role before, during, and after combat operations, across the spectrum of conflict. In doing so, the manual focuses the efforts of military forces appropriately in support of the other instruments of national and international power; thus, the manual defines a comprehensive approach to stability operations in a complex and uncertain future. For Army forces, those efforts are fundamental to full spectrum operations.

The essential nature of stability operations in this era of persistent conflict became increasingly clear following combat operations in Afghanistan and Iraq. Recognizing this shift in focus, the Department of Defense (DOD) implemented DODD 3000.05 in November 2005. The directive emphasized that stability operations were no longer secondary to combat operations, stating:

> *Stability operations are a core U.S. military mission that the Department of Defense shall be prepared to conduct and support. They shall be given priority comparable to combat operations and be explicitly addressed and integrated across all DOD activities including doctrine, organizations, training, education, exercises, materiel, leadership, personnel, facilities, and planning.*

The directive further stressed that stability operations were likely more important to the lasting success of military operations than traditional combat operations. Thus, the directive elevated stability operations to a status equal to that of the offense and defense. That fundamental change in emphasis sets the foundation for this doctrine.

This manual addresses military stability operations in the broader context of United States Government reconstruction and stabilization efforts. It describes the role of military forces in supporting those broader efforts by leveraging the coercive and constructive capabilities of the force to establish a safe and secure environment; facilitate reconciliation among local or regional adversaries; establish political, legal, social, and economic institutions; and help transition responsibility to a legitimate civil authority operating under the rule of law. This transition is fundamental to the shift in focus toward long-term developmental activities where military forces support broader efforts in pursuit of national and international objectives. Success in these endeavors typically requires a long-term commitment by external actors and is ultimately determined by the support and participation of the host-nation population.

However, this manual also provides doctrine on how those capabilities are leveraged to support a partner nation as part of peacetime military engagement. Those activities, executed in a relatively benign security environment as an element of a combatant commander's theater security cooperation plans, share many of the same broad goals as stability operations conducted after a conflict or disaster. Such activities aim to build partner capacity, strengthen legitimate governance, maintain rule of law, foster economic growth, and help to forge a strong sense of national unity. Ideally, these are addressed before, rather than after, conflict. Conducted within the context of peacetime military engagement, they are essential to sustaining the long-term viability of host nations and provide the foundation for multinational cooperation that helps to maintain the global balance of power.

Through a comprehensive approach to stability operations, military forces establish conditions that enable the efforts of the other instruments of national and international power. By providing the requisite security and control to stabilize an operational area, those efforts build a foundation for transitioning to civilian control, and eventually to the host nation. Stability operations are usually conducted to support a host-nation government or a transitional civil or military authority when no legitimate, functioning host-nation government exists. Generally, military forces establish or restore basic civil functions and protect them until a civil authority or the host nation is capable of providing these services for the local populace. They perform specific functions as part of a broader response effort, supporting the complementary activities of other agencies, organizations, and the private sector. When the host nation or other agency cannot fulfill their role, military forces may be called upon to significantly increase its role, including providing the basic civil functions of government.

By nature, stability operations are typically lengthy endeavors. All tasks must be performed with a focus toward maintaining the delicate balance between long-term success and short-term gains. Ultimately, stability operations do not necessarily aim to reduce the military presence quickly but to achieve broader national policy goals that extend beyond the objectives of military operations. The more effective those military efforts are at setting conditions that facilitate the efforts of the other instruments of national power, the more likely it is that the long-term commitment of substantial military forces will not be required.

To that end, military forces have to operate with the other instruments of national power to forge unity of effort through a whole of government approach. This approach accounts for a wider range of considerations beyond those of the military instrument, ensuring that planning accounts for broader national policy goals and interests. For the commander and staff, this may mean planning and executing operations within an environment of political ambiguity. As a result, the potentially slow development process of government reconstruction and stabilization policy may frustrate flexible military plans that adapt to the lethal dynamics of combat operations. Thus, integrating the planning efforts of all the agencies and organizations involved in a stability operation is essential to long-term peace and stability.

Chapter 1

The Strategic Context

It is needless to say that Charles Gordon held a totally different view of the soldier's proper sphere of action, and with him the building part of the soldier's profession was far more important than the breaking part.... The nation that will insist upon drawing a broad line of demarcation between the fighting man and the thinking man is liable to find its fighting done by fools and its thinking by cowards.

Colonel Sir William F. Butler
Charles George Gordon

THE AMERICAN EXPERIENCE WITH STABILITY

1-1. During the relatively short history of the United States, military forces have fought only eleven wars considered conventional. From the American Revolution through Operation Iraqi Freedom, these wars represented significant or perceived threats to national security interests, where the political risk to the nation was always gravest. These were the wars for which the military traditionally prepared; these were the wars that endangered America's very way of life. Of the hundreds of other military operations conducted in those intervening years, most are now considered stability operations, where the majority of effort consisted of stability tasks. Contrary to popular belief, the military history of the United States is one characterized by stability operations, interrupted by distinct episodes of major combat.

1-2. America's experience with stability operations began with the *Royal Proclamation of 1763*. King George III of Great Britain issued it after the British acquired French territory in North America following the French and Indian War. Intended to stabilize relations with Native Americans, the proclamation established British foreign policy to regulate trade, settlement, and land purchases on the British Empire's vast western frontier. The proclamation also limited expansion of the thirteen colonies, essentially outlawing them from purchasing or settling territory west of the Appalachian Mountains. With the Proclamation, King George III authorized the British military to execute colonial policy in the Americas, including the ability to detain and arrest those who violated the proclamation.

1-3. Shortly after the signing of the Treaty of Paris on 3 September 1783, Congress appointed military commissioners to negotiate peace treaties and land purchases with native tribes. However, Congress had no means of enforcing the policy. In 1786, it passed *The Ordinance for the Regulation of Indian Affairs* and placed the program under Secretary of War Henry Knox. Secretary Knox directed the commanders of the frontier posts to support the Indian superintendents in settling disputes, regulating trade, adjusting land claims, and enforcing the law. Later, President George Washington tasked Secretary Knox with developing and implementing a military plan to prevent hostilities against settlers on former Indian lands. This experience continued in the trans-Mississippi West for the rest of the nineteenth century, where military forces enforced treaty agreements while protecting settlers moving into the western United States.

1-4. During the occupation of central Mexico from 1846 to 1848, General Winfield Scott quickly achieved the support of the local populace through programs focused on their immediate needs. His forces protected the goods and trade routes of local merchants, allowing markets to reopen quickly in the aftermath of operations. He instituted local programs to remove accumulated garbage and the obvious signs of war. Finally, he established civilian jobs programs that infused much needed cash into the local economies.

1-5. During Reconstruction following the Civil War, military forces maintained order and provided security. These forces also initiated comprehensive measures to establish new state governments, hold elections, ensure the well-being of freed slaves, and provide for economic and social development. Military forces assumed three roles during Reconstruction in the South:

- As an occupation force following the war, supporting a Presidential-appointed civilian government.
- As a military government under the Reconstruction Acts of 1867.
- As a supporting force to elected state governments until 1877.

1-6. In the aftermath of the Spanish-American War, the United States conducted a number of small-scale military operations around the world. It imposed a military government in Cuba, initiating free elections; reform of the security sector; and health, sanitation, and public works programs. A similar effort in the Philippines, however, resulted in a nationalist uprising that evolved into an insurgency lasting more than a decade. When President Woodrow Wilson ordered American forces into the Mexican coastal city of Veracruz in 1914, Soldiers soon found themselves performing the same humanitarian, governmental, economic, and security tasks performed in Cuba and the Philippines 15 years earlier. In 1915, the Marine Corps began a series of Caribbean interventions in Haiti, the Dominican Republic, and Nicaragua. However, they faced constant armed, irregular opposition from the local populace and had little success establishing effective constitutional governments using the lessons of the past.

1-7. The occupations of Germany and Japan following World War II serve as models for modern post-conflict stability operations as the Army reorganized and retrained its forces for a peacetime role focused on the reconstruction and development of war-torn nations. The postwar occupation of Japan provides similar lessons. The initial 60 days of occupation focused on disarmament and demobilization, essential to the demilitarization of the Japanese military complex and the democratization of Japanese society. In 1958, following the overthrow and murder of the pro-American Iraqi royal government, President Dwight Eisenhower ordered military forces to conduct a show of force to help quell civil unrest in Lebanon, providing much-needed stability to the Beirut government.

1-8. Vietnam earned America invaluable experience with the complexity of conducting operations *among the people*. Military forces contended with an established insurgency while working alongside the other instruments of national power to bring peace and stability to South Vietnam. Through the Civil Operations and Revolutionary Development Support (known as CORDS), the efforts of the Departments of State and Defense were integrated under a "single manager concept" that effectively achieved the civil-military unity of effort vital to success. While the overall war effort was ultimately unsuccessful, Civil Operations and Revolutionary Development Support provided valuable lessons that helped shape contemporary approaches to stability operations.

1-9. Following the end of the Cold War, the Army began reducing force structure while preparing to reap the benefits of a new era of peace. The benefits of this "peace dividend" were never realized. The strategic environment evolved from one characterized by the bipolar nature of the relationship between the world's dominant powers to one of shared responsibility across the international community. In the decade after the fall of the Berlin Wall, the Army led or participated in more than 15 stability operations, intervening in places such as Haiti, Liberia, Somalia, and the Balkans. Many of these efforts continued into the new century, and incursions into Afghanistan and Iraq revealed a disturbing trend throughout the world: the collapse of established governments, the rise of international criminal and terrorist networks, a seemingly endless array of humanitarian crises, and grinding poverty. The global implications of such destabilizing forces proved staggering.

THE STRATEGIC APPROACH

1-10. In the complex, dynamic strategic environment of the 21st century, significant challenges to sustainable peace and security persist across the spectrum of conflict. In this world of sovereign states, unequal in development and resources, tension and conflict are ubiquitous. Sources of instability that push parties toward open conflict, known as drivers of conflict, include religious fanaticism, global competition for resources, climate change, residual territorial claims, ideology, ethnic tension, elitism, greed, and the desire for power. The drivers of conflict emerge as numerous symptoms of crises worldwide. In this era of persistent conflict, rapidly evolving terrorist structures, transnational crime, and ethnic violence continue to complicate international relations. These conditions create belts of state fragility and instability that present a grave threat to national security. While journeying into this uncertain future, leaders will increasingly call on stability operations to reduce the drivers of conflict and instability and build local institutional capacity to forge sustainable peace, security, and economic growth.

1-11. Any integrated approach to stability operations requires a framework that applies across the spectrum of conflict, from stable peace to general war. It must frame purposeful intervention at any point along that spectrum, reflecting the execution of a wide range of stability tasks performed under the umbrella of various operational environments—

- To support a partner nation during peacetime military engagement.
- After a natural or man-made disaster as part of a humanitarian-based limited intervention.
- During peace operations to enforce international peace agreements.
- To support a legitimate host-nation government during irregular warfare.
- During major combat operations to establish conditions that facilitate post-conflict activities.
- In a post-conflict environment following the general cessation of organized hostilities.

1-12. In each instance, the roles and responsibilities of the various actors—civilian and military—vary according to the threat, stability of the environment, viability of the host-nation government, and several other factors. When the situation requires intervention, posturing such an effort for success necessitates a detailed conflict assessment; this assessment provides a thorough measure of those factors and helps to appropriately delineate roles and responsibilities among the actors involved. This assessment also serves as the basis for planning, which links the broad strategic goals to a realizable end state, supporting objectives, and discreet, executable tasks. The resulting plan nests these together into a coherent framework optimally suited to address the conditions of the operational environment identified by the initial conflict assessment. (See chapter 4 for a discussion of planning consideration in stability operations; see FM 5-0 for doctrine on planning.)

1-13. For many agencies and organizations, stability operations are considered as part of broader efforts to reestablish enduring peace and stability following the cessation of open hostilities. For military forces, however, stability tasks are executed continuously throughout all operations. Executed early enough and in support of broader national policy goals and interests, stability operations provide an effective tool for reducing the risk of politically motivated violence. It does this by addressing the possible drivers of conflict long before the onset of hostilities. Providing the authority and resources to conduct these stability operations as part of peacetime military engagement may be the most effective and efficient method to mitigate the risk of lengthy post-conflict interventions.

UNITY OF EFFORT

1-14. Uniting all of the diverse capabilities necessary to achieve success in stability operations requires collaborative and cooperative paradigms that focus those capabilities toward a common goal. Where military operations typically demand unity of command, the challenge for military and civilian leaders is to forge unity of effort among the diverse array of actors involved in a stability operation. This is the essence of *unified action*: the synchronization, coordination, and/or integration of the activities of governmental and nongovernmental entities with military operations to achieve unity of effort (JP 1). *Unity of effort* is the coordination and cooperation toward common objectives, even if the participants are not necessarily part of the same command or organization—the product of successful unified action (JP 1). Unity of effort is fundamental to successfully incorporating all the instruments of national power in a collaborative approach to stability operations.

1-15. Unity of effort is the foundation of success for operations that require integrating the capabilities of all the instruments of national power, as well as those of other nations, nongovernmental organizations, intergovernmental organizations, and the private sector. However, many actors, particularly nongovernmental organizations, participate in unified action at their own discretion. Their roles are often defined by competing interests and governed by differences in policy; in the case of nongovernmental organizations, their activities are driven by fundamental humanitarian principles and may have goals separate from the United States Government (USG) or the international community. (See appendix E for additional detail on humanitarian response principles.)

1-16. Therefore, unity of effort in such complex endeavors is often the operational norm. Unity of effort leverages the ability of various actors to achieve a cooperative environment that focuses effort toward a common goal, regardless of individual command or organizational structures. The mechanisms for achieving unity of effort are maximized when a legitimate, functioning host-nation government exists. Military forces coordinate their efforts through host-nation civilian agencies and the county team to sustain the host nation's legitimacy, build capacity, and foster sustainability. However, if the state has failed through military action or other socioeconomic factors, then a transitional authority must assume responsibility for governing. This can be a transitional civil authority typically authorized by the United Nations and under international lead, or a transitional military authority. (Chapter 5 discusses transitional military authority.)

A Whole of Government Approach

1-17. A *whole of government approach* is an approach that integrates the collaborative efforts of the departments and agencies of the United States Government to achieve unity of effort toward a shared goal. A whole of government approach is vital to achieving the balance of resources, capabilities, and activities that reinforce progress made by one of the instruments of national power while enabling success among the others. It relies on interagency coordination among the agencies of the USG, including the Department of Defense, to ensure that the full range of available capabilities are leveraged, synchronized, and applied toward addressing the drivers of conflict and reinforcing local institutions to facilitate achieving sustainable peace. Success in this approach depends upon the ability of civilians and military forces to plan jointly and respond quickly and effectively through an integrated, interagency approach to a fundamentally dynamic situation. Accomplishing this requires a willingness and ability to share resources among USG agencies and organizations while working toward a common goal. These resources—financial, military, intelligence, law enforcement, diplomatic, developmental, and strategic communications—are often limited in availability and cannot be restricted to use by a single agency, Service, or entity. To achieve the broad success envisioned in a whole of government engagement, all must be integral to unified action. All are elements of the whole of government approach.

1-18. To that end, all actors involved in unified action are integrated into the operation from the onset of planning. Together, they complete detailed analysis of the situation and operational environment, develop integrated courses of action, and continuously assess the situation throughout execution. These actions ensure that the various capabilities and activities focus on achieving specific conflict transformation goals in cooperation with host-nation and international partners. (See paragraph 1-23.) A coherent whole of government approach requires early and high-level participation of both national and multinational civilian and military participants. This process necessitates active dialog and reciprocal information sharing with intergovernmental and nongovernmental organizations, the host-nation government, and the private sector, when necessary.

1-19. A primary challenge for integrating civilian and military efforts into a whole of government approach is the differing capacities and cultures in civilian agencies compared to those of military forces. A successful whole of government approach requires that all actors—

- Are represented, integrated, and actively involved in the process.
- Share an understanding of the situation and problem to be resolved.
- Strive for unity of effort toward achieving a common goal.
- Integrate and synchronize capabilities and activities.
- Collectively determine the resources, capabilities, and activities necessary to achieve their goal.

A Comprehensive Approach

1-20. A *comprehensive approach* **is an approach that integrates the cooperative efforts of the departments and agencies of the United States Government, intergovernmental and nongovernmental organizations, multinational partners, and private sector entities to achieve unity of effort toward a shared goal**. A comprehensive approach is founded in the cooperative spirit of unity of effort. It is common in successful operations involving actors participating at their own discretion or present in the operational area but not acting as a member of a coalition. Integration and collaboration often elude the diverse array of actors involved; a comprehensive approach achieves unity of effort through extensive cooperation and coordination to forge a shared understanding of a common goal. A comprehensive approach is difficult to sustain but still critical to achieving success in an operation with a wide representation. See figure 1-1.

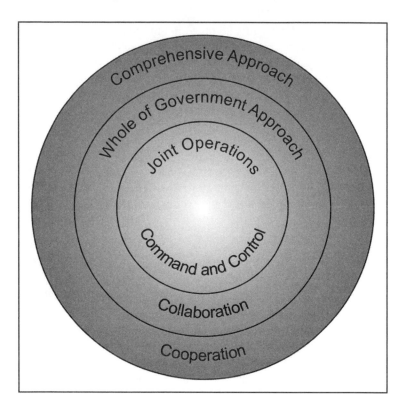

Figure 1-1. Comprehensive approach to stability operations

1-21. Forging a comprehensive approach is necessary to leverage the capabilities of the disparate actors present to achieve broad conflict transformation goals and attain a sustainable peace. Unlike a whole of government approach, which aims for true interagency integration toward those ends, a comprehensive approach requires a more nuanced, cooperative effort. In a comprehensive approach, actors are not compelled to work together toward a common goal; instead, they participate out of a shared understanding and appreciation for what that goal represents. Achieving the end state is in the best interests of the actors participating;

the actors recognize that fact forges the bonds that allow them to achieve unity of effort. Some groups, such as nongovernmental organizations, must retain independence of action. Reconciling that independence with the mission requirements may pose specific challenges to unity of effort and must be considered throughout the operations process.

1-22. A comprehensive approach is framed by four underlying tenets:

- **Accommodate**. The approach accommodates the concerns and contributions of all participants; it determines appropriate priorities for resourcing and sets support relationships as required to deconflict activities.

- **Understand**. The approach leverages a shared understanding of the situation toward a common goal. Understanding does not imply conformity; each actor contributes a distinct set of professional, technical, and cultural disciplines, values, and perceptions. Together they provide breadth, depth, and resilience to assessment, planning, and execution.

- **Base on purpose**. The approach focuses cooperative effort toward a common, purpose-based goal. The approach links discreet, yet interrelated, tasks and objectives to conditions that comprise the desired end state.

- **Cooperate**. The approach is based on a cooperative effort reinforced by institutional familiarity, trust, and transparency. Communities of practice that provide forums for information sharing and concept development support cooperation among the actors involved.

CONFLICT TRANSFORMATION

1-23. Conflict transformation focuses on converting the dynamics of conflict into processes for constructive, positive change. *Conflict transformation* **is the process of reducing the means and motivations for violent conflict while developing more viable, peaceful alternatives for the competitive pursuit of political and socioeconomic aspirations.** It aims to set the host nation on a sustainable positive trajectory where transformational processes can directly address the dynamics causing civil strife or violent conflict. It seeks to resolve the root causes of conflict and instability while building the capacity of local institutions to forge and sustain effective governance, economic development, and the rule of law.

1-24. Addressing the drivers of violent conflict begins with a detailed conflict assessment and thorough analysis of the conditions of the operational environment. This ensures planning focuses on the root causes of conflict or strife and prescribes integrated approaches to resolution. (See chapter 4 for a discussion of assessment and planning.) The active and robust presence of external military forces may be required to help shape the environment and reduce the drivers of violent conflict, in partnership and cooperation with a sizable international civilian presence. Together, efforts are directed toward imposing order, reducing violence, delivering essential services, moderating political conflict, and instituting an acceptable political framework pursuant to a peace accord. Peace becomes sustainable when the sources of conflict have been reduced to such an extent that they can be largely managed by developing host-nation institutions. This facilitates the subsequent reduction of external actors to levels that foster the development effort with minimal outside presence.

1-25. Ultimately, conflict transformation aims to shift the responsibility for providing security and stability from the international community to the host nation, with a sustainable level of continuing support from external actors. Conflict transformation recognizes that conflict is a normal and continuous social dynamic within human relationships and seeks to provide effective peaceful means of resolution. Conflict transformation is based in cultural astuteness and a broad understanding of the dynamics of conflict. Success depends on building creative solutions that improve relationships; it necessitates an innate understanding of underlying relational, social, and cultural patterns. Success relies heavily on understanding, recognizing that conflict can potentially stimulate growth and to leverage that potential to spur constructive change. This understanding is based on:

- The intellectual capacity to envision conflict positively, as a natural social phenomenon with inherent potential for positive change.
- The flexibility to adapt approaches to respond in ways that maximize this potential for constructive growth.

1-26. It exploits the opportunity within a conflict to achieve positive change. It aims to reduce the motivations and means for violent conflict. At the same time, conflict transformation develops more attractive, peaceful alternatives for the competitive pursuit of political and economic goals. This entails addressing the drivers of conflict while assisting in developing or supporting local institutions that have both legitimacy and the capacity to provide basic services, economic opportunity, public order, and security. It derives its long-term success from shaping the environment so the local populace can actively check the state's abuse of power.

1-27. Successful conflict transformation relies on the ability of intervening actors to identify and resolve the primary sources of conflict and instability in the host nation. These efforts reflect the constant tension between the time commitment required to achieve sustainable progress and the need to quickly build momentum to lessen the drivers of conflict and instability. National interest and resources are finite; therefore, conflict transformation efforts must focus on the underlying sources, not the visible symptoms, of conflict and instability. In countries seeking to transition from war to peace, often a limited window of opportunity exists to reshape structures to address these drivers. This may include deterring adversaries and mitigating their effects on local populaces and institutions, as well as developing approaches that include marginalized groups, consensus-building mechanisms, checks and balances on power, and transparency measures.

LEGITIMACY

1-28. Legitimacy is central to building trust and confidence among the people. Legitimacy is a multifaceted principle that impacts every aspect of stability operations from every conceivable perspective. Within national strategy, legitimacy is a central principle for intervention: both the legitimacy of the host-nation government and the legitimacy of the mission. The legitimacy of the government has many facets. It generally represents the legitimacy of the supporting institutions and societal systems of the host-nation. Legitimacy derives from the legal framework that governs the state and the source of that authority. It reflects not only the supremacy of the law, but also the foundation upon which the law was developed: the collective will of the people through the consent of the governed. It reflects, or is a measure of, the perceptions of several groups: the local populace, individuals serving within the civil institutions of the host nation, neighboring states, the international community, and the American public.

1-29. Ultimately, a legitimate government does not go to war against its population or instigate unwarranted hostilities with its neighbors. A legitimate government acts in accordance with human rights laws and ensures that citizens have access to state resources in a fair and equitable manner. It respects the rights and freedoms reflected in the Universal Declaration of Human Rights and abides by human rights treaties to which it is a party. In addition, *The National Security Strategy of the United States of America* (known as the *National Security Strategy*) lists four traits that characterize a legitimate, effective state in which the consent of the governed prevails:

- **Honors and upholds basic human rights and fundamental freedoms**. Respects freedom of religion, conscience, speech, assembly, association, and press.

- **Responds to their citizens**. Submits to the will of the people, especially when people vote to change their government.
- **Exercises effective sovereignty**. Maintains order within its own borders, protects independent and impartial systems of justice, punishes crime, embraces the rule of law, and resists corruption.
- **Limits the reach of government**. Protects the institutions of civil society, including the family, religious communities, voluntary associations, private property, independent businesses, and a market economy.

1-30. The legitimacy of the mission is as sensitive to perceptions as it is dependent upon the support and participation of the local populace in the processes that comprise the mission. *Ownership*, a central tenet of successful stability operations that capitalizes on that support and participation, is fundamental to legitimacy. (See appendix C for a discussion of the principle of ownership.) The legitimacy of the mission includes four distinct factors:

- Mandate.
- Manner.
- Consent.
- Expectations.

1-31. The mandate or authority that establishes the intervention mission often determines the initial perceptions of legitimacy. Multilateral missions with the broad approval of the international community have a higher degree of legitimacy than unilateral missions. These might include missions conducted by a coalition under a United Nations' mandate.

1-32. The credible manner in which intervening forces conduct themselves and their operations builds legitimacy as the operation progresses. Highly professional forces are well disciplined, trained, and culturally aware. They carry with them an innate perception of legitimacy that is further strengthened by consistent performance conforming to the standards of national and international law. For military forces, a clearly defined commander's intent and mission statement are critical to establishing the initial focus that drives the long-term legitimacy of the mission.

1-33. Consent is essential to the legitimacy of the mission. Generally, no mission is perceived as legitimate without the full consent of the host nation or an internationally recognized mandate. In addition, host-nation consent must extend to external actors with a vested interest in the intervention. An exception is an intervention to depose a regime that significantly threatens national or international security or willfully creates conditions that foment humanitarian crises. However, such missions are only perceived as legitimate with the broad approval of the international community; unilateral missions to impose regime change are rarely perceived as legitimate however well intentioned.

1-34. Expectations are the final arbiter of legitimacy. Realistic, consistent, and achievable expectations—in terms of goals, time, and resources—help to ensure legitimacy during a lengthy operation. Progress is a measure of expectations and an indirect determinant of will; missions that do not achieve a degree of progress consistent with expectations inevitably sap the will of the host nation, the international community, and the American people. Without the sustained will of the people, the legitimacy of any mission gradually decreases.

CAPACITY BUILDING

1-35. Building institutional capacity in the host nation is fundamental to success in stability operations. *Capacity building* **is the process of creating an environment that fosters host-nation institutional development, community participation, human resources development, and strengthening managerial systems.** It includes efforts to improve governance capacity, political moderation, and good governance—ethos as well as structure—as part of broader capacity-building activities within a society. Supported by appropriate policy and legal frameworks, capacity building is a long-term, continuing process, in which all actors contribute to enhancing the host nation's human, technological, organizational, institutional, and resource capabilities.

1-36. Capacity-building activities may support a partner-nation leadership or build on existing capacities; it may focus on reforming extant capacity or developing a new capability and capacity altogether. To some degree, local capacity always exists; capacity-building activities aim to build, nurture, empower, and mobilize that capacity. Those efforts can be facilitated through groups or individuals. They can be broad, long-term efforts or targeted to specific responsibilities or functions to achieve decisive results sooner. Initial response actions reestablish a safe, secure environment and provide for the immediate humanitarian needs of the local populace. All following efforts aim to build partner capacity across the five stability sectors defined in chapter 2 and the Department of State publication, *Post-Conflict Reconstruction Essential Tasks*. (See chapter 2 for a detailed description and discussion of these tasks.)

1-37. Capacity-building activities develop and strengthen skills, systems, abilities, processes, and resources. Host-nation institutions and individuals need to adapt these activities to dynamic political and societal conditions within the operational environment. Most capacity building focuses on long-term technical assistance programs, which may include—

- Human resource development.
- Organizational development.
- Institutional and legal framework development.

1-38. Human resource development is the process of equipping individuals with the understanding, skills, and access to information, knowledge, and training that enables them to perform effectively. Human resource development is central to capacity building. Education and training lie at the heart of development efforts; most successful interventions require human resource development to be effective. Human resource development focuses on a series of actions directed at helping participants in the development process to increase their knowledge, skills, and understanding, and to develop the attitudes needed to bring about the desired developmental change.

1-39. Organizational development is the creation or adaptation of management structures, processes, and procedures to enable capacity building. This includes managing relationships among different organizations and sectors (public, private, and community). Institutional and legal framework development makes the legal and regulatory changes necessary to enable organizations, institutions, and individuals at all levels and in all sectors to perform effectively and to build their capacities.

RULE OF LAW

1-40. During stability operations, it is imperative that the local populace have confidence that they will be treated fairly and justly under the law. They must also believe that they will have access to justice, have an open and participatory government, and trust that all persons, entities, and institutions—public and private—are accountable to the law. *Rule of law* **is a principle under which all persons, institutions, and entities, public and private, including the state itself, are accountable to laws that are publicly promulgated, equally enforced, and independently adjudicated, and that are consistent with international human rights principles.** It also requires measures to ensure adherence to the principles of supremacy of law, equality before the law, accountability to the law, fairness in applying the law, separation of powers, participation in decisionmaking, and legal certainty. Such measures also help to avoid arbitrariness as well as promote procedural and legal transparency.

1-41. Rule of law establishes principles that limit the power of government by setting rules and procedures that prohibit the accumulation of autocratic or oligarchic power. It dictates government conduct according to prescribed and publicly recognized regulations while protecting the rights of all members of society. It also provides a vehicle to resolve disputes nonviolently and in a manner integral to establishing enduring peace and stability. In general terms, rule of law exists when:

- The state monopolizes the use of force in the resolution of disputes.
- Individuals are secure in their persons and property.
- The state is bound by law and does not act arbitrarily.
- The law can be readily determined and is stable enough to allow individuals to plan their affairs.
- Individuals have meaningful access to an effective and impartial justice system.
- The state protects basic human rights and fundamental freedoms.
- Individuals rely on the existence of justice institutions and the content of law in the conduct of their daily lives.

1-42. Typically, operations conducted to support rule of law are part of broader interagency and multinational efforts. Within the USG, the Department of State leads and coordinates reconstruction and stabilization operations, including activities to establish and support the rule of law. The primary U.S. interagency partners for these efforts are the Department of State, the U.S. Agency for International Development, and the Department of Justice. Operations that support rule of law are planned and executed with these interagency partners, but will normally include representation from other organizations, agencies, and multinational partners, when applicable.

1-43. Effective rule of law establishes authority vested in the people, protects rights, exerts a check on all branches of government, and complements efforts to build security. It accounts for the customs, culture, and ethnicity of the local populace. Adherence to the rule of law is essential to legitimate and effective governance. Rule of law enhances the legitimacy of the host-nation government by establishing principles that limit the power of the state and by setting rules and procedures that prohibit accumulating autocratic or oligarchic power. It dictates government conduct according to prescribed and publicly recognized regulations while protecting the rights of all members of society. It also provides a vehicle for resolving disputes nonviolently and in a manner integral to establishing enduring peace and stability.

FRAGILE STATES

1-44. The United States has a long history of assisting other nations. This assistance may come as humanitarian aid, development assistance, free trade agreements, or military assistance. Fragile states, however, pose a particularly complicated challenge. The weakness of these states, especially with respect to governance institutions, threatens the success of any development effort. Development activities within weak states require extended time commitments to build partner capacity in key institutions and to improve the lives of their citizens.

1-45. A *fragile state* **is a country that suffers from institutional weaknesses serious enough to threaten the stability of the central government.** These weaknesses arise from several root causes, including ineffective governance, criminalization of the state, economic failure, external aggression, and internal strife due to disenfranchisement of large sections of the population. Fragile states frequently fail to achieve any momentum toward development. They can generate tremendous human suffering, create regional security challenges, and collapse into wide, ungoverned areas that can become safe havens for terrorists and criminal organizations.

1-46. The term fragile state refers to the broad spectrum of failed, failing, and recovering states. The distinction among them is rarely clear, as fragile states do not travel a predictable path to failure or recovery. The difference between a recovering and failed state may be minimal, as the underlying conditions, such as insurgency or famine, may drive a state to collapse in a relatively short period. It is far more important to understand how far and quickly a state is moving from or toward stability. The fragile states framework, developed by the U.S. Agency for International Development, provides a model for applying U.S. development assistance in fragile states. This framework serves to inform understanding for intervening actors, providing a graphic tool that describes the conditions of the operational environment. (See figure 1-2 on page 1-17.) National Security Presidential Directive 44 frames this spectrum as "foreign states and regions at risk of, in, or in transition from conflict or civil strife." (Paragraph 1-65 discusses this policy directive in detail.)

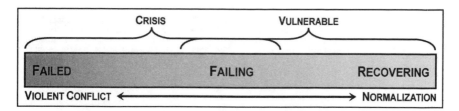

CRISIS   VULNERABLE

FAILED   FAILING   RECOVERING

VIOLENT CONFLICT ⟵——————————⟶ NORMALIZATION

Figure 1-2. The fragile states framework

1-47. Fragile states can be defined as either vulnerable or in crisis. A *vulnerable state* **is a nation either unable or unwilling to provide adequate security and essential services to significant portions of the population.** In vulnerable states, the legitimacy of the central government is in question. This includes states that are failing or recovering from crisis. **A *crisis state* is a nation in which the central government does not exert effective control over its own territory.** It is unable or unwilling to provide security and essential services for significant portions of the population. In crisis states, the central government may be weak, nonexistent, or simply unable or unwilling to provide security or basic services. This includes states that are failing or have failed altogether, where violent conflict is a reality or a great risk.

NATIONAL STRATEGY

1-48. National strategy is based on a distinctly American policy of internationalism that reflects the interests and values of the country. It clearly aims to make the world a safer, better place, where a community of nations lives in relative peace. To that end, the *National Security Strategy* and subordinate supporting strategies focus on a path to progress that promotes political and economic freedom, peaceful relations with other nations, and universal respect for human dignity.

1-49. The body of security strategy that shapes the conduct of stability operations includes the *National Security Strategy*, the *National Defense Strategy*, and *The National Military Strategy of the United States of America* (known as the *National Military Strategy*). Related strategies include the *National Strategy for Combating Terrorism*, the *National Strategy for Homeland Security*, and the *National Strategy to Combat Weapons of Mass Destruction*. Together with national policy, strategy provides the broad direction necessary to conduct operations to support national interests. (See figure 1-3 on page 1-18.)

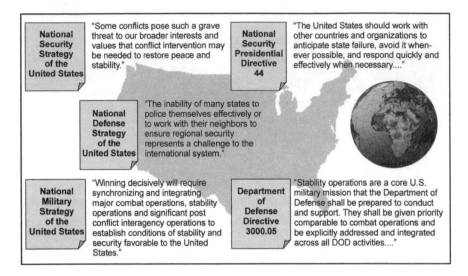

National Security Strategy of the United States: "Some conflicts pose such a grave threat to our broader interests and values that conflict intervention may be needed to restore peace and stability."

National Security Presidential Directive 44: "The United States should work with other countries and organizations to anticipate state failure, avoid it whenever possible, and respond quickly and effectively when necessary...."

National Defense Strategy of the United States: "The inability of many states to police themselves effectively or to work with their neighbors to ensure regional security represents a challenge to the international system."

National Military Strategy of the United States: "Winning decisively will require synchronizing and integrating major combat operations, stability operations and significant post conflict interagency operations to establish conditions of stability and security favorable to the United States."

Department of Defense Directive 3000.05: "Stability operations are a core U.S. military mission that the Department of Defense shall be prepared to conduct and support. They shall be given priority comparable to combat operations and be explicitly addressed and integrated across all DOD activities...."

Figure 1-3. Strategy and policy references for stability operations

NATIONAL SECURITY STRATEGY

1-50. Fragile states tend to attract destabilizing forces, manifesting the potentially dangerous effects of rapid globalization. This poses a national security challenge unforeseen even a decade ago yet central to today's strategic environment. While the phenomenon of fragile states is not new, the need to provide a stabilizing influence is more critical than ever. This challenge is at the core of the current *National Security Strategy*. Essentially, national strategy aims to—

- Promote freedom, justice, and human dignity while working to end tyranny, to promote effective democracies, and to extend prosperity through free trade and wise development policies.
- Confront challenges of the strategic environment by leading a growing community of nations to defeat the threats of pandemic disease, the proliferation of weapons of mass destruction, terrorism, international crime, human trafficking, and natural disasters.

1-51. The *National Security Strategy* outlines the President's vision for providing enduring security for the American people in a volatile, uncertain, and complex strategic environment. It sets a course for statecraft, providing the broad national strategy for applying the instruments of national power to further U.S. interests globally. At the heart of this strategy is the nation's approach to stability operations: to help create a world of legitimate, well-governed states that can meet the needs of their citizens and conduct themselves responsibly in the international system.

1-52. The *National Security Strategy* addresses stability operations within the broad engagement strategy for regional conflict. These regional conflicts significantly threaten national security; they rarely remain isolated and often devolve into humanitarian tragedy or anarchy. External actors exploit them to further their own ends, as Al Qaeda continues to do in Afghanistan and Pakistan. Even when a particular conflict does not directly affect national security, the long-term interests of the Nation often are affected. For this reason, the national strategy identifies three levels of engagement for addressing regional conflict:

- Conflict prevention and resolution.
- Conflict intervention.
- Post-conflict reconstruction and stabilization.

1-53. The most effective long-term measure for conflict prevention and resolution is the promotion of democracy and economic development. Effective democracies generally resolve disputes through peaceful means, either bilaterally or through other regional states or international institutions. Stability tasks executed as part of a theater security cooperation plan under the operational theme of peacetime military engagement generally fall in this category.

1-54. Conflicts that threaten the Nation's security, interests, or values may require direct intervention to restore peace and stability. Stability tasks executed at the higher end of the spectrum of conflict, typically under the operational themes of major combat operations or irregular warfare, fall into this category.

1-55. While military involvement may be necessary to end a conflict, peace and stability endure when follow-on efforts succeed. Such efforts aim to restore order and rebuild infrastructure, governance, and civil society institutions. Success depends on the early establishment of strong local institutions such as effective police forces and functioning justice and penal systems. This governance capacity is critical to establishing rule of law and a market economy that ensure lasting stability and prosperity. At the same time, reconstruction and stabilization efforts rely heavily on the early involvement and support of the local populace with identifying and rebuilding critical infrastructure. Such infrastructure helps societies and institutions to function effectively. In this category, stability tasks generally characterize the overall mission, regardless of the predominant operational theme.

1-56. *Reconstruction* **is the process of rebuilding degraded, damaged, or destroyed political, socioeconomic, and physical infrastructure of a country or territory to create the foundation for long-term development.** *Stabilization* **is the process by which underlying tensions that might lead to resurgence in violence and a breakdown in law and order are managed and reduced, while efforts are made to support preconditions for successful long-term development.** Together, reconstruction and stabilization comprise the broad range of activities defined by the Department of Defense as stability operations.

NATIONAL DEFENSE STRATEGY

1-57. Reinforcing the direction of the *National Security Strategy*, the *National Defense Strategy* emphasizes the threat to national security posed by the inability of fragile states to police themselves or to work in cooperation with neighbor states to ensure long-term security. These states often undermine regional stability, threatening broader national interests. The *National Defense Strategy* recognizes the need for building partner capacity in these states. Built on the understanding that the national security of the United States closely ties to security within the broader international system, the *National Defense Strategy* focuses on the use of programs to build partnerships that strengthen the host nation's ability to confront security challenges. Security cooperation, the principal vehicle for building security capacity, supports these states by—

- Encouraging partner nations to assume lead roles in areas that represent the common interests of the United States and the host nation.
- Encouraging partner nations to increase their capability and willingness to participate in a coalition with U.S. forces.
- Facilitating cooperation with partner militaries and ministries of defense.
- Spurring the military transformation of allied partner nations by developing multinational command and control, training and education, concept development and experimentation, and security assessment framework.

1-58. The *National Defense Strategy* also recognizes the need to foster interagency coordination and integration in these efforts. Such efforts draw a vital link between the Department of Defense and Department of State in the conduct of stability operations. The *National Defense Strategy* emphasizes the need to establish conditions of enduring security to support stability operations, necessary to the success of the other instruments of national power. Unless the security environment supports using civilian agencies and organizations, military forces must be prepared to perform those nonmilitary tasks normally the responsibility of others. Thus, the *National Defense Strategy* clearly establishes the intent of the Secretary of Defense to focus efforts on tasks directly associated with establishing favorable long-term security conditions.

NATIONAL MILITARY STRATEGY

1-59. Prepared by the Chairman of the Joint Chiefs of Staff, the *National Military Strategy* is consistent with the *National Security Strategy* and *National Defense Strategy*. It specifies the ends, ways, and means necessary to ensure national security and interests, and to pursue national interests at home and abroad. It also describes and analyzes the strategic environment as it affects military operations, as well as the most significant threats in that environment.

1-60. The *National Military Strategy* echoes the *National Defense Strategy* on the necessity of interagency integration, emphasizing the role of interagency partners and nongovernmental organizations in achieving lasting success in stability operations. It establishes the requirement for the joint force to retain the capability to conduct full spectrum operations, combining offensive, defensive, and stability tasks simultaneously and to seamlessly transition between them. Finally, it highlights the need to integrate conflict termination measures with the other instruments of national power, ensuring unity of effort toward a common set of national objectives. (See appendix A for a discussion of interagency, intergovernmental, and nongovernmental organizations in stability operations.)

NATIONAL AND DEFENSE POLICIES

1-61. Consistent with the national strategy, U.S. policy focuses on achieving unity of effort through an integrated approach to intervention. This approach, echoed throughout defense policy, is fundamental to unified action. Through this approach, the nation synchronizes, coordinates, and integrates activities of governmental and nongovernmental agencies and organizations toward a common goal. As expressed in the *National Security Strategy*, American foreign policy adopts this approach to help fragile, severely stressed states. It helps their governments avoid failure or recover from devastating disasters by reestablishing or strengthening the institutions of governance and society that represent an effective, legitimate state.

1-62. Interagency cooperation and coordination has long been a goal of national policy. From the post-World War II administration of President Harry Truman through the current administration, every president has prioritized improving the interagency integration process. When Congress passed the National Security Act of 1947, it included formal interagency consultative structures to coordinate national intelligence and policy, ensuring the presence of seasoned government experience to provide advice on presidential decisions. President Dwight Eisenhower's experience as a military commander led him to establish interagency structures to oversee the development and implementation of policy.

1-63. In 1962, President John Kennedy signed National Security Action Memorandum 182 to ensure unity of effort in interagency operations outside the United States. Seven years later, President Nixon signed National Security Decision Memorandum 3 assigning authority and responsibility for directing, coordinating, and supervising interagency operations overseas. In addition, in 1997, President Clinton implemented Presidential Decision Directive 56 creating formal interagency planning processes to support future contingency operations.

1-64. Ultimately, every presidential administration in the past 60 years has implemented some form of policy directive in an attempt to spur cooperation and collaboration among government agencies. Some have been more successful than others have, but none has survived a change in administration. As long as this trend continues, true integration across the interagency will remain elusive.

NATIONAL SECURITY PRESIDENTIAL DIRECTIVE 44

1-65. In 2005, President George Bush signed National Security Presidential Directive 44 (NSPD-44). NSPD-44 outlines the President's vision for promoting the security of the United States through improved coordination, planning, and implementation of reconstruction and stabilization assistance. This policy is significant for two reasons: it was his administration's first attempt at defining national policy for interagency integration, and it was the first time that any administration implemented interagency policy focused on stability operations. In addition, NSPD-44 formally acknowledged that the stability of foreign states served the broader national interests of the United States, recognizing stability operations as a necessary capability of the Federal government.

1-66. NSPD-44 assigns lead agency responsibility to the Department of State for these operations, directing the Secretary of State to coordinate and lead integrated USG efforts and activities. These efforts and activities involve all U.S. departments and agencies with relevant capabilities, to prepare, plan for, and conduct reconstruction and stabilization activities. It also mandated the Secretary of State to coordinate with the Secretary of Defense to ensure the integration and synchronization of any planned or ongoing U.S. military operations across the spectrum of conflict. The policy also authorized the Secretary of State to delegate that authority to the coordinator for reconstruction and stabilization to—

- Lead USG development of a civilian response capability for stability operations.
- Develop strategies and plans for stability operations.
- Coordinate USG responses, including foreign assistance and foreign economic cooperation, in stability operations.
- Ensure coordination among the USG agencies.
- Coordinate USG stability operations with foreign governments, international and regional organizations, nongovernmental organizations, and private sector entities.
- Develop plans to build partner capacity for security.

1-67. To assist the Secretary of State, NSPD-44 called on an interagency office within the Department of State specifically created to enhance the nation's institutional capacity to respond to crises involving fragile states. Based on an April 2004 decision of the National Security Council principals committee, former Secretary of State Colin Powell created the Department of State, Office of the Coordinator for Reconstruction and Stabilization (S/CRS) in July 2004. This office leads, coordinates, and institutionalizes the USG civilian capacity for reconstruction and stabilization and conflict transformation. It is designed to create mechanisms, tools, and processes to help reconstruct and stabilize societies in countries at risk of, in, or in transition from, violent conflict or civil strife, so they can reach a sustainable path toward peace, democracy, and a market economy. S/CRS is the first USG entity specifically created to address stability operations.

1-68. To establish a stable and lasting peace based on the fundamentals of conflict transformation, stability operations capitalize on coordination, cooperation, integration, and synchronization among military and nonmilitary organizations. To that end, S/CRS has led interagency partners by developing three distinct yet tightly linked capabilities that can be customized in scale and scope. These capabilities are composed of the Interagency Management System (IMS) for reconstruction and stabilization, the whole of government planning framework, and the Civilian Response Corps (CRC).

1-69. The IMS is a management structure designed to assist policymakers, chiefs of mission, and military commanders who manage complex reconstruction and stabilization activities. This structure assists them by ensuring coordination among all USG stakeholders at the strategic, operational, and tactical levels. It consists of three structures flexible in size and composition to meet the particular requirements of the situation and integrate personnel from all relevant agencies:

- The country reconstruction and stabilization group is a Washington-based decisionmaking body with an executive secretariat that serves as the central coordinating body for the USG effort.

- The integration planning cell is established and deployed to integrate and synchronize civil-military planning processes.

- An advance civilian team supports or establishes new field operations by rapidly deploying cross-functional teams of USG civilians in an expeditionary environment. It also conducts implementation planning and operations. The team may deploy one or more field advance civilian teams to plan and implement reconstruction and stabilization activities at a provincial or local level.

1-70. The role of the IMS is to prepare and implement whole of government strategic and implementation plans as governed by the USG planning framework for reconstruction and stabilization and conflict transformation. The IMS also is tasked to integrate and synchronize the management of the interagency process at strategic, operational, and tactical levels. The planning framework facilitates assessment and planning for complex crises that require significant and complex security, reconstruction, governance, and economic efforts utilizing all of the instruments of national power. The CRC stabilization initiative provides a standing civilian response capability with the training, equipment, and resources necessary for successful planning and the conduct of operations in the field. The CRC comprises the "civilian forces" that populate the IMS. (See appendix B for additional detail on the Interagency Management System.)

1-71. This system ensures three capabilities to limit duplication of effort. First, USG reconstruction and stabilization participants at all levels have a common operational picture. Second, the chief of mission possesses a coherent framework for decisionmaking and implementation. Third, all agency activities are synchronized in time, space, and purpose. Together, these capabilities comprise the current USG approach to achieving and maintaining stability in a complex crisis. The principles and foundations of these components are approved at senior levels of government, and refinement is expected to continue under NSPD-44.

DEPARTMENT OF DEFENSE DIRECTIVE 3000.05

1-72. Also in 2005, the Secretary of Defense signed DODD 3000.05 providing the military force with definitive guidance to conduct stability operations. It outlines Department of Defense policy and assigns responsibility for planning, preparing for, and executing stability operations. It is part of a broader USG and international effort to establish or maintain order in states and regions while supporting national interests. Most importantly, however, it establishes stability operations as a core military mission on par with combat operations.

1-73. DODD 3000.05 also emphasizes that many of the tasks executed in a stability operation are best performed by host-nation, foreign, or USG civilian personnel, with military forces providing support as required. However, the directive clearly states that, in the event civilians are not prepared to perform those tasks, military forces will assume that responsibility. Finally, the directive describes the comprehensive purposes supporting these tasks:

- Rebuild host-nation institutions, including various types of security forces, correctional facilities, and judicial systems necessary to secure and stabilize the environment.
- Revive or build the private sector, including encouraging citizen-driven, bottom-up economic activity and constructing necessary infrastructure.
- Develop representative government institutions.

1-74. In addition, DODD 3000.05 defines the goals for stability operations. The immediate goal, consistent with initial response efforts, is to provide the local populace with security, restore essential services, and meet humanitarian needs. Long-term goals that reflect transformation and foster sustainability efforts include developing host-nation capacity for securing essential services, a viable market economy, rule of law, legitimate and effective institutions, and a robust civil society.

1-75. The directive also stresses the importance of civil-military teaming in stability operations. It lists the wide array of actors that assume an active role in an intervention, as well as others—often referred to as *stakeholders*—that have an expressed interest in the outcome of that intervention but may not participate in the operation:

- The host nation.
- Relevant USG departments and agencies (interagency partners).
- Foreign governments and forces (multinational partners).
- Global and regional international and intergovernmental organizations.
- International, national, and local nongovernmental organizations.

- Nongovernmental humanitarian agencies.
- Community and civil society organizations.
- Private sector individuals and for-profit companies (private sector).
- Enemies and potential adversaries opposed to intervention.

1-76. These civil-military teams are a critical USG tool in stability operations. DODD 3000.05 directs that military forces work closely with other actors and stakeholders to establish the broad conditions that represent mission success.

STRATEGY FOR STABILITY OPERATIONS

1-77. To achieve conditions that ensure a stable and lasting peace, stability operations capitalize on coordination, cooperation, integration, and synchronization among military and nonmilitary organizations. These complementary civil-military efforts aim to strengthen legitimate governance, restore or maintain rule of law, support economic and infrastructure development, and foster a sense of national unity. These complementary efforts also seek to reform institutions to achieve sustainable peace and security and create the conditions that enable the host-nation government to assume responsibility for civil administration.

1-78. Successful efforts require an overarching framework that serves as a guide to develop strategy in pursuit of broader national or international policy goals. The following purpose-based framework, derived from ongoing work within the USG and led by the United States Institute of Peace, is founded on five broad conditions that describe the desired end state of a successful stability operation. In turn, a series of objectives link the execution of tactical tasks to that end state.

1-79. This framework provides the underpinnings for strategic, whole of government planning, yet also serves as a focal point for integrating operational- and tactical-level tasks. It is flexible and adaptive enough to support activities across the spectrum of conflict but relies on concrete principles and fundamentals in application. Within the framework, the end state conditions include the following:

- A safe and secure environment.
- Established rule of law.
- Social well-being.
- Stable governance.
- A sustainable economy.

SAFE AND SECURE ENVIRONMENT

1-80. In the aftermath of conflict or disaster, conditions often create a significant security vacuum within the state. The government institutions are either unwilling or unable to provide security. In many cases, these institutions do not operate within internationally accepted norms. They are rife with corruption, abusing the power entrusted to them by the state. Sometimes these institutions actually embody the greatest threat to the populace. These conditions only serve to ebb away at the very foundation of the host nation's stability.

1-81. Security is the most immediate concern of the military force, a concern typically shared by the local populace. A safe and secure environment is one in which these civilians can live their day-to-day lives without fear of being drawn into violent conflict or victimized by criminals. Achieving this condition requires extensive collaboration with civil authorities, the trust and confidence of the people, and strength of perseverance.

1-82. The most immediate threat to a safe and secure environment is generally a return to fighting by former warring parties. However, insurgent forces, criminal elements, and terrorists also significantly threaten the safety and security of the local populace. The following objectives support a safe and secure environment:

- Cessation of large-scale violence enforced.
- Public security established.
- Legitimate monopoly over means of violence established.
- Physical protection established.
- Territorial security established.

ESTABLISHED RULE OF LAW

1-83. While military forces aim to establish a safe and secure environment, the rule of law requires much more: security of individuals and accountability for crimes committed against them. These basic elements are critical for a broader culture of rule of law to take hold in a society emerging from conflict. This typically requires a broad effort that integrates the activities of a wide array of actors, focusing civilian and military law and order capabilities to support host-nation civil institutions in establishing and supporting the rule of law. These functions must be rooted in a shared sense of confidence among the population that the justice sector is oriented toward serving the public rather than pursuing narrow interests. Planning, preparing, and executing the transfer of responsibility from military to host-nation control for rule of law, although critical for building public confidence is often the most difficult and complex transition conducted in a stability operation. Failure to ensure continuity of rule of law through this transition threatens the safety and security of the local populace, erodes the legitimacy of the host nation, and serves as an obstacle to long-term development and achieving the desired end state.

1-84. Establishing effective rule of law typically requires an international review of the host-nation legal framework, a justice reform agenda, and general justice reform programs. Many societies emerging from conflict will also require a new constitution. All efforts to establish and support the rule of law must take into account the customs, culture, and ethnicity of the local populace. The following objectives support rule of law:

- Just legal frameworks established.
- Law and order enforced.
- Accountability to the law.
- Access to justice ensured.
- Citizen participation promoted.
- Culture of lawfulness promoted.
- Public security established.

SOCIAL WELL-BEING

1-85. The most immediate needs of a host-nation population emerging from conflict or disaster are generally clear: food, water, shelter, basic sanitation, and health care. International aid typically responds quickly in most situations, often due to their presence in, or proximity to, the affected area. If allowed, and once the situation is relatively stable and secure, local and international aid organizations can provide for the immediate humanitarian needs of the people, establish sustainable assistance programs, and assist with dislocated civilians.

1-86. However, attention must also be paid to long-term requirements: developing educational systems, addressing past abuses, and promoting peaceful coexistence among the host-nation people. These requirements are most appropriately supported by the efforts of civilian actors, including other government agencies, intergovernmental organizations, and nongovernmental organizations. Resolving issues of truth and justice are paramount to this process, and systems of compensation and reconciliation are essential. The following objectives support social well-being:

- Access to and delivery of basic needs ensured.
- Right of return ensured.
- Transitional justice promoted.
- Peaceful coexistence supported.

STABLE GOVERNANCE

1-87. Since the end of the Cold War, all international interventions have aimed to establish stable governments with legitimate systems of political representation at the national, regional, and local levels. In a stable government, the host-nation people regularly elect a representative legislature according to established rules and in a manner generally recognized as free and fair. Legislatures must be designed consistently with a legal framework and legitimate constitution. Officials must be trained, processes created, and rules established.

1-88. Typically, early elections in a highly polarized society empower elites, senior military leaders, and organized criminal elements. However, the local populace will likely seek early and visible signs of progress; therefore, reform processes should begin at the provincial or local level to minimize the likelihood of national polarization and reemergence of violent divisions in society. This allows popular leaders, capable of delivering services and meeting the demands of their constituents, and effective processes to emerge.

1-89. To be successful, stable governments also require effective executive institutions. Such capacity building generally requires a long-term commitment of effort from the international community to reestablish effective ministries and a functional civil service at all levels of government. Stable governments also require free and responsible media, multiple political parties, and a robust civil society. The following objectives support a stable government:

- Accountability of leadership and institutions promoted.
- Stewardship of state resources promoted.
- Civic participation and empowerment encouraged.
- Provision of government services supported.

SUSTAINABLE ECONOMY

1-90. Following conflict or a major disaster, economies tend toward a precarious state. They often suffer from serious structural problems that must be addressed immediately. However, they also possess significant growth potential. Commerce—both legitimate and illicit—previously inhibited by circumstances emerges quickly to fill market voids and entrepreneurial opportunities. International aid and the requirements of intervening military forces often infuse the economy with abundant resources, stimulating rapid growth across the economic sector. However, much of this growth is temporary. It tends to highlight increasing income inequalities, the government's lagging capacity to manage and sustain growth, and expanding opportunities for corruption.

1-91. Rather than focus efforts toward immediately achieving economic growth, intervening elements aim to build on those aspects of the economic sector that enable the economy to become self-sustaining. These include physical infrastructure, sound fiscal and economic policy, an effective and predictable regulatory and legal environment, a viable workforce, business development and increased access to capital, and effective management of natural resources. The following objectives support a sustainable economy:

- Macroeconomic stabilization supported.
- Control over illicit economy and economic-based threats to peace enforced.
- Market economy sustainability supported.
- Individual economic security supported.
- Employment supported.

1-92. Whether stability operations are led by an international body, a coalition of nations, or the domestic leaders of the affected nation, dynamic, transformational leadership is central to any successful effort. It is the catalyst that drives broad success in any operation. Effective leadership inspires and influences others to work together toward a common goal; this is the essence of unity of effort. Through unity of effort, leaders leverage diverse agencies and organizations to pursue complementary actions, focus discreet activities, and shape decisions to support a shared understanding and recognition of the desired end state.

1-93. This framework is not intended to be all-inclusive; no two situations are exactly the same and the development of strategy must be adapted to the specific conditions of the operational environment. A detailed conflict assessment and thorough analysis provide the foundation upon which to build a strategy for engagement. That assessment and analysis underpins conflict transformation efforts, addressing the root causes of conflict while building host-nation institutional capacity to sustain effective governance, economic development, and rule of law.

Chapter 2

Stability in Full Spectrum Operations

Repeating an Afghanistan or an Iraq—forced regime change followed by nation-building under fire— probably is unlikely in the foreseeable future. What is likely though, even a certainty, is the need to work with and through local governments to avoid the next insurgency, to rescue the next failing state, or to head off the next humanitarian disaster.

Correspondingly, the overall posture and thinking of the United States armed forces has shifted—away from solely focusing on direct American military action, and towards new capabilities to shape the security environment in ways that obviate the need for military intervention in the future.

Robert M. Gates
Secretary of Defense

FULL SPECTRUM OPERATIONS

2-1. Full spectrum operations apply to the joint force as well as Army forces. The foundations for Army operations conducted outside the United States and its territories are reflected in the elements of full spectrum operations: continuous, simultaneous combinations of offensive, defensive, and stability tasks. These combinations are manifested in operations designed to seize, retain, and exploit the initiative using the mutually supporting lethal and nonlethal capabilities of Army forces. This is the essence of full spectrum operations, representing the core of Army doctrine. In full spectrum operations, the emphasis on the individual elements changes with echelon, time, and location. (See figure 2-1 on page 2-2.) No single element is more important than another is; simultaneous combinations of the elements, constantly adapted to the dynamic conditions of the operational environment, are key to successful operations. (See FM 3-0 for doctrine on full spectrum operations.)

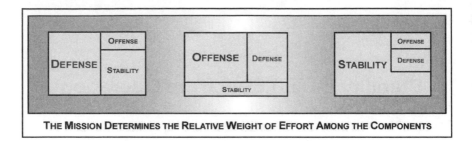

THE MISSION DETERMINES THE RELATIVE WEIGHT OF EFFORT AMONG THE COMPONENTS

Figure 2-1. Full spectrum operations

2-2. This is the essence of full spectrum operations: Army forces combine offensive, defensive, and stability or civil support operations simultaneously as part of an interdependent joint force to seize, retain, and exploit the initiative, accepting prudent risk to create opportunities to achieve decisive results. Army forces employ synchronized action—lethal and nonlethal—proportionate to the mission and informed by a thorough understanding of all dimensions of the operational environment. Mission command that conveys intent and an appreciation of all aspects of the situation guides the adaptive use of Army forces. Offensive and defensive tasks focus on the destructive effects of combat power; stability tasks emphasize constructive effects.

OFFENSIVE AND DEFENSIVE OPERATIONS

2-3. Offensive and defensive operations emphasize employing the lethal effects of combat power against an enemy force, yet they are also critical to success in stability operations. Speed, surprise, and shock are the hallmarks of combat operations; the side better able to leverage these effects defeats its opponent quickly and incurs fewer losses. Such victories create opportunities for exploitation. In some operations, the effects of speed, surprise, and shock suffice to collapse organized resistance. Such a collapse occurred in the offensive phase of Operation Iraqi Freedom in 2003.

2-4. Offensive operations compel the enemy to react, creating or revealing weaknesses that the attacking force can exploit. Successful offensive operations tremendously pressure defenders, creating a cycle of deterioration that can lead to their disintegration. Against a capable, adaptive enemy, the offense is the most direct and sure means of seizing, retaining, and exploiting the initiative. Seizing, retaining, and exploiting the initiative is the essence of the offense. Offensive operations seek to throw enemy forces off balance, overwhelm their capabilities, disrupt their defenses, and ensure their defeat or destruction by maneuver and fires.

2-5. Defensive operations counter the offensive actions of enemy or adversary forces. They defeat attacks, destroying as much of the attacking enemy as possible. They also preserve control over land, resources, and populations. Defensive operations retain terrain, guard populations, and protect critical capabilities and resources. They can be used to gain time through economy of force so offensive and stability tasks can be executed elsewhere.

STABILITY OPERATIONS

2-6. Stability operations leverage the coercive and constructive capabilities of the military force to establish a safe and secure environment; facilitate reconciliation among local or regional adversaries; establish political, legal, social, and economic institutions; and facilitate the transition of responsibility to a legitimate civil authority. Through stability operations, military forces help to set the conditions that enable the actions of the other instruments of national power to succeed in achieving the broad goals of conflict transformation. Providing security and control stabilizes the area of operations. These efforts then provide a foundation for transitioning to civilian control and, eventually, to the host nation. Stability operations are usually conducted to support a host-nation government. However, stability operations may also support the efforts of a transitional civil or military authority when no legitimate government exists.

2-7. Generally, the responsibility for providing for the basic needs of the people rests with the host-nation government or designated civil authorities, agencies, and organizations. When this is not possible, military forces provide essential civil services to the local populace until a civil authority or the host nation can provide these services. In this capacity, military forces perform specific functions as part of a broader response effort, supporting the activities of other agencies, organizations, and institutions.

2-8. In certain circumstances, stability operations may involve activities associated with combating weapons of mass destruction. These activities may include actions applicable across the three strategic pillars to combat weapons of mass destruction: nonproliferation, counterproliferation, and weapons of mass destruction consequence management. Military forces may be directed to conduct weapons of mass destruction elimination operations; chemical, biological, radiological, and nuclear (CBRN) passive defense; or CBRN consequence management. Military forces receive their direction through interagency coordination or from the joint force commander in an effort to reduce the threat or in response to a CBRN incident.

INITIATIVE

2-9. Initiative embodies the offensive spirit of the military force. This spirit is fundamental to how the force operates in any situation and serves to guide leaders in performing their duties. The force embraces risk to create opportunities to gain the initiative. It relentlessly sets the tone and tempo of operations to ensure decisive results. Seizing the initiative within the context of a fragile state or after a disaster requires an appropriately sized expeditionary force with a broad mix of capabilities applicable to the situation. That expeditionary force may require the capability and capacity to either provide support to a civil administration or institute a transitional military authority and the support structure to provide for the well-being of the population.

2-10. Success in stability operations depends on military forces seizing the initiative. In fragile states, the sudden appearance of military forces typically produces a combination of shock and relief among the local populace. Resistance is unorganized and potential adversaries are unsure of what course of action to take. This malleable situation following in the wake of conflict, disaster, or internal strife provides the force with the greatest opportunity to seize, retain, and exploit the initiative. By quickly dictating the terms of action and driving positive change in the environment, military forces improve the security situation and create opportunities for civilian agencies and organizations to contribute. Immediate action to stabilize the situation and provide for the immediate humanitarian needs of the people begins the processes that lead to a lasting peace. Failing to act quickly may create a breeding ground for dissent and possible recruiting opportunities for enemies or adversaries.

2-11. Stability operations rely on military forces quickly seizing the initiative to improve the civil situation while preventing conditions from deteriorating further. Through the initiative, friendly forces dictate the terms of action and drive positive change. Initiative creates opportunities to rapidly stabilize the situation and begin the process that leads to a lasting peace. In turn, this improves the security environment, creating earlier opportunities for civilian agencies and organizations to contribute. Understanding is vital to retaining the initiative; commanders must remain responsive to a dynamic environment while anticipating the needs of the local populace. By acting proactively to positively influence events, Army forces exploit the initiative to ensure steady progress toward conditions that support a stable, lasting peace.

2-12. Stability operations are conducted among the people, within the lens of the media. Therefore, during stability operations, effective information engagement is inseparable from initiative. Information engagement enhances the success of each primary stability task, reinforcing and complementing actions on the ground with supporting messages. The efficacy of seizing, retaining, and exploiting the initiative often depends on the perceptions of various audiences. Through effective information engagement, Army forces seize, retain, and exploit the initiative, drawing on cultural understanding and media engagement to achieve decisive results. They communicate with the local populace in an honest, consistent fashion while providing fair and open access to media representatives. As much as practical, commanders provide the news media with factual information to facilitate prompt, accurate reporting. (See paragraph 2-71 for a detailed discussion of information engagement.)

LETHAL AND NONLETHAL ACTIONS

2-13. In the conduct of full spectrum operations, an inherent, complementary relationship exists between lethal and nonlethal actions; every situation requires a different combination of violence and restraint. Lethal actions are critical to accomplishing offensive and defensive missions. They leverage swift, decisive force to impose friendly will on enemy forces. Nonlethal actions are vital contributors to all operations but are typically decisive only in the execution of stability tasks. Determining the appropriate combination of lethal and nonlethal actions necessary to accomplish the mission is an important consideration for every commander. Every situation is unique and requires a careful balance between lethal and nonlethal actions to achieve success.

2-14. Generally, stability operations require a greater emphasis on nonlethal actions. Nonlethal actions expand the options available to commanders to achieve their objectives. Conditions may limit the conduct of lethal actions, and forces must be organized appropriately to reflect this change in emphasis. Nonlethal actions range from constructive activities focused on building institutional capacity and social well-being to coercive activities intended to compel certain behaviors. They may include a wide range of intelligence-gathering, disruptive, and other activities. They may also include aspects of command and control warfare, nonlethal fires, or other technological means that aim to alter the behavior of an adversary or impair, disrupt, or delay hostile forces, functions, and facilities. By using nonlethal actions, forces can shape the broader situation to maintain or reestablish a safe and secure environment.

2-15. Sometimes, just the threat of violent action is enough to compel the enemy to yield to friendly will and force a settlement. In stability operations, military forces combine various lethal and nonlethal actions to accomplish the mission; within the security sector, for example, lethal action is often critical to overcoming violent opposition, yet enduring success is generally achieved through nonlethal activities. Stability operations emphasize nonlethal, constructive actions by military forces operating among the local populace; however, the more coercive aspects of nonlethal actions may prove equally critical to success.

2-16. Well-trained, equipped, and led forces represent a potent combination of lethal and nonlethal capabilities. Often, the presence of military forces alone influences human behavior; demonstrating the potential for lethal action helps to maintain order. Maintaining order is vital to establishing a safe, secure environment. Even though stability operations emphasize nonlethal actions, the ability to engage potential enemies with decisive lethal force remains a sound deterrent and is often a key to success. The successful application of lethal capabilities in stability operations requires a thorough understanding of when the escalation of force is necessary and when it might be counterproductive. It requires sound judgment supported by constant assessment of the security situation and an intuitive sense of timing with respect to the actions of enemies and adversaries. Adversaries may curtail their activities to avoid being engaged by military forces that they perceive to be capable and willing to use lethal force. This allows military forces to extend the scope and tempo of nonlethal actions.

2-17. Perception is also a major factor for military forces; the actions of Soldiers, both positive and negative, influence how the local populace perceives the military. Therefore, in all actions, leaders focus on managing expectations and informing the people about friendly intentions and actions. This is accomplished through specific nonlethal means: information engagement. Commanders use information engagement to inform, influence, and persuade the populace within limits prescribed by international law. In this way, commanders enhance the legitimacy of the operation and the credibility of friendly forces. (See chapter 3 for additional detail concerning information engagement tasks.)

2-18. Effective, accurate, and timely intelligence is essential to successful full spectrum operations. This is especially true in stability operations where the ultimate success or failure of the mission often depends on the effectiveness of the intelligence effort. In operations conducted among the people, tailored intelligence facilitates understanding of the operational environment while emphasizing the local populace, the host-nation government, and the security apparatus of the state. Commanders require accurate and timely intelligence to retain the initiative during stability operations.

LINKING MILITARY AND CIVILIAN EFFORTS

2-19. The integrated approach necessary to achieve true unity of effort in a comprehensive approach to stability operations is attained through close, continuous coordination and cooperation among the actors involved. This is necessary to overcome internal discord, inadequate structures and procedures, incompatible or underdeveloped communications infrastructure, cultural differences, and bureaucratic and personnel limitations. Within the United States Government, the *National Security Strategy* guides the development, integration, and coordination of all the instruments of national power to achieve national objectives.

2-20. At the national level, the Department of State leads the effort to support interagency coordination and integration. (See appendix A for a discussion of interagency, intergovernmental, and nongovernmental organizations in stability operations.) During stability operations, the essential stability task matrix facilitates coordination by providing a means of integrating activities by various actors at the tactical level. In turn, this helps attain unity of effort across the stability sectors, focusing all activities toward a common set of objectives and a shared understanding of the desired end state. The end state focuses on the conditions required to support a secure, lasting peace; a viable market economy; and a legitimate host-nation government capable of providing for its populations' essential needs. Together, the stability sectors and the primary tasks that comprise the stability element of full spectrum operations constitute a single, integrated model essential to achieving unity of effort. (See figure 2-2.)

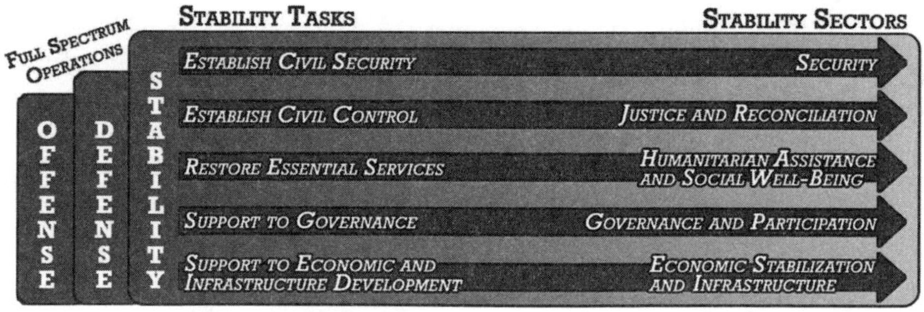

Figure 2-2. An integrated approach to stability operations

2-21. Linking the basic military and civilian task frameworks creates a single model that forms the basis for developing lines of effort. (See chapter 4 for detail on using lines of effort in stability operations.) This model serves as the underpinning for an integrated approach to stability operations founded on unity of effort and coordinated engagement. Thus, the conduct of full spectrum operations to support a broader effort contributes toward the shared end state established by the actors involved. On a fundamental level, the execution of discreet military tasks is linked to a coordinated, comprehensive effort. This ensures that the efforts of military forces are integral to broader engagement activities. These efforts unite in the pursuit of a common goal and shared understanding of the desired end state. A clear delineation and understanding of the formal lines of authority enhances unity of effort. Together with the activities of the other participants, these tasks contribute to unity of effort with the diverse array of actors involved in any collaborative effort.

DEPARTMENT OF STATE POST-CONFLICT RECONSTRUCTION ESSENTIAL TASKS

2-22. While national policy charges the Department of State to lead stability operations on behalf of the Federal government, the Department of State's Office of the Coordinator for Reconstruction and Stabilization (S/CRS) serves as the office for the Department of State designated to coordinate United States Government (USG) efforts in these operations. To that end, S/CRS developed a detailed list of stability-focused, post-conflict reconstruction essential tasks (hereafter referred to as the essential stability task matrix). The essential stability task matrix is an evolving interagency document to help planners identify specific requirements to support countries in transition from armed conflict or civil strife to sustaining stability. It serves as a detailed planning tool and will continue to develop as it is implemented during operations.

2-23. The essential stability task matrix divides the tasks conducted during stability operations and their relative time frame for execution across five broad technical areas. These areas, often referred to as *stability sectors*, may be involved in an intervention (see figure 2-2):

- Security.
- Justice and reconciliation.
- Humanitarian and social well-being.
- Governance and participation.
- Economic stabilization and infrastructure.

2-24. These sectors, which are similar in purpose and application to lines of effort, help to focus and unify reconstruction and stabilization efforts within specific functional areas of society. (See chapter 4 for a discussion on the use of lines of effort in stability operations.) They define and encompass integrated task areas across a broad spectrum of interagency engagement, including the Department of Defense. The essential stability task matrix addresses many of the requirements necessary to support countries in transition from armed conflict or civil strife. It serves as a means to leverage functional knowledge and systemic thinking into planning, preparation, execution, and assessment. The essential stability task matrix ensures that—

- The execution of tasks is focused toward achieving the desired end state.
- Tasks that should be executed by actors outside the USG are highlighted and responsibility for them within the international community is identified.
- Sector specialists understand the diversity of tasks in other sectors and the interdependence among the sectors.

2-25. While the assignment of specific tasks and prioritization among them depends on the conditions of the operational environment, the essential stability task matrix provides a tool to help visualize the conduct of an operation, sequence necessary activities within an operation, and develop appropriate priorities for those activities and resource allocation. Depending on the scope, scale, and context of the operation, those priorities help to deconflict activities, focus limited resources, and delineate specific responsibilities. Detailed planning is necessary to integrate and synchronize activities in time and space, identify complementary and reinforcing actions, and prioritize efforts within and across the stability sectors.

2-26. The essential stability task matrix provides a foundation for thinking systemically about stability operations. Many of the tasks are "crosscutting" and create effects across multiple sectors. In this respect, the essential stability task matrix facilitates integration by allowing sector specialists to establish and understand links among the stability sectors. In cases where the intervening actors lack the capability or capacity to perform certain functions, the essential stability task matrix facilitates identifying gaps that require building or leveraging specific capabilities within the international community.

2-27. The stability sectors form a framework for executing stability tasks that represent the five key areas in which civil-military efforts focus on building host-nation capacity. Individually, they encompass the distinct yet interrelated tasks that constitute reform activities in a functional sector. Collectively, they are the pillars upon which the government frames the possible reconstruction tasks required for nations torn by conflict or disaster. Although some tasks are executed sequentially, success necessitates an approach that focuses on simultaneous actions across the operational area. These tasks are inextricably linked; positive results in one sector depend upon the successful integration and synchronization of activities across the other sectors.

SECURITY

2-28. Efforts in the security sector focus on establishing a stable security environment and developing legitimate institutions and infrastructure to maintain that environment. Security encompasses the provision of individual and collective security and is the foundation for broader success across the other sectors. While securing the lives of local civilians from the violence of conflict and restoring the territorial integrity of the state, intervening forces stabilize the security environment. This stability allows for comprehensive reform efforts that are best accomplished by civilian personnel from other stakeholder agencies and organizations.

2-29. In the most pressing conditions, expeditionary forces assume responsibility for all efforts in the security sector. These efforts typically assemble under the activities reflected in the primary stability task, *establish civil security*, but also complement and reinforce parallel efforts in other sectors. Ultimately, for the results of these efforts to be lasting, host-nation forces—acting on behalf of the host nation and its people— must provide security.

JUSTICE AND RECONCILIATION

2-30. The justice and reconciliation sector encompasses far more than policing, civil law and order, and the court systems of a state. Within the sector, efforts provide for a fair, impartial, and accountable justice system while ensuring an equitable means to reconcile past crimes and abuse arising from conflict or disaster. Tasks most closely associated with justice focus on reestablishing a fair and impartial judiciary and effective justice system. This system ensures public safety and helps to resolve disputes and enforce established contracts. Those tasks relating to reconciliation address grievances and crimes, past and present, in hopes of forging a peaceful future for an integrated society.

2-31. An integrated approach to justice and reconciliation is central to broader reform efforts across the other sectors. The justice and reconciliation sector is supported by eight key elements:

- Effective and scrupulous law enforcement institutions responsive to civil authority and respectful of human rights and dignity.
- An impartial, transparent, and accountable judiciary and justice system.
- A fair, representative, and equitable body of law.

- Mechanisms for monitoring and upholding human rights.
- A humane, reform-based corrections system.
- Reconciliation and accountability mechanisms for resolving past abuses and grievances arising from conflict.
- An effective and ethical legal profession.
- Public knowledge and understanding of rights and responsibilities under the law.

2-32. Successful interventions address the most critical gaps in capability and capacity as soon as possible. Initial response forces that immediately account for vital issues of justice and reconciliation typically maintain the initiative against subversive and criminal elements seeking to fill those gaps. Host-nation involvement in planning, oversight, and monitoring of justice and reconciliation sector reforms is essential. Generally, intervention in the justice and reconciliation sector encompasses three categories:

- Initial response activities to institute essential interim justice measures that resolve the most urgent issues of law and order until host-nation processes and institutions are restored.
- An established system of reconciliation to address grievances and past atrocities.
- Long-term actions to establish a legitimate, accountable host-nation justice system and supporting infrastructure.

2-33. The justice and reconciliation sector closely relates to the security and governance sectors; activities in one sector often complement or reinforce efforts in another. These relationships are further reinforced by the inseparable nature of the tasks subordinate to each sector, which reflects the dynamic interaction between security and justice. Due to the close relationships among the activities and functions that comprise the security, governance, and justice and reconciliation sectors, failure to act quickly in one sector can lead to the loss of momentum and gains in the other sectors.

HUMANITARIAN ASSISTANCE AND SOCIAL WELL-BEING

2-34. Conflict and disaster significantly stress how well the state can provide for the essential, immediate humanitarian needs of its people. The institutions of security and governance that enable the effective functioning of public services often fail first, leading to widespread internal strife and humanitarian crisis. In some areas, the intense competition for limited resources may explode into full-blown conflict, possibly leaving pervasive starvation, disease, and death as obvious outward indications of a fragile state in crisis. (See appendix E for a discussion of humanitarian assistance principles.)

2-35. Any intervention effort is incomplete if it fails to alleviate immediate suffering. Generally, this suffering is understood to include the immediate need for water, food, shelter, emergency health care, and sanitation. However, solutions that focus on ensuring sustainable access to these basic needs are also necessary to prevent the recurrence of systemic failures while assuring the social well-being of the people. These sustainable solutions establish the foundation for long-term development. They address the root or underlying causes of a conflict that result in issues such as famine, dislocated civilians, refugee flows, and human trafficking. It also ensures the lasting effects of the intervention effort by institutionalizing positive change in society.

GOVERNANCE AND PARTICIPATION

2-36. Tasks in the governance and participation sector address the need to establish effective, legitimate political and administrative institutions and infrastructure. *Governance* **is the state's ability to serve the citizens through the rules, processes, and behavior by which interests are articulated, resources are managed, and power is exercised in a society, including the representative participatory decisionmaking processes typically guaranteed under inclusive, constitutional authority.** Effective governance involves establishing rules and procedures for political decisionmaking, strengthening public sector management and administrative institutions and practices, providing public services in an effective and transparent manner, and providing civil administration that supports lawful private activity and enterprise. Participation includes procedures that actively, openly involve the local populace in forming their government structures and policies that, in turn, encourage public debate and the generation and exchange of new ideas.

2-37. Efforts to strengthen civil participation foster achieving positive, lasting change in society. Achieving this change enables the people to influence government decisionmaking and hold public leaders accountable for their actions. Activities that develop social capital help local communities influence policies and institutions at local, regional, and national levels. With this assistance, communities establish processes for problem identification, development of proposals to address critical issues, capability and capacity building, community mobilization, rebuilding social networks, and advocacy. These social capital development activities are founded on three pillars:

- **Human rights** by promoting and protecting social, economic, cultural, political, civil, and other basic human rights.

- **Equity and equality** by advancing equity and equality of opportunity among citizens in terms of gender, social and economic resources, political representation, ethnicity, and race.

- **Democracy and self-determination** by supporting participation and involvement in public forums and self-determination in human development.

2-38. Response efforts that seek to build local governance and participation capacity ensure host-nation responsibility for these processes. Even when civilians are deprived of authority or the right to vote, they must be encouraged to take the lead in rebuilding their own government. This lead is essential to establishing successful, enduring host-nation government institutions. Even when external actors perform certain governance functions temporarily, this process to build host-nation capacity—complemented by a comprehensive technical assistance program—is vital to long-term success.

2-39. Military forces may assume the powers of a sovereign governing authority under two conditions: when military forces intervene in the absence of a functioning government or when military operations prevent a government from administering to the public sector and providing public services. Transitional military authority is an interim solution. It is intended to continue only until the host-nation institutions and infrastructure can resume their functions and responsibilities. (Chapter 5 has a detailed discussion of transitional military authority during stability operations.)

ECONOMIC STABILIZATION AND INFRASTRUCTURE

2-40. Much of the broader success achieved in stability operations begins at the local level as intervening actors engage the populace with modest economic and governance programs. These programs set the building blocks for comprehensive national reform efforts. These efforts aim to build the institutions and processes to ensure the sustained viability of the state. To support the progress of the state from disarray to development, external actors and the host nation—

- Establish the policies and regulatory framework that supports basic economic activity and development.

- Secure and protect the natural resources, energy production, and distribution infrastructure of the host nation.

- Engage and involve the private sector in reconstruction.

- Implement programs that encourage trade and investment with initial emphasis on host-nation and regional investors, followed at a later stage by foreign investors.

- Rebuild or reform essential economic governance institutions.
- Reconstruct or build essential economic infrastructure.

2-41. Although conflict and disaster cause significant economic losses and disrupt economic activity, they also create opportunities for economic reform and restructuring. In fragile states, elites who benefit from the existing state of the economic situation can discourage the growth of trade and investment, stifle private sector development, limit opportunities for employment and workforce growth, and weaken or destroy emerging economic institutions. Intervening actors work to legitimize the host nation's economic activities and institutions. Such legitimate institutions provide an opportunity to stimulate reconstruction and stabilization by facilitating assistance from the international community. This community helps develop comprehensive, integrated humanitarian and economic development programs required to achieve sustained success. Ultimately, such success can reduce the likelihood of a return to violent conflict while restoring valuable economic and social capital to the host nation.

2-42. The economic recovery of the host nation is tied directly to effective governance. Sound economic policy supported by legitimate, effective governance fosters recovery, growth, and investment. Recovery begins at the local level as markets and enterprises are reestablished, the workforce is engaged, and public and private investment is restored. These events help to stabilize the host-nation currency and reduce unemployment, thus providing the tax base necessary to support the recovery of the host nation's treasury. In turn, this enables the host-nation government to fund the public institutions and services that provide for the social and economic well-being of the people.

PRIMARY STABILITY TASKS

2-43. Stability operations consist of the five primary tasks shown in figure 2-2. The primary tasks correspond to the five stability sectors adopted by S/CRS. Together, they provide a mechanism for interagency tactical integration, linking the execution of discreet tasks among the instruments of national power. The subordinate tasks performed by military forces under the primary stability tasks directly support broader efforts within the stability sectors executed as part of unified action. (Chapter 3 addresses the relationship between the stability sectors and the primary stability tasks.)

2-44. None of these primary tasks is performed in isolation. When integrated within their complementary stability sectors, they represent a cohesive effort to reestablish the institutions that provide for the civil participation, livelihood, and well-being of the citizens and the state. At the operational level, the primary stability tasks may serve as lines of effort or simply as a guide to action, ensuring broader unity of effort across the stability sectors. (See chapter 4 for a discussion on the use of lines of effort in stability operations.) Each primary task and stability sector contains a number of related subordinate tasks. In any operation, the primary stability tasks, and the subordinate tasks included within each area, are integrated with offensive and defensive tasks under full spectrum operations. (See FM 3-0 for more information on full spectrum operations.)

2-45. The primary stability tasks are fundamental to full spectrum operations and are conducted across the spectrum of conflict, from stable peace to general war. They may be executed before, during, or after conflict. They may be executed to support a legitimate host-nation government, to assist a fragile state, or in the absence of a functioning civil authority. Each situation is unique. Planning and execution must be supported by thorough assessment and analysis to determine the ends, ways, and means appropriate to the conditions of the operational environment.

ESTABLISH CIVIL SECURITY

2-46. Establishing civil security involves providing for the safety of the host nation and its population, including protection from internal and external threats; it is essential to providing a safe and secure environment. Civil security includes a diverse set of activities. These range from enforcing peace agreements to conducting disarmament, demobilization, and reintegration. Until a legitimate civil government can assume responsibility for the security sector, military forces perform the tasks associated with civil security. At the same time, they help develop host-nation security and police forces. Normally, the responsibility for establishing and maintaining civil security belongs to military forces from the onset of operations through transition, when host-nation security and police forces assume this role. (Chapter 4 includes additional detail on the role of transitions in stability operations.)

2-47. Civil security is resource intense; as a primary stability task, *establish civil security* requires more manpower, materiel, and monetary support than any other task. However, civil security is a necessary precursor to success in the other primary stability tasks. Civil security provides the foundation for unified action across the other stability sectors. Well-established and maintained civil security enables efforts in other areas to achieve lasting results.

2-48. Establishing a safe, secure, and stable environment for the local populace is a key to obtaining their support for the overall stability operation. Such an environment facilitates introducing civilian agencies and organizations whose efforts ensure long-term success. When the people have confidence in the security sector providing for their safety, they cooperate. Military forces need this cooperation to control crime and subversive behavior, defeat insurgents, and limit the effects of adversary actions. For political and economic reform efforts to be successful, people, goods, and livestock must be able to circulate within the region.

2-49. Establishing or reestablishing competent host-nation security forces is fundamental to providing lasting safety and security of the host nation and its population. These forces are developed primarily to counter external threats. However, they may also assist in other key missions including disaster relief, humanitarian assistance, and in special cases countering certain internal military threats. Developing host-nation security forces is integral to successful stability operations and includes organizing, training, equipping, rebuilding, and advising various components of host-nation security forces. (See chapter 6 for a detailed discussion of security force assistance.)

ESTABLISH CIVIL CONTROL

2-50. Establishing civil control is an initial step toward instituting rule of law and stable, effective governance. Although establishing civil security is the first responsibility of military forces in a stability operation, this can only be accomplished by also restoring civil control. Internal threats may manifest themselves as an insurgency, subversive elements within the population, organized crime, or general lawlessness. Each constitutes a significant threat to law and order and therefore to the overall effort to establish a secure, stable peace. Civil control centers on justice reform and the rule of law, supported by efforts to rebuild the host-nation judiciary, police, and corrections systems. It encompasses the key institutions necessary for a functioning justice system, including police, investigative services, prosecutorial arm, and public defense. It includes helping the state select an appropriate body of laws to enforce; usually this is the host nation's most recent criminal code, purged of blatantly abusive statutes.

2-51. In a fragile state, the justice system may have ceased to function altogether with absent judges and legal professionals, looted or destroyed courts and prisons, damaged or destroyed records, and any surviving vestiges of the justice system stripped of essentials. If transitional military authority is instituted, intervening forces may perform both judicial and correctional functions. A key to promoting the rule of law in these cases is ensuring that military forces themselves abide by the law and are held accountable for any crimes committed. (See chapter 5 for a discussion of rule of law under transitional military authority.)

2-52. To provide for the safety and security of the populace successfully, an effective judiciary branch and a functioning corrections system must complement the state's security institutions. Together with governance and civil security, civil control is a core element of security sector reform. This reform sets the foundation for broader government and economic reform and successful humanitarian relief and social development. Establishing civil control protects the integrity of the security sector reform program. Civil control tasks prevent corruption that threatens security institutions when they lack the support of judges to apply the law and prisons to incarcerate the convicted.

2-53. Building host-nation capacity for civil control is paramount to establishing the foundation for lasting civil order. Community-oriented police services under civilian control that clearly separate the roles of the police and military are essential to success. As with host-nation security forces, the development of police forces proves integral to providing a safe, secure environment for the local populace. Military forces may first need to restore and then maintain civil order until formed police units trained in stability policing skills are available to perform these functions and begin training host-nation police forces. In some cases, military forces may also be tasked to train, or oversee the training of, host-nation police forces.

2-54. In some cases, host-nation justice system actors may have been part of a corrupt or authoritarian regime, and their continued service in such capacities is inconsistent with institutional reform programs. As with other elements of the civil security and governance sectors, an appropriate authority vets the judiciary, police, and corrections staffs and oversees their activities as part of the security sector reform program. Conducted in parallel with other reform processes, near-term efforts focus on building host-nation capacity by restoring the components of the justice system. Long-term development aims to institutionalize a rule of law culture within the government and society. Establishing this culture often relies on the delicate balance between retribution and reconciliation in a state recovering from the effects of collapse. Successful development depends on the ability of the host nation to reconcile with its past—determining whom to punish, whom to forgive, whom to exclude, and whom to accept within the new order of the state. (See chapter 6 for a discussion of security sector reform and its relationship to justice reform.)

RESTORE ESSENTIAL SERVICES

2-55. Efforts to restore essential services ultimately contribute to achieving a stable democracy, a sustainable economy, and the social well-being of the population. In the aftermath of armed conflict and major disasters, military forces support efforts to establish or restore the most basic civil services: the essential food, water, shelter, and medical support necessary to sustain the population until local civil services are restored. Military forces also protect them until transferring responsibility to a transitional civil authority or the host nation. In addition, these efforts typically include providing or supporting humanitarian assistance, providing shelter and relief for dislocated civilians, and preventing the spread of epidemic disease. The immediate humanitarian needs of the local populace are always a foremost priority.

2-56. However, activities associated with this primary stability task extend beyond simply restoring local civil services and addressing the effects of humanitarian crises. While military forces generally center their efforts on the initial response tasks that provide for the immediate needs of the populace, other civilian agencies and organizations focus on broader humanitarian issues and social well-being. Typically, local and international aid organizations are already providing assistance, although the security situation or obstacles to free movement may limit their access to all populations. By providing a secure environment, military forces enable these organizations to expand their access to the entire populace and ease the overall burden on the force to provide this assistance in isolation.

SUPPORT TO GOVERNANCE

2-57. Military efforts to support governance help to build progress toward achieving effective, legitimate governance. Military support to governance focuses on restoring public administration and resuming public services while fostering long-term efforts to establish a functional, effective system of political governance. The support provided by military forces helps to shape the environment for extended unified action by other partners. Their efforts eventually enable the host nation to develop an open political process, a free press, a functioning civil society, and legitimate legal and constitutional frameworks.

2-58. Ultimately, the goal in a stability operation is to leave a society at peace with itself and its regional neighbors, sustainable by the host nation without the support of external actors. Governance is the process, systems, institutions, and actors that enable a state to function; effective, legitimate governance ensures that these are transparent, accountable, and involve public participation. Democratization, while often an end state condition in planning, does not ensure these outcomes. In societies already divided along ethnic, tribal, or religious lines, elections may further polarize factions. Generally, representative institutions based on universal suffrage offer the best means of reconstituting a government acceptable to the majority of the citizens. This is the broad intent of developing host-nation governance.

2-59. Although the United States has a secular, representative government that clearly separates church and state, other states have varying degrees of religious participation in their governments. Countries such as Iran and Saudi Arabia have codified versions of Shari'a (Islamic legislation). Shari'a uses the Quran as the foundation for the national constitution. Religion is often a central defining characteristic in some forms of government and cannot be discounted by external actors. Ultimately, the form of government adopted must reflect the host-nation customs and culture rather than those of the intervening actors.

SUPPORT TO ECONOMIC AND INFRASTRUCTURE DEVELOPMENT

2-60. Military tasks executed to support the economic sector are critical to sustainable economic development. The economic viability of a state is among the first elements of society to exhibit stress and ultimately fracture as conflict, disaster, and internal strife overwhelms the government. Signs of economic stress include rapid increases in inflation, uncontrolled escalation of public debt, and a general decline in the state's ability to provide for the well-being of the people. Economic problems are inextricably tied to governance and security concerns. As one institution begins to fail, others are likely to follow.

2-61. Infrastructure development complements and reinforces efforts to stabilize the economy. It focuses on the society's physical aspects that enable the state's economic viability. These physical aspects of infrastructure include construction services, engineering, and physical infrastructure in the following sectors:

- Transportation, such as roads, railways, airports, ports, and waterways.
- Telecommunications.
- Energy, such as natural resources, the electrical power sector, and energy production and distribution.
- Municipal and other public services.

2-62. Accurate, detailed assessment is a key to formulating long-term plans for infrastructure development. Military forces often possess the capability to conduct detailed reconnaissance of the state's physical infrastructure and can effectively inform planning efforts. Infrastructure reconnaissance gathers technical information on the status of large-scale public systems, services, and facilities necessary for economic activity. This task facilitates restoring essential services as well as spurring economic and infrastructure development. Infrastructure reconnaissance is accomplished in two stages: infrastructure assessment—associated with the restoration of essential services—and infrastructure survey—that supports economic and infrastructure development. Infrastructure reconnaissance supports the operations process by providing vital information on the quality of the local infrastructure or problems within it. It also supports how those infrastructure issues impact military operations and the population. (FM 3-34.170 contains doctrine on infrastructure assessment.)

STABILITY OPERATIONS FRAMEWORK

2-63. During stability operations, engagement and intervention activities are better defined in terms of the progress toward stabilizing the operational environment. Using the spectrum that describes fragile states, figure 2-3 illustrates conditions that characterize an operational environment during stability operations. (See chapter 1 for a discussion of fragile states.) This spectrum also defines the environment according to two quantifiable, complementary scales: decreasing violence and increasing normalization of the state, the fundamental measures of success in conflict transformation. Although fragile states do not recover from conflict or disaster according to a smooth, graduated scale, this spectrum provides a means with which to gauge conditions of an operational environment, formulate an engagement methodology, and measure progress toward success.

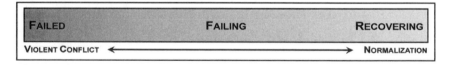

Figure 2-3. The fragile states spectrum

2-64. Military forces can engage at any point along this spectrum. In each case, achieving the end state requires quickly reducing the level of violence while creating conditions that support safely introducing other government agencies and intergovernmental organizations while securing critical humanitarian access for nongovernmental organizations. Military operations focus on stabilizing the environment and transforming conditions of the environment and the state toward normalization. In a failed or failing state, conditions typically require more coercive actions to eliminate threats and reduce violence. As conditions of the environment begin to improve, the constructive capabilities of military forces focus toward building host-nation capacity and encouraging sustained development.

PHASING INTERVENTION

2-65. The failed states spectrum is also a critical tool for understanding and prioritizing the broad range of activities that embody unity of effort in an operational environment characterized by a fragile state. These activities occur within distinct phases—categorized in the S/CRS essential stability task matrix as initial response, transformation, and fostering sustainability—that collectively represent the post-conflict actions necessary to achieve security and reestablish stable, lasting peace. Together, the failed states spectrum and the essential stability task matrix phases provide a basic framework for stability operations. This framework characterizes the operational environment, identifies distinct phases for intervention activities, defines the types and ranges of tasks performed in that environment, and provides a tool with which to measure progress toward the desired end state. (See figure 2-4.)

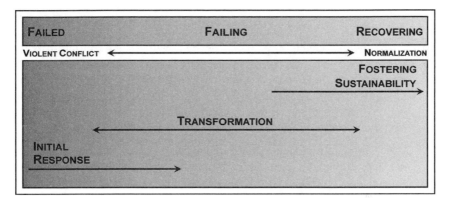

Figure 2-4. The stability operations framework

2-66. This framework encompasses all the tasks performed by military and civilian actors during stability operations. It guides the understanding of the effort and commitment necessary to rebuild a nation torn by conflict or disaster while providing a tool to shape activities during peacetime military engagement. The intervention phases during a stability operation include the following:

- Initial response phase.
- Transformation phase.
- Fostering sustainability phase.

2-67. The initial response phase generally reflects tasks executed to stabilize the operational environment in a crisis state. During this phase, military forces perform stability tasks during or directly after a conflict or disaster where the security situation hinders the introduction of civilian personnel. Activities during the initial response phase aim to provide a safe, secure environment; they allow the force to attend to the immediate humanitarian needs of the host-nation population. They support efforts to reduce the level of violence and human suffering while creating conditions that enable other actors to participate safely in ongoing efforts.

2-68. The transformation phase represents the broad range of post-conflict reconstruction, stabilization, and capacity-building tasks. These tasks are performed in a relatively secure environment free from most wide-scale violence, often to support broader civilian efforts. Transformation phase tasks may be executed in either crisis or vulnerable states. These tasks aim to build host-nation capacity across multiple sectors. While establishing conditions that facilitate broad unified action to rebuild the host nation and its supporting institutions, these tasks are essential to ensuring the continued stability of the environment.

2-69. Fostering sustainability phase encompasses long-term efforts that capitalize on capacity-building and reconstruction activities to establish conditions that enable sustainable development. Usually military forces perform fostering sustainability phase tasks only when the security environment is stable enough to support efforts to implement the long-term programs that commit to the viability of the institutions and economy of the host nation. Often military forces conduct these long-term efforts to support broader, civilian-led efforts.

2-70. The stability operations framework helps to emphasize the training and organization of forces prior to initial deployment and later during force generation. It spurs design and planning, serving as an engagement paradigm. This paradigm frames response efforts and scopes the tasks to accomplish the mission. In the simplest terms, it is a guide to action in stability operations.

INFORMATION ENGAGEMENT IN STABILITY

2-71. Successfully executing essential stability tasks also depends on informing the local populace and influencing attitudes. Although there are more tangible objectives that mark the success of a stability operation, the final measure of success or failure often rests with the perceptions of the people. Military forces must go beyond defeating the enemy. They must secure the trust and confidence of the population. This requires a mastery of *information engagement*: the integrated employment of public affairs to inform United States and friendly audiences; psychological operations, combat camera, USG strategic communication and defense support to public diplomacy, and other means necessary to influence foreign audiences; and, leader and Soldier engagements to support both efforts (FM 3-0). Since stability operations are conducted within a broader global and regional context, success often depends on the integration of information engagement efforts among military forces and the various agencies and organizations participating in the operation. Information engagement efforts must support and complement those of higher headquarters, national interests, and broader USG policy. (When updated, FM 3-13 will include doctrine on information engagement.)

2-72. In stability operations, leader and Soldier engagement may be the most critical component of information engagement. It is the sustained engagement of the host-nation population that most directly influences the attitudes and shapes the perceptions of the people. Leader and Soldier engagement amplifies positive actions, counters enemy propaganda, and increases support among the host-nation population. It begins with the direct interaction between Soldiers and the local populace, where the consistency between words and deeds is most important. It includes meetings conducted with key communicators, civilian leaders, or others whose perceptions, decisions, and actions will affect mission accomplishment. Conducted with detailed preparation and planning, both activities often prove crucial in building local support for military operations, providing an opportunity for persuasion, and reducing friction and mistrust. This is essential to gaining the trust and confidence of the local populace.

2-73. Psychological operations exert significant influence on foreign target audiences and are often the primary capability for affecting behaviors among these audiences. During stability operations, psychological operations forces also advise the commander and staff on the psychological effects of their operations, provide public information to the target audience to support humanitarian assistance, and assess adversary propaganda. Effective psychological operations can support communications with the local populace, reduce civil interference with military operations, support efforts to establish and maintain rule of law, and influence the host-nation attitude toward external actors. The approved objectives and themes of psychological operations are integrated through the operations process to ensure forces effectively and efficiently apply limited resources.

2-74. Stability operations are conducted among the people, in the spotlight of international news media, and under the umbrella of international law. The actions of Soldiers communicate American values and beliefs more effectively than words alone. Therefore, military forces ensure consistency in their actions and messages. They provide the media with prompt, factual information to quell rumors and misinformation. They grant media representatives access to information within the limits of operations security. Finally, they understand the culture of each audience and tailor the message appropriately.

2-75. No other military activity has as significant a human component as operations that occur among the people. With urbanization, these operations will be increasingly conducted among concentrations of people and thus significantly affect their psyche. Human beings capture information and form perceptions based on inputs received through all the senses. They see actions and hear words. They compare gestures and expressions with the spoken word. They weigh the messages presented to them with the conditions that surround them. When the local and national news media are unavailable or unreliable, people often rely on "word of mouth" to gain information or turn to the Internet, where unverified information flows freely at unimaginable speeds. To the people, perception equals reality. Creating favorable perceptions requires an understanding of the psychological motivations of the populace and shaping messages according to how people absorb and interpret information to ensure broad appeal and acceptance.

Chapter 3

Essential Stability Tasks

Many stability operations tasks are best performed by indigenous, foreign, or U.S. civilian professionals. Nonetheless, U.S. military forces shall be prepared to perform all tasks necessary to establish or maintain order when civilians cannot do so. ... The long-term goal is to help develop indigenous capacity for securing essential services, a viable market economy, rule of law, democratic institutions, and a robust civil society.

Department of Defense Directive 3000.05

IDENTIFYING ESSENTIAL TASKS

3-1. Military forces are organized, trained, and equipped to be modular, versatile, and rapidly deployable. They are tailored for expeditionary operations, easily task-organized, and continuously self-sufficient. These unique expeditionary capabilities allow for prompt movement into any operational environment, even the most austere regions. Expeditionary military forces can conduct operations without delay; they can deliver decisive combat power with little advance warning.

3-2. In an operational environment with unstable security conditions in which the host-nation government has either failed or is unable to function effectively, a military force may be the only substantial stabilizing presence. In these conditions, the force must be prepared to perform all the tasks essential to establishing and maintaining security and order while providing for the essential needs of the populace. In most situations, local and international aid organizations will be present in the operational area but may have limited access to the population. Military forces can significantly contribute to increasing the access of these aid organizations, allowing them to provide essential humanitarian assistance to the civilian population. In turn, this reduces a substantial logistic burden on military forces, allowing them to focus on providing a safe, secure environment.

3-3. Success in stability operations often depends on the commander's ability to identify the tasks essential to mission success. Success also depends on the commander's ability to prioritize and sequence the execution of those tasks with available combat power, the diverse array of actors participating, and the ability of the host nation to accept change. Even more so than in the offense and defense, stability operations require commanders to demonstrate cultural astuteness and a clear understanding of the myriad stability tasks to determine which are truly essential to mission success.

3-4. The commander and staff identify essential stability tasks based on due consideration of the relevant mission variables. (See FM 3-0 for a discussion of mission variables.) Essential stability tasks are those that the force must successfully execute to accomplish the specific mission. These essential tasks may include specified and implied tasks required to establish the end state conditions that define success. They include stability tasks and supporting information engagement tasks that inform and influence a wide array of audiences. In addition, they include any essential offensive and defensive tasks associated with the defeat of an enemy force. Typically, these are initial response tasks for which military forces retain primary responsibility. Other tasks may be included that are not the primary responsibility of military forces. Some tasks are executed simultaneously and some sequentially.

3-5. For the commander and staff, stability operations require a unique combination of knowledge and understanding, the ability to achieve unity of effort, and a thorough depth of cultural astuteness. A finite amount of combat power is available to apply against the essential tasks associated with a given stability operation. Essential stability tasks lay the foundation for success of the other instruments of national power. This foundation must sustain the burdens of governance, rule of law, and economic development that represent the future viability of a state. Establishing this foundation depends on applying combat power to the essential stability tasks identified during the initial assessment of the situation and the framing of the basic problem. Decisions about using combat power are more than a factor of the size of the force deployed, its relative composition, and the anticipated nature and duration of the mission. Ensuring a state's long-term stability depends on applying combat power to those tasks that are, in fact, essential.

PRIMARY STABILITY TASKS

3-6. Stability operations aim to stabilize the environment enough so the host nation can begin to resolve the root causes of conflict and state failure. These operations establish a safe, secure environment that facilitates reconciliation among local or regional adversaries. Stability operations aim to establish conditions that support the transition to legitimate host-nation governance, a functioning civil society, and a viable market economy.

3-7. The size of the force and combination of tasks necessary to stabilize conditions depend on the situation in the operational area. When a functional, effective host-nation government exists, military forces work through and with local civil authorities. Together they restore stability and order and may be required to reform the security institutions that foster long-term development. In this situation, the size of the force and the scope of the mission are more limited. However, in a worst-case engagement scenario, the security environment is in chaos, and the state is in crisis or has failed altogether. In this situation, international law requires the military force to focus on essential tasks that establish a safe, secure environment and address the immediate humanitarian needs of the local populace. This requires a force capable of securing borders, protecting the population, holding individuals accountable for criminal activities, regulating the behavior of individuals or groups that pose a security risk, reestablishing essential civil services, and setting conditions in the operational area that enable the success of other actors.

3-8. Military forces provide support to facilitate the execution of tasks for which the host nation is normally responsible. Typically, these tasks have a security component ideally performed by military forces or a private security company. However, military forces sometimes provide logistic, medical, or administrative support to enable the success of civilian agencies and organizations. These tasks generally fall into one of three categories, representing the collective effort associated with a stability operation:

- Tasks for which military forces retain primary responsibility.
- Tasks for which civilian agencies or organizations likely retain responsibility, but military forces are prepared to execute.
- Tasks for which civilian agencies or organizations retain primary responsibility.

3-9. This chapter only addresses those essential tasks for which military forces retain primary responsibility or must be prepared to execute. Within each stability sector, the primary stability tasks focus effort toward the desired end state conditions for a specific execution time frame. For example, initial response tasks executed in the security sector typically focus on establishing a safe, secure environment. Finally, the five primary stability tasks are broken down into major subcategories that facilitate integration and synchronization of related activities.

3-10. The primary stability tasks reflect a myriad of interrelated activities conducted across the five stability sectors. Tasks executed in one sector inevitably create related effects in another; planned and executed appropriately, carefully sequenced activities complement and reinforce these effects. Achieving a specific objective or establishing certain conditions often requires performing a number of related tasks among different stability sectors. An example of this is the effort required to provide a safe, secure environment for the local populace. Rather than the outcome of a single task focused solely on the local populace, safety and security are broad effects. Military forces achieve them by ending hostilities, isolating belligerents and criminal elements, demobilizing armed groups, eliminating explosives and other hazards, and providing public order and safety. Sustaining that security over time requires the execution of even more tasks across all the stability sectors.

ESTABLISH CIVIL SECURITY

3-11. Within the security sector, initial response tasks aim to establish a safe and secure environment; transformation tasks focus on developing legitimate and stable security institutions; and fostering sustainability tasks consolidate host-nation capacity-building activities. These conditions define success within the sector but also reflect the end state that ensures the foundation for enduring stability and peace.

Enforce Cessation of Hostilities, Peace Agreements, and Other Arrangements

3-12. The tasks associated with this subcategory contribute to providing security and stability after an armed conflict while setting the conditions necessary to begin disarmament, demobilization, and reintegration. These tasks are critical to providing effective security for the local populace by reducing their exposure to the threat of violent conflict. The tasks help military forces establish a sustained peace by focusing on processes and activities fundamental to conflict transformation. The list of essential tasks may include—

- An initial response in which military forces—
  - Enforce ceasefires.
  - Supervise disengagement of belligerent forces.
  - Identify and neutralize potential adversaries.
  - Provide security for negotiations.
- Transformation in which military forces establish and control buffers, including demilitarized zones.

Determine Disposition and Constitution of National Armed and Intelligence Services

3-13. The tasks within this subcategory establish the conditions for successful security sector reform. These tasks focus on the security and intelligence institutions that form the underpinnings of an effective security sector based in a clearly defined legal framework. They provide the broad guidance and direction for the training and advising effort central to security sector reform. The list of essential tasks may include—

- An initial response in which military forces—
  - Implement a plan for disposition of host-nation forces, intelligence services, and other national security institutions.
  - Identify future roles, missions, and structure.
  - Vet senior officers and other individuals for past abuses and criminal activity.
- Transformation in which military forces—
  - Conduct security force assistance.
  - Build host-nation capacity to protect military infrastructure.
  - Establish defense institutions.
- Fostering sustainability in which military forces establish military-to-military programs with host-nation forces and services.

Conduct Disarmament, Demobilization, and Reintegration

3-14. A disarmament, demobilization, and reintegration program is fundamental to most efforts to establish stability and lasting peace. It includes physically disbanding armed groups, removing the means of combat from former combatants and belligerents, and reintegrating the latter two into society. The groups include men, women, and children. Many do not carry weapons; however, they support the fighting forces. Their communities and families perceive them as part of an armed group. Together, the tasks of disarmament, demobilization, and reintegration reduce a potential resurgence of armed conflict. Additionally, these tasks provide a means for these individuals and groups to reenter society as contributing members.

3-15. While the tasks that support the disarmament, demobilization, and reintegration program generally fall under civil security, the program itself represents one element of comprehensive security sector reform. (See chapter 6 for a detailed discussion of security sector reform.) The list of essential tasks may include—

- An initial response in which military forces—
  - Negotiate arrangements with belligerents.
  - Establish and enforce weapons control programs, including collection and destruction.
  - Provide reassurances and incentives for disarmed factions.
  - Establish a monitoring program.
  - Establish demobilization camps.
  - Ensure adequate health, food, and security for belligerents.
- Transformation in which military forces—
  - Disarm former combatants and belligerents.
  - Reduce availability of unauthorized weapons.
  - Ensure safety of quartered personnel and families.
  - Reintegrate former combatants and dislocated civilians into society.
- Fostering sustainability in which military forces—
  - Secure, store, and dispose of weapons.
  - Develop host-nation arms control capacity.

Conduct Border Control, Boundary Security, and Freedom of Movement

3-16. A central component of civil security is the ability of the state to monitor and regulate its borders. Generally, border and coast guard forces secure national boundaries while customs officials regulate the flow of people, animals, and goods across state borders. These border controls are necessary to regulate immigration, control the movements of the local populace, collect excise taxes or duties, limit smuggling, and control the spread of disease vectors through quarantine. The list of essential tasks may include—

- An initial response in which military forces—
  - Establish border control and boundary security.
  - Establish and disseminate rules relevant to movement.
  - Dismantle roadblocks and establish checkpoints.
  - Ensure freedom of movement.
- Transformation in which military forces train and equip border control and boundary security forces.

Support Identification

3-17. Identification programs complement efforts to vet host-nation personnel, encourage participation in representative government, resolve property disputes, and validate professional credentials. Although vital to other programs for rebuilding a functioning civil society, identification programs are equally important to civil security. After the collapse of an authoritarian or hostile regime, these programs ensure that potential adversaries do not inadvertently reintegrate into society. Thus, they are deprived of the ability to provide the seeds for future organized sabotage, subversion, or insurgency. The list of essential tasks may include—

- An initial response in which military forces—
  - Secure documents relating to personal identification, property ownership, court records, voter registries, professional certificates, birth records, and driving licenses.
  - Establish identification program.
  - Ensure individuals have personal forms of identification.
- Transformation in which military forces develop mechanisms for long-term dispute resolution.

Protect Key Personnel and Facilities

3-18. When required, military forces may extend protection and support to key civilian personnel to ensure their continued contribution to the overall stability operation. In the interest of transparency, military forces specifically request and carefully negotiate this protection. Similarly, the long-term success of any intervention often relies on the ability of external actors to protect and maintain critical infrastructure until the host nation can resume that responsibility. The list of essential tasks may include—

- An initial response in which military forces—
  - Protect government-sponsored civilian reconstruction and stabilization personnel.
  - Protect contractor and civilian reconstruction and stabilization personnel and resources.
  - Provide emergency logistic support, as required.
  - Protect and secure places of religious worship and cultural sites.
  - Protect and secure critical infrastructure, natural resources, civil registries, and property ownership documents.

- Protect and secure strategically important institutions (such as government buildings; medical and public health infrastructure; the central bank, national treasury, and integral commercial banks; museums; and religious sites).
- Protect and secure military depots, equipment, ammunition dumps, and means of communications.
- Identify, secure, protect, and coordinate disposition for stockpiles of munitions and chemical, biological, radiological, and nuclear (CBRN) materiel and precursors; facilities; and adversaries with technical expertise.
- Transformation in which military forces—
  - Build host-nation capacity to protect civilian reconstruction and stabilization personnel.
  - Build host-nation capacity to protect infrastructure and public institutions.
  - Build host-nation capacity to protect military infrastructure.

Clear Explosive and CBRN Hazards

3-19. In a state already burdened by collapsed institutions of central government, the presence of explosive hazards (including minefields and unexploded explosive ordnance) and CBRN hazards (resulting from intentional or accidental release) inflicts stress that the surviving institutions cannot bear. These hazards restrict freedom of movement, hinder international trade, and detract from the ability of a fragile state to secure its borders and boundaries. Military forces may clear unexploded explosive ordnance and other explosive hazards to facilitate capacity-building activities. Removing these hazards ensures the safety, security, and well-being of the local populace. (FM 3-34.210 includes tactics, techniques, and procedures for clearing explosive hazards.) The list of essential tasks may include—

- An initial response in which military forces—
  - Establish an explosive hazards coordination cell.
  - Conduct emergency clearing of mines, unexploded explosive ordnance, and other explosive hazards.
  - Map, survey, and mark mined areas, unexploded explosive ordnance, and other explosive hazards.
  - Remediate hazards remaining from the release of CBRN hazards and radiological fallout, as well as provide decontamination support.
- Transformation in which military forces—

- Create host-nation capacity to conduct demining.
- Build host-nation capability to export demining expertise.

3-20. The John Warner National Defense Authorization Act limits the assistance that military forces may provide with respect to demining. Military forces may assist and train others in demining techniques and procedures. However, no member of the armed forces—while providing humanitarian demining assistance—will engage in the physical detection, lifting, or destroying of landmines or other explosive remnants of war (unless the member does so for the concurrent purpose of supporting a U.S. military operation). Nor will any member provide such assistance as part of a military operation that does not involve the armed forces.

ESTABLISH CIVIL CONTROL

3-21. Civil control regulates selected behavior and activities of individuals and groups. It reduces risk to individuals or groups and promotes security. Within the justice and reconciliation stability sector, initial response tasks aim to develop interim mechanisms for establishing rule of law. Transformation tasks focus on restoring the justice system and processes for reconciliation. Fostering sustainability tasks serve to establish a legitimate, functioning justice system founded on international norms. These conditions define success within the sector while reflecting the end state necessary to ensure the foundation for enduring stability and peace.

Establish Public Order and Safety

3-22. The tasks within this category provide a broad range of activities to protect the civilian populace, provide interim policing and crowd control, and secure critical infrastructure. These essential tasks represent actions that must occur during and after direct armed conflict to ensure the long-term sustainability of any reform efforts. The speed and effectiveness in performing these tasks directly correlates with the length of time required to return the host nation to a normal state. Executing these tasks as soon as practical after intervening reduces the time required for related efforts and allows the mission to be accomplished far sooner. However the military's legal authorities for all activities in the justice sector, particularly involving enforcement and adjudication of the law, must be clear. The list of essential tasks may include—

- An initial response in which military forces—
  - Protect vulnerable elements of the population (such as dislocated civilians).
  - Ensure humanitarian aid and security forces have access to endangered populations and refugee camps.

- Perform civilian police functions, including investigating crimes and making arrests.
- Locate and safeguard key witnesses, documents, and other evidence related to key ongoing or potential investigations and prosecutions.
- Control crowds, prevent looting, and manage civil disturbances.
- Secure facilities, records, storage equipment, and funds related to criminal justice and security institutions.

- Transformation in which military forces—
  - Build host-nation capacity to protect military infrastructure.
  - Build host-nation capacity to protect infrastructure and public institutions.
  - Build host-nation capacity for emergency response.
- Fostering sustainability in which military forces identify modernization needs and the means to achieve them.

Establish Interim Criminal Justice System

3-23. When conditions require the restoration of governance, establishing an interim justice system is a prerequisite. This restoration requires a wide range of skilled professionals working under a clearly defined legal authority: judges, prosecutors, court administrators, defense lawyers, corrections personnel, law enforcement, and investigators. These personnel—and the institutions they represent—provide a temporary respite allowing the host nation to restore its capacity. The list of essential tasks may include an initial response in which military forces—

- Assess the current legal framework and the need for modifications or adoption of internationally accepted codes.
- Deploy interim justice personnel to complement host-nation criminal justice system.
- Establish mechanisms to review the legality of detentions and minor cases to minimize pretrial detention.
- Enact interim legal codes and procedures permitted by international law.
- Assess host-nation capacity to combat crime.

Support Law Enforcement and Police Reform

3-24. Integral to establishing civil control is the support military forces provide to law enforcement and policing operations. Host-nation civilian law enforcement agencies and organizations may provide this capability if the security environment permits. However, in a fragile state, these institutions may have become corrupt or failed altogether. In failed states, especially during and immediately after conflict, military police forces are the only organizations able to fill this void. At times, civilian law enforcement personnel augment military forces.

3-25. The preferred providers of civilian law enforcement services are civilian police, augmented as required by military and paramilitary police units with stability policing capabilities. Civilian agencies typically provide training and capacity-building support for law enforcement services. However, military forces may be required to perform these services on an interim basis, until the situation permits the transition of this function to civilian agencies or organizations. The list of essential tasks may include—

- An initial response in which military forces—
  - Identify, secure, and preserve evidence of war crimes, crimes against humanity, corruption, and transnational crime (terrorism, organized crime, human trafficking, and narcotics).
  - Identify and detain perpetrators of these offenses.
  - Support vetting, credentialing, and accounting for host-nation police forces.
  - Deploy police trainers and advisors.
  - Inventory and assess police facilities and systems.
- Transformation in which military forces—
  - Train and advise host-nation police forces.
  - Establish police academies.
  - Develop community interface forums.
  - Rehabilitate or construct necessary facilities.

Support Judicial Reform

3-26. The reform of judicial bodies is integral to rule of law and provides the necessary framework for broader security sector reform. The support provided to judicial institutions parallels efforts with police and security forces to enhance the state's capability to maintain civil control and security. Under most circumstances, other agencies and organizations typically support the development of the judicial branch of government. In a failed state, however, military forces may initially perform these functions until they can be transitioned to an appropriate civilian agency or organization. The list of essential tasks may include—

- An initial response in which military forces—
  - Identify host-nation legal professionals.
  - Identify actual and potential leaders to incorporate into reform process.
  - Determine gaps or inconsistencies with international human rights norms in legal framework.
  - Establish vetting criteria.
  - Educate criminal justice personnel on interim legal codes and international human rights standards.
  - Inventory and assess courts, law schools, legal libraries, and bar associations.
  - Deploy judicial advisors and liaisons.
- Transformation in which military forces—
  - Rehabilitate or construct necessary facilities.
  - Support vetting of host-nation legal professionals.

Support Property Dispute Resolution Processes

3-27. One of the most vital services provided by the judiciary branch is the resolution of property disputes. In a fragile state, long-standing disputes over ownership and control of property are common. Authorities must implement dispute resolution mechanisms. This prevents the escalation of violence that can occur in the absence of law and order as people seek resolution on their own terms. Typically, the military's role in resolving disputes is limited to transitional military authority where these mechanisms are implemented in the absence of a functioning host-nation government. The list of essential tasks may include an initial response in which military forces—

- Implement mechanisms to prevent unauthorized occupation or seizure of land or property.
- Publicize dispute resolution process.
- Coordinate dispute resolution process to deter violence and retribution.

Support Justice System Reform

3-28. Justice system reform, much like other reform processes, is integral to a comprehensive rule of law program and is necessary for successful security sector reform. Within the justice system, reform activities aim to reorganize basic structures, update legal statutes, encourage citizen participation, protect human rights, and ultimately achieve broad institutional reform. These activities are instrumental to establishing a justice system the local populace perceives as legitimate, fair, and effective. Although other civilian agencies typically lead reform efforts, military forces may conduct some critical tasks to establish the conditions necessary to facilitate future efforts. The list of essential tasks may include an initial response in which military forces—

- Support the development of a host-nation strategy to rebuild the justice system.
- Determine local due process norms and expectations.
- Develop awareness of notice and comment forums.
- Review current laws and resolve questions of applicability.
- Abolish provisions incompatible with international standards of human rights.
- Assess court administration capabilities and resources.

Support Corrections Reform

3-29. As with other reform processes, corrections reform is an integral component of broader security sector reform. Corrections reform tasks focus on building host-nation capacity in the penal system, restoring the institutional infrastructure, and providing oversight of the incarceration process. Tasks also include a comprehensive assessment of the prisoner population to help reintegrate political prisoners and others unjustly detained or held without due process. The list of essential tasks may include—

- An initial response in which military forces—
  - Identify and register all detention, correction, or rehabilitative facilities.
  - Preserve and secure penal administrative records and reports.
  - Inventory and assess prison populations and conditions.
  - Implement humanitarian standards in prisons.
  - Provide emergency detention facilities.
  - Vet corrections personnel.
  - Deploy penal trainers and advisors.
  - Refurbish prison facilities at key sites.
  - Coordinate jurisdiction and handover.
  - Facilitate international monitoring.
- Transformation in which military forces—
  - Rebuild corrections institutions.
  - Train and advise corrections personnel to internationally accepted standards.

■ Develop reconciliation, parole, and reintegration mechanisms.

Support War Crimes Courts and Tribunals

3-30. While the military government operates military commissions and provost courts, the international community oversees the conduct of war crimes courts and tribunals. As part of the broad processes that represent justice system reform, military forces identify, secure, and preserve evidence for courts and tribunals of war crimes and crimes against humanity. However, military forces also provide support in other forms, to include helping to establish courts and tribunals, supporting the investigation and arrest of war criminals, and coordinating efforts with other agencies and organizations. The list of essential tasks may include—

- An initial response in which military forces—
    ■ Acquire secure facilities.
    ■ Establish an atrocity reporting system.
    ■ Document and preserve evidence of mass atrocities.
    ■ Publish progress reports.
- Transformation in which military forces—
    ■ Assist in investigation, arrest, and transfer of suspected war criminals to international courts.
    ■ Support witness protection.
    ■ Support media access.

Support Public Outreach and Community Rebuilding Programs

3-31. Public outreach and community rebuilding programs are central to the reconciliation process and to promoting public respect for the rule of law. They provide the local populace with a means to form a cohesive society. While these programs generally do not involve substantial military involvement, some activities require the force's support to achieve success. The list of essential tasks may include an initial response in which military forces—

- Establish broad public information programs to promote reconciliation efforts.
- Develop public access to information.
- Assess needs of vulnerable populations.

RESTORE ESSENTIAL SERVICES

3-32. The activities associated with this primary stability task extend beyond simply restoring local civil services and addressing the effects of humanitarian crises. While military forces generally center efforts on the initial response tasks for immediate needs of the populace, other civilian agencies and organizations focus on broader humanitarian issues and social well-being. Transformation tasks establish the foundation for long-term development, resolving the root causes of conflict that lead to events such as famine, dislocated civilians, refugee flows, and human trafficking. Fostering sustainability tasks ensures the permanence of those efforts by institutionalizing positive change in society.

3-33. Normally, military forces support host-nation and civilian relief agencies with these efforts. However, when the host nation cannot perform its roles, military forces may execute these tasks directly or to support other civilian agencies and organizations. It is imperative that these activities are properly scaled to local capacity for sustainment. Proper scaling also creates the best opportunity for the local populace to create small-scale enterprises to provide as many of these essential services as possible through the private economy. Large-scale projects that require complicated host-nation efforts to sustain should not be initiated until the necessary infrastructure is in place to support such effort.

Provide Essential Civil Services

3-34. Although closely related to establishing and supporting effective local governance, efforts to provide essential civil services to the host-nation people involve developing the capacity to operate, maintain, and improve those services. This broader focus involves a societal component that encompasses long-range education and training, employment programs, and economic investment and development.

3-35. At the tactical level, activities of military forces to provide essential civil services are often defined in terms of the immediate humanitarian needs of the people: providing the food, water, shelter, and medical support necessary to sustain the population until local civil services are restored. Once their immediate needs are satisfied, efforts to restore basic services and transition control to civil authorities typically progress using lines of effort based on the memory aid, SWEAT-MSO (sewage, water, electricity, academics, trash, medical, safety, and other considerations). These lines of effort are vital to integrating efforts to reestablish local civil services with similar, related actions to establish a safe, secure environment. Military forces, specifically functional units or functional specialists, may support the effort to provide essential civil services by conducting detailed infrastructure reconnaissance. The list of essential tasks may include—

- An initial response in which military forces—
  - Provide for immediate humanitarian needs of the population (food, water, shelter, and medical support).
  - Ensure proper sanitation, purification, and distribution of drinking water.
  - Provide interim sanitation, wastewater, and waste disposal services.
- Transformation in which military forces build host-nation capacity to operate and maintain essential civil services.

Tasks Related to Civilian Dislocation

3-36. The following three task subcategories share similar characteristics related to the challenges associated with dislocated civilians. Intergovernmental and nongovernmental organizations, as well as other humanitarian actors, are best equipped and trained to manage the human crises associated with dislocated civilians. Intergovernmental organizations may include the United Nations and the International Organization for Migration. Nongovernmental organizations may include groups such as Cooperative Assistance for Relief Everywhere (known as CARE). Humanitarian actors may include the International Committee of the Red Cross, a well-known international organization.

3-37. The presence and uncontrolled flow of dislocated civilians can threaten the success of any stability operation. Dislocated civilians are symptoms of broader issues such as conflict, insecurity, and disparities among the population. How displaced populations are treated can either foster trust and confidence—laying the foundation for stabilization and reconstruction among a traumatized population—or create resentment and further chaos. Local and international aid organizations are most often best equipped to deal with the needs of the local populace but require a secure environment in which to operate. Through close cooperation, military forces can enable the success of these organizations by providing critical assistance to the populace.

3-38. Nearly 80 percent of all dislocated civilians are women or children. Most suffer from some form of posttraumatic stress disorder, and all require food, shelter, and medical care. Following a major disaster, humanitarian crisis, or conflict, providing adequate support to dislocated civilians often presents a challenge beyond the capability of available military forces. Therefore, military forces offer vital support—coordinated with the efforts of other agencies and organizations—to provide humanitarian assistance to the general population. The list of essential tasks includes—

- Assist dislocated civilians.
- Support assistance to dislocated civilians.
- Support security to dislocated civilians camps.

Assist Dislocated Civilians

3-39. When assisting dislocated civilians, military forces—

- Ensure humanitarian aid organizations have access to populations in need.
- Estimate food aid needs for affected populations.
- Assess the adequacy of local physical transport, distribution, and storage.

Support Assistance to Dislocated Civilians

3-40. When supporting efforts to assist dislocated civilians, the list of essential tasks may include—

- An initial response in which military forces—
  - Estimate food aid needs for dislocated civilians.
  - Assess the adequacy of local physical transport, distribution, and storage.
  - Establish camps for dislocated civilians.
  - Provide emergency food, water, shelter, sanitation, and medical care to dislocated civilians.
- Transformation in which military forces—
  - Ensure access to basic services, including education and health care.
  - Clear damaged and destroyed housing and assess damage.

Support Security to Dislocated Civilians Camps

3-41. When supporting dislocated civilians camp security, the list of essential tasks may include—

- An initial response in which military forces—
  - Assess conditions of temporary shelters and camps for dislocated civilians.
  - Ensure adequate protection and monitoring of camps.
  - Ensure access of humanitarian aid organizations and security forces to camps.
- Transformation in which military forces assist in establishing and maintaining order in camps.

Support Famine Prevention and Emergency Food Relief Programs

3-42. Famine-prone countries are a unique subcategory of fragile states and require special focus. Without exception, weak and failing economic, governance, health, and food systems at the national level increase famine vulnerability. The combination of weak institutions, poor policies, and environmental change often results in famine. Famine may result in food insecurity, increased poverty, morbidity, malnutrition, and mortality. Government agencies—such as the U.S. Agency for International Development—numerous nongovernmental organizations, and the United Nations are instrumental to response efforts in famine-prone states. They oversee the major relief programs that provide emergency food aid to suffering populations.

3-43. Military support of these efforts is minimal but vital to the overall success of the operation. The list of essential tasks may include—

- An initial response in which military forces—
  - Monitor and analyze food security and market prices.
  - Predict the effects of conflict on access to food.
  - Estimate total food needs.
  - Assess the adequacy of local physical transport, distribution, and storage of food.
  - Deliver emergency food aid to most vulnerable populations.
- Transformation in which military forces ensure safe access to transportation and distribution networks.

Support Nonfood Relief Programs

3-44. Military forces offer significant support capability to the broader effort to provide nonfood relief during humanitarian crises. Any support provided for nonfood relief programs for dislocated civilians should be closely coordinated with the relevant host-nation ministry, United Nations agency, and appropriate aid organizations. Although the related tasks are minimal, they greatly influence the long-term success of these efforts. The list of essential tasks may include—

- An initial response in which military forces—
  - Secure emergency nonfood relief distribution networks.
  - Deliver emergency nonfood items.
- Transformation in which military forces clear devastated housing and assess damage.

Support Humanitarian Demining

3-45. Humanitarian demining is related to the subordinate task *clear explosive and CBRN hazards* under the primary stability task *establish civil security*; however, this task focuses on supporting the humanitarian aspects of demining, while the task *clear explosive and CBRN hazards* is generally considered a protection-related task. In fragile states, vast minefields and unexploded explosive ordnance pose a significant hazard to freedom of movement. Marking and removing these hazards initiates long-term recovery, especially along major transport routes and in critical public facilities. In comprehensive demining programs, much of the effort focuses on educating the local populace on how to recognize, avoid, and report the presence of mines and unexploded explosive ordnance. The list of essential tasks may include—

- An initial response in which military forces—
  - Map and survey mined areas.
  - Mark minefields.
  - Treat initial injuries.
- Transformation in which military forces—
  - Educate the local populace to recognize and avoid mines.
  - Build host-nation capacity to conduct demining.

Support Human Rights Initiatives

3-46. Often, forces that intervene after conflict or disaster encounter conditions of human suffering beyond their ability to resolve. Such situations require the dedicated support of intergovernmental and nongovernmental organizations able to provide long-term solutions to complex humanitarian issues. The military contribution to these efforts generally involves preventing further abuse of vulnerable populations and establishing conditions that support long-term development. These conditions enable the success of the agencies and organizations that provide for the long-term well-being of these populations. Military forces play a critical role in promoting the rule of law in preventing human rights abuses within its own ranks. The list of essential tasks may include an initial response in which military forces monitor vulnerable groups, provide information and referrals to groups whose rights may be violated, and act preemptively to deter human rights abuses.

Support Public Health Programs

3-47. The military contribution to the public health sector, especially early in an operation, enables the complementary efforts of local and international aid organizations. The initial efforts of military forces aim to stabilize the public health situation within the operational area. These efforts may include assessments of the civilian medical and public health system such as infrastructure, medical staff, training and education, medical logistics, and public health programs. Following these initial response tasks, civilian organizations tailor their efforts to reforming the public health sector through health systems strengthening and other public health capacity-building activities. Health systems strengthening involves reducing bureaucracy by streamlining management, increasing cost-effectiveness, improving efficiency through reorganized services, decentralizing health systems, and allocating resources to better address the needs of the population. Achieving measurable progress requires early coordination and constant dialog with other actors; ultimately, this also facilitates a successful transition from military-led efforts to civilian organizations or the host nation.

3-48. The tasks performed to support public health programs closely relate to the tasks required to restore essential services. In many cases, they complement and reinforce those efforts. The list of essential tasks may include—

- An initial response in which military forces—
  - Assess public health hazards within their area of operations and area of interest including malnutrition, water sources, and sewer and other sanitation services.
  - Assess existing medical infrastructure including preventative and veterinary services, health—physical and psychological—care systems, and medical logistics.
  - Evaluate the need for additional medical capabilities.
  - Repair existing civilian clinics and hospitals.
  - Operate or augment the operations of existing civilian medical facilities.
  - Prevent epidemics through immediate vaccinations.
- Transformation in which military forces—
  - Support improvements to local waste and wastewater management capacity.
  - Promote and enhance the host-nation medical infrastructure.

Support Education Programs

3-49. Military activities to support education programs generally focus on physical infrastructure. In some cases, trained personnel with appropriate civilian backgrounds provide additional services such as administrative or educational expertise. The efforts of civilian organizations aim to improve adult literacy, train teachers and administrators, develop curricula, and improve school-age access to education. The list of essential tasks may include—

- An initial response in which military forces repair and reopen schools as quickly as possible.
- Transformation in which military forces build schools.

SUPPORT TO GOVERNANCE

3-50. When a legitimate and functional host-nation government is present, military forces operating to support the state have a limited role. However, if the host-nation government cannot adequately perform its basic civil functions—whatever the reason—some degree of military support to governance may be necessary. A state's legitimacy among its people is tied in part to its perceived ability to provide these essential services. In extreme cases, where civil government is completely dysfunctional or absent altogether, international law requires the military force to provide the basic civil administration functions of the host-nation government under the auspices of a transitional military authority. (See chapter 5 for a detailed discussion of transitional military authority.)

Support Transitional Administrations

3-51. When the host-nation government has collapsed or been deposed, initial response efforts focus on immediately filling the void in governance. In either situation, the reliability and trustworthiness of local officials is suspect; due care and prudence are necessary to avoid empowering officials whose interests and loyalties are inconsistent with those of the occupying force. The list of essential tasks may include—

- An initial response in which military forces—
  - Vet host-nation officials.
  - Reconstitute leadership at multiple levels of government.
  - Establish interim legislative processes.
- Transformation in which military forces advise and assist transitional administrations.

Support Development of Local Governance

3-52. Establishing effective governance at the local level is necessary before developing governance institutions and processes throughout the state. Initially, effective local governance almost depends entirely on the ability to provide essential civil services to the people; restoring these services is also fundamental to humanitarian relief efforts. (See paragraph 2-55 for additional discussion on the primary stability task, *restore essential services*.) Most stability tasks require an integrated and synchronized effort across all sectors to achieve the desired end state. The list of essential tasks may include—

- An initial response in which military forces—
  - Establish mechanisms for local-level participation.
  - Identify, secure, rehabilitate, and maintain basic facilities for the local government.
  - Restore essential local public services.
  - Provide resources to maintain essential local public services.
- Transformation in which military forces advise local legislatures and civil servants during administrative actions.

Support Anticorruption Initiatives

3-53. Providing legal guidance and assistance to the transitional government mitigates the near-term effects of corruption. Long-term measures ensure lasting success. Corruption and graft can hinder efforts to establish governance, restore rule of law, or institute economic recovery. While some level of corruption is common to many cultures, its existence can unhinge reform efforts and put the entire mission at risk. The list of essential tasks may include an initial response in which military forces create mechanisms to curtail corruption across government institutions. The list of essential tasks may include an initial response in which military forces—

- Implement or reaffirm government employee oaths of office.
- Develop and disseminate ethical standards for civil servants.
- Ensure transparency in the dispersal of government resources.
- Implement reporting procedures for corruption and intimidation.
- Support witness protection programs.

Support Elections

3-54. The ability of the state and its local subdivisions to stage fair and secure elections is a significant milestone toward establishing legitimate, effective governance. While civilian agencies and organizations that maintain strict transparency guide the elections process, military forces provide the support that enables broad participation by the local populace. The list of essential tasks may include—

- An initial response in which military forces—
  - Determine identification requirements for voter registration.
  - Establish or verify voter registry.
- Transformation in which military forces provide security to ensure free and fair elections.

SUPPORT TO ECONOMIC AND INFRASTRUCTURE DEVELOPMENT

3-55. Sound economic policies promote equitable, sustainable growth. It is the key to remedying underlying tensions in society. This allows the state to progress toward recovery and eventually long-term economic development. Therefore, any effort to establish economic stabilization is closely linked to similar efforts in other stability sectors. Linking these efforts expands the possibilities for changing the underlying social, economic, and political conditions that led to the collapse of the state. Synchronizing reform efforts among the economic, governance, and security sectors decreases the chance of continued or renewed conflict.

3-56. Building capacity within the economic sector requires an integrated approach to achieve sustainable growth. Appropriate civilian or host-nation organizations can accomplish much of this effort at the macro level through development mechanisms but may look to the military for security or other types of assistance. Despite this, military forces must maintain an understanding of the economic sector, the impact of their activities on the economy, and the proper method to lay a stabilizing foundation that will support future sustainability and development.

3-57. At the local level, military forces play a significant role in supporting economic stabilization and infrastructure development. The building blocks for broad national recovery and development are set at the local level. At the local level, emphasis is on generating employment opportunities, infusing monetary resources into the local economy, stimulating market activity, fostering recovery through microeconomics, and supporting the restoration of physical infrastructure. However, military forces must avoid causing unintended disruptions to the local markets by suddenly stimulating the economy. Unanticipated demand on local markets may cause prices to spike, thus making products cost prohibitive for the people. This may cause resentment and undermine broader efforts, particularly if the military force is only in the area for a short time and a sudden collapse in market activity occurs after its departure. Thus, it is critical that members of the force understand the economic fundamentals of the area—key markets, revenue producers, and price trends—to gauge the impact of military activities.

3-58. At the regional or national level, efforts focus on comprehensive infrastructure improvements, such as rebuilding a national electrical grid system or on supporting the efforts of other agencies to strengthen the economy or foster development. Intergovernmental organizations such as the World Bank, the International Monetary Fund, and the Organisation for Economic Co-operation and Development help set sound economic policies and establish conditions for long-term development and investment. (See *The [Organisation for Economic Co-operation and Development Development Assistance Committee] Handbook on Security System Reform (SSR): Supporting Security and Justice* for more information.)

Support Economic Generation and Enterprise Creation

3-59. Economic recovery begins with an actively engaged labor force. When a military force occupies an operational area, the demand for local goods, services, and labor creates employment opportunities for the local populace. Local projects, such as restoring public services, rebuilding schools, or clearing roads, offer additional opportunities for the local labor pool. Drawing on local goods, services, and labor presents the force with the first opportunity to infuse cash into the local economy, which in turn stimulates market activity. However, this initial economic infusion must be translated into consistent capital availability and sustainable jobs programs. Thus, short-term actions are taken with an eye towards enabling financial self-reliance and the creation of a durable enterprise and job market.

3-60. The local economy requires this stimulus to sustain economic generation and enterprise creation. It includes efforts to execute contracting duties; identify, prioritize, and manage local projects; and implement employment programs. Often, such programs reinforce efforts to establish security and civil order by providing meaningful employment and compensation for the local populace. The assessment of the economic sector must include developing knowledge and understanding of local pay scales; this is essential to establishing jobs programs with appropriately wages. Inflated pay scales may divert critical professionals from their chosen field in pursuit of short-term financial gains from new jobs created by the force. Establishing appropriate pay scales is also significant when the environment includes illicit actors willing to pay for actions or services in direct conflict with the aims of the force. Adversaries can easily exploit relatively low pay scales and quickly undermine efforts to build positive perceptions among the people.

3-61. Host-nation enterprise creation is an essential activity whereby the local people organize themselves to provide valuable goods and services. In doing so, they create jobs for themselves, their families, and neighbors that are inherently sustainable after the departure of other actors. Host-nation enterprises may provide various goods and services, including essential services such as small-scale sewerage, water, electricity, transportation, health care, and communications. The availability of financing through banking or microfinance institutions is essential to enterprise creation.

3-62. Local jobs programs require a complementary vetting program to ensure the reliability of the workforce, especially if the labor pool draws from a population that includes former combatants. Linking vetting tasks with efforts to support economic generation mitigates risk to the force and the local populace. The list of essential tasks may include—

- An initial response in which military forces—
  - Implement initiatives to provide immediate employment.
  - Create employment opportunities for all ages and genders.
  - Assess the labor force for critical skills requirements and shortfalls.
  - Assess market sector for manpower requirements and pay norms.
- Transformation in which military forces—
  - Implement public works projects.
  - Support establishment of a business registry to register lawful business activity at the local or provincial level.
  - Provide start-up capital for small businesses through small-scale enterprise grants.
  - Encourage the creation of small lending institutions.
  - Enable the development of financial institutions.

Support Monetary Institutions and Programs

3-63. At the operational level, the military force focuses on supporting the strengthening of the national economy, including the central bank, which acts as the physical repository of government funds and maintains the stability of the currency and financial (banking) systems of the country. Normally, other agencies lead this effort while the military provides support to ensure the broad success of the mission. Efforts include selecting a national currency, working through the central bank to ensure the solvency of commercial financial institutions, and balancing government expenditures and revenue. Organizations such as the Department of the Treasury, World Bank, and the International Monetary Fund provide the means and expertise to establish or reform the central bank. The Department of the Treasury possesses the capability to dispatch civilian experts along with or immediately after military forces to ensure adequate crisis management. In some instances, international institutions can provide the fiscal resources to manage the currency while maintaining the national budget. The list of essential tasks may include an initial response in which military forces—

- Facilitate assessment of capabilities of central bank and ministry of finance.
- Assist in the distribution of currency to key banking outlets.
- Initiate immediate capacity in the central bank to conduct essential operations.

Support National Treasury Operations

3-64. In most nations, the finance ministry is the central authority for establishing fiscal policy regarding the use of government resources. In fragile states, this ministry is often among the first institutions to collapse, resulting in high unemployment, uncontrolled inflation, and other financial crises. Restoring the payment programs of the national treasury ministry, identifying and renewing sources of revenue, and developing the host nation's fiscal capacity are central to reestablishing the economic viability of the state. The Department of the Treasury, U.S. Agency for International Development, and international organizations can provide assistance in these areas. In states suffering from economic collapse, the failure of the national treasury may leave essential regional or local public services without a paid work force. Reestablishing government payment programs complements efforts to restore and maintain these vital public works. The list of essential tasks may include an initial response in which military forces—

- Reestablish government payment mechanisms to fulfill recurrent and emergency expenditures.
- Establish simple and reliable capacity to process, record, and report payments.
- Facilitate assessment of revenue-generating activities for the national treasury.
- Identify tax structure and sources of revenue.
- Facilitate establishment of basic audit functions to ensure officials use local government resources appropriately.

Support Public Sector Investment Programs

3-65. Although organizations such as U.S. Agency for International Development usually manage public sector investment in a fragile state, the military force also can influence success in these programs. Public sector investment ensures the long-term viability of public education, health care, and mass transit. It also provides for development in industries—such as mining, oil, and natural gas—and hydroelectricity. At the local level, military forces may spur investment through grant programs or direct public investment projects. The list of essential tasks may include—

- An initial response in which military forces—
  - Prioritize public investment needs.
  - Develop plans to allocate available resources.
  - Pay civil service debts.
- Transformation in which military forces invest in critical projects neglected by the private sector.

Support Private Sector Development

3-66. Developing the private sector typically begins with employing large portions of the labor force. In addition to acquiring goods and services from the local economy, the tasks that support private sector development infuse much-needed cash into local markets and initiate additional public investment and development. Even in the most remote, austere regions of the world, local markets offer unique entrepreneurial opportunities, as well as services often considered vital to the economies of developed countries. The list of essential tasks may include—

- An initial response in which military forces—
  - Assess the depth of the private sector and enterprise creation.
  - Identify obstacles to private sector development.
- Transformation in which military forces—
  - Facilitate access to markets.
  - Strengthen the private sector through contracting and outsourcing.
  - Provide investors with protection and incentives.
  - Facilitate access to credit for legitimate banking and financial activity.

Protect Natural Resources and Environment

3-67. Protecting a nation's natural resources is an extension of the requirement to secure and protect other institutions of the state. Additionally, it preserves the long-term economic development and investment capacity of a fragile state. This capacity includes the revenues generated by the storage, distribution, and trade in natural resources. Rival factions often target these resources to finance illegitimate interests. The list of essential tasks may include—

- An initial response in which military forces assess and secure access to vital natural resources.
- Transformation in which military forces prevent the illicit generation of revenues from natural resources.

Support Agricultural Development Programs

3-68. The agricultural sector is a cornerstone of a viable market economy, providing crops and livestock vital to local markets and international trade. The development of this sector may be hindered by property disputes, difficulty accessing nearby markets, poor irrigation, animal disease, minefields, or unexploded explosive ordnance. Therefore, development agencies prioritize and integrate projects with related tasks in other stability sectors to establish and institutionalize practical solutions to the long-term growth of the agricultural sector. The military contribution to agricultural development parallels related efforts to spur economic growth in local communities. Together, they draw on local labor pools to help reestablish basic services central to the agricultural sector. The list of essential tasks may include—

- An initial response in which military forces—
  - Assess the state of agricultural sector.
  - Secure and protect postharvest storage facilities.
  - Rebuild small-scale irrigation systems.
  - Establish work programs to support agricultural development.
- Transformation in which military forces—
  - Protect water sources.
  - Identify constraints to production.
  - Assess health, diversity, and numbers of animals.
  - Channel food aid to promote market activity.
  - Establish transportation and distribution networks.
  - Encourage host-nation enterprise creation to provide goods and services to the agricultural sector.
  - Ensure open transit and access to local markets.

Restore Transportation Infrastructure

3-69. Restoring the transportation and distribution capability of the state is central to economic recovery. An underdeveloped or incapacitated transportation infrastructure limits freedom of movement, trade, social interaction, and development. Military forces often initiate immediate improvement to the transportation and distribution networks of the host nation. These networks enable freedom of maneuver, logistic support, and the movement of personnel and materiel to support ongoing operations. Transportation infrastructure improvements help to ease the transportation challenges common to relief efforts in fragile states. These improvements facilitate the vital assistance efforts of civilian agencies and organizations that follow in the wake of military forces. The list of essential tasks may include an initial response in which military forces—

- Assess overall condition of national transportation infrastructure (airports, roads, bridges, railways, and coastal and inland ports, harbors, and waterways), including facilities and equipment.
- Determine and prioritize essential infrastructure programs and projects.
- Conduct expedient repairs or build new facilities to facilitate commercial trade.

Restore Telecommunications Infrastructure

3-70. The telecommunications infrastructure of the state exists to support every element of a society, from the government to the financial sector, and from the media to the local populace. The failure of this infrastructure accelerates the collapse of the state, isolates the state and the populace from the outside world, and hampers development efforts. The military contribution to reconstruction efforts in the telecommunications infrastructure is limited; normally, few essential tasks exist in this area. The list of essential tasks may include an initial response in which military forces—

- Assess overall condition of the national telecommunications infrastructure.
- Determine and prioritize essential infrastructure programs and projects.

Support General Infrastructure Reconstruction Programs

3-71. General infrastructure reconstruction programs focus on rehabilitating the state's ability to produce and distribute fossil fuels, generate electrical power, exercise engineering and construction support, and provide municipal and other services to the populace. The United States Army Corps of Engineers and Field Force Engineering have the expertise to support host-nation capacity building in many of these areas. Such capacity building spurs rehabilitation efforts that establish the foundation for long-term development. As with the restoration of essential services, support to general infrastructure programs requires a thorough understanding of the civil component of the operational area. Civil affairs (CA) personnel support this information collection to help prioritize programs and projects.

3-72. The forward engineer support team, part of the United States Army Corps of Engineers, provides detailed infrastructure reconnaissance in the operational area. These efforts are central to understanding the needs of the state and prioritizing programs and projects. In a fragile state, fuels, energy, engineering, and construction industries represent the difference between a primitive tribal state and a developing country with a vibrant, functioning society. The list of essential tasks may include an initial response in which military forces—

- Assess overall condition of national energy infrastructure.
- Determine and prioritize essential infrastructure programs and projects.
- Assess conditions of existing power generation and distribution facilities.
- Assess conditions of existing natural resources conversion and distribution facilities.
- Assess conditions of existing facilities integral to effectively execute essential tasks in other sectors.
- Assess conditions of existing local, municipal facilities that provide essential services.
- Conduct expedient repairs or build new facilities to support local populace (such as schools, medical clinics, and municipal buildings).

INFORMATION ENGAGEMENT TASKS

3-73. Although not considered stability tasks, information engagement tasks are fundamental to each stability sector. Information engagement tasks are deliberately integrated with activities in each stability sector and primary stability task to complement and reinforce the success of operations. This integration is vital to success; information engagement tasks must be carefully sequenced with other tasks and supported with thorough risk assessments. Exploiting or ceding the initiative within the information domain is often a matter of precise timing and coordination. Combined with broad efforts to reduce the drivers of conflict and build host-nation capacity, information engagement is essential to achieving decisive results: the recovery of the host-nation government and the attainment of a lasting, stable peace. Figure 3-1 on page 3-31 illustrates the relationship between information engagement and each of the primary stability tasks.

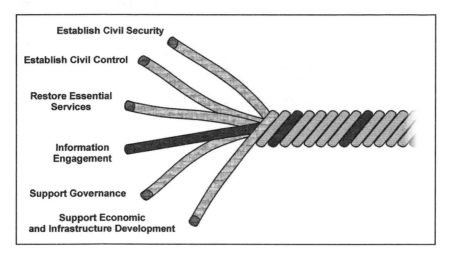

Figure 3-1. Relating information engagement to the primary stability tasks

3-74. In executing stability operations, the military force focuses on people. They aim to gain the cooperation and support of the populace. Stability tasks that improve their safety, security, and livelihood help to shape their perceptions that supporting the objectives of the operation are in their best interest. Shaping perceptions that the operation is legitimate will increase support for it. Executing the following essential tasks can further the populace's and the international community's understanding of the commander's objectives:

- Identify or establish outlets for international, national, and local news media.
- Provide factual, accurate information to the media to control rumors and disinformation.
- Issue effective press releases and prompt information in local languages.
- Assist transitional civil or military authorities with public information programs.
- Synchronize messages with operations; ensure messages are consistent with actions.
- Assess media capability and capacity of the host nation; tailor information engagement strategy to the ability of the local populace to receive messages.

- Integrate cultural understanding with information engagement strategy.

THE ROLE OF CIVIL AFFAIRS IN STABILITY OPERATIONS

3-75. CA forces support full spectrum operations in every environment across the spectrum of conflict, from stable peace to general war. They are essential to the conduct of successful stability operations. CA personnel provide unique area and linguistic orientation, cultural astuteness, advisory capabilities, and civilian professional skills that generally parallel those of host-nation governments. They provide the commander with specialized expertise on the civil component of the operational environment. The commander draws on this expertise to analyze and influence the human dimension through specific processes and dedicated resources and personnel.

THE CIVIL AFFAIRS MISSION

3-76. The mission of CA forces is to engage and influence the local populace by planning, executing, and transitioning CA operations in Army, joint, interagency, and multinational operations. These forces conduct CA operations that support and are nested within the overall operation. CA forces support these operations by addressing civil considerations within the operational area before, during, or after a conflict or disaster. CA forces help to shape the operational environment by interacting with the local populace to facilitate military operations. A supportive local populace can provide valuable resources and critical information that supports friendly operations. A hostile local populace threatens the immediate success of military operations and may undermine domestic public support for those operations. When executed properly, CA operations reduce the friction between the local populace and the military force.

CIVIL AFFAIRS OPERATIONS

3-77. During full spectrum operations, CA forces conduct operations that support and are nested within the overall mission and commander's intent. CA operations improve the relationship between military forces and host-nation authorities in areas in which the military force operates. They involve applying CA functional specialty skills to areas normally under the responsibility of a host-nation government. CA operations establish, maintain, influence, or exploit relationships between military forces and all levels of host-nation governments and officials. These operations are fundamental to executing stability tasks successfully.

3-78. CA organizations and personnel develop detailed assessments based on civil considerations. These include information about infrastructure, civilian institutions, and attitudes and activities of civilian leaders, the local populace, and host-nation organizations. These assessments may reveal that a viable host-nation government does not exist or cannot perform its basic civil functions. In such cases, military forces may support or implement transitional military authority until a legitimate host-nation government is established. (JP 3-57 and FMs 3-05.40 and 3-05.401 provide doctrine on CA.)

3-79. CA operations help to ensure the sustained legitimacy of the mission and the transparency and credibility of the military force. This is accomplished by minimizing the effects of military operations on the local populace, limiting how civilians impact those military operations, and providing sound advice to the commander on the legal and moral obligations of the force as it conducts operations. The key to successful CA operations is in leveraging the relationship between the military force and every individual, group, and organization in the operational area.

3-80. CA personnel help the commander to understand and visualize the civil component of the operational area. They provide detailed analysis based on careful consideration of operational and mission variables. (See FM 3-0 for doctrine for the operational and mission variables.) This analysis is critical to determining the following within the supported unit's operational area:

- The root causes of instability and civil strife.
- The requirement for civil-military operations centers to facilitate communications and coordinate with civilian agencies and organizations.
- The need to use liaison teams to enhance communications and coordination with civilian agencies and organizations to facilitate operations at all echelons.
- What, when, where, and why civilians might be encountered; what ongoing or planned military operations might impact the activities of those civilians; what activities those civilians are engaged in that might affect military operations; and what actions the military force must take to mitigate the effects of those civilians.
- Measures of performance and measures of effectiveness for CA operations to support the larger military operation.

MISSION-ESSENTIAL TASKS IN STABILITY OPERATIONS

3-81. A mission-essential task is a collective task a unit must be capable of performing successfully to accomplish its mission. Since organizations must be able to conduct full spectrum operations, they cannot afford to focus training exclusively on one element of full spectrum operations at the expense of the other elements. Yet they also cannot conceivably maintain proficiency on all tasks across the spectrum of conflict. Therefore, commanders use the mission-essential task list to focus organizational training. There are three types of mission-essential task lists:

- Joint mission-essential task list derived from the Universal Joint Task List.
- Core mission-essential task list (CMETL) standardized for brigades and above units by the Department of the Army.
- Directed mission-essential task list (DMETL) developed by a commander.

3-82. Units train on only a single mission-essential task list at any given time but may be required to report readiness on more than one mission-essential task list.

CORE MISSION-ESSENTIAL TASK LIST

3-83. An organization's CMETL is a list of the tasks derived from a unit's specific capabilities based on the organization, mission, and doctrine for that unit. A CMETL reflects the tasks the organization was designed to perform and general tasks applicable to all organizations, regardless of type. The CMETL consists of general mission-essential tasks and core capabilities mission-essential tasks. Each mission-essential task is comprised of task groups of related collective tasks that support a specific portion of a mission capability. (See FM 7-0 for a detailed discussion of general mission-essential tasks and core capabilities mission-essential tasks.)

3-84. For stability operations, the specific focus of the CMETL will typically vary between echelons and organizations and will be regulated by procedures outlined in FM 7-0. However, for all echelons, CMETL will aim for proficiency in those tasks most likely during or immediately after a violent conflict or disaster. Divisions and corps will orchestrate a broad range of missions and must maintain proficiency in selected primary stability tasks during training. Since CMETLs are reviewed periodically by Headquarters, Department of the Army, those lists and their associated task groups are subject to change. For division and corps headquarters, an example of the task groups underpinning the core capabilities mission-essential task of *conduct stability operations* could include the following:

- *Establish civil security.*
- *Establish civil control.*
- *Restore essential services.*

3-85. For brigade-level headquarters, the focus of the CMETL varies according to the type of brigade, its mission, and established doctrine. The CMETL only trains brigades to minimum capability. In stability operations, the brigade combat team remains the principal means of executing the broad range of tasks required for success. Other brigade-level organizations, such as the maneuver enhancement brigade, play a significant role in stability operations; these brigades provide the force with significant capabilities to conduct a wide array of stability tasks. For these support brigades, the CMETL will likely focus training on providing their core capabilities mission-essential tasks during full spectrum operations, including the stability element. For example, an aviation brigade may provide specific support focused on stability tasks performed by other elements of the force.

3-86. Functional brigades, like the support brigades, have a subordinate organizational structure that may vary considerably among brigades of the same type. Unlike the support brigades, however, functional brigades typically operate under theater army control and depend on theater-level elements for signal and other support. The theater army may task-organize them to corps or division headquarters. For functional brigades, the core capabilities mission-essential tasks reflect the most likely tasks according to its organization, mission, and doctrine.

DIRECTED MISSION-ESSENTIAL TASK LIST

3-87. When an organization is assigned a specific mission, the focus of organizational training shifts from CMETL to a DMETL and training conditions that realistically portray mission conditions. The commander develops a list of the tasks required to accomplish that mission. This list, a unit's DMETL, is based on a thorough mission analysis and, once established, forms the new foundation and focus for unit training until mission accomplishment. When developing the DMETL, commanders may capture a broad range of stability tasks required for the directed mission, possibly expanding on the CMETL significantly.

3-88. Analysis of the situation and conditions within the operational area helps determine the DMETL with respect to specific stability tasks. The DMETL for stability operations may remain consistent with a unit's CMETL, assume a broader focus on tasks that encompass reconstruction activities, or focus on stability tasks conducted during peacetime military engagement. For division and corps headquarters, the DMETL may expand to include the primary stability tasks *support to governance* and *support to economic and infrastructure development.* (See FM 7-0 for doctrine on CMETL and DMETL development.)

3-89. For brigade-level organizations, the DMETL may expand to include various tasks that support the efforts of the other instruments of national power, the host nation, and other actors and stakeholders. In operations where host-nation security forces cannot provide security adequately for the state and its people, brigade combat teams may be assigned the mission of conducting security force assistance. Though not integral to the CMETL of these organizations, security force assistance draws on many skills already resident in these organizations, as well as the developed command and control infrastructure to coordinate the broad and often dispersed efforts involved. (See chapter 6 for a discussion of security force assistance.)

Chapter 4

Planning for Stability Operations

A plan, like a tree, must have branches—if it is to bear fruit. A plan with a single aim is apt to prove a barren pole.

Captain Sir Basil Liddell Hart
Thoughts on War

PLANNING FUNDAMENTALS

4-1. For every operation, commanders develop personal, detailed understanding of the situation and operational environment. They then visualize a desired end state and craft a broad concept for shaping the current conditions toward that end state. Finally, they describe their visualization through the commander's intent, planning guidance, and concept of operations, setting formal planning processes in motion. Thus, planning is an adaptive process that ebbs and flows with the situation; as understanding of the situation evolves, planners develop branches and sequels to account for such evolution. Planning is a continuous activity, constantly adapting as the conditions of the operational environment are shaped by activities, both natural and human. Since planning is an ongoing process, the resultant plan is an interim product of deliberate thought, based on knowledge and understanding at a specific point in time and space. The truest measure of a good plan is not whether execution occurs as planned, but whether the plan fosters flexibility, initiative, and adaptability in the face of unforeseen events.

4-2. Planning consists of two separate, but closely related aspects: a conceptual component, represented by the less tangible aspects of visualization, and a detailed component, which introduces specificity to the plan through a deliberate process. During planning these activities overlap; there is no clear delineation between either. As commanders conceptualize the operation, their vision informs the staff to add detail to the plan. As the plan increases in detail, it helps to refine the commander's visualization. This chapter addresses the conceptual component of planning.

REDUCE COMPLEXITY

4-3. Conflict, by nature, is a complex endeavor; it is fundamentally human in character and, as such, is inherently unpredictable in nature. Uncertainty, chance, and friction are ubiquitous. This is the essence of complexity. In an era of persistent conflict, human interaction, globalization, and technological diffusion characterize an increasingly complex global security environment. Planning provides the tools necessary to understand this environment and to minimize the adverse effects of complexity on operations.

4-4. Given the inherently uncertain nature of war, the object of planning is not to eliminate or minimize uncertainty but to foster decisive and effective action in the midst of such uncertainty. Planning does not aim to predict the future but contains an element of forecasting. Effective planning provides an informed forecast of how future events are likely to unfold based on understanding the current situation and conditions of the operational environment. This forecast accounts for the uncertainty, chance, and friction innate to complex situations. Commanders express it through planning as flexibility and adaptability.

4-5. Simplicity is central to reducing complexity in planning. The most effective plans are clear, concise, and direct. Simplicity fosters a shared understanding of the situation, the problem, and the solution. It counters the effects of complexity by encouraging Soldiers to exercise initiative, accept prudent risks, and seize opportunities. A well-conceived plan accounts for risk and spurs initiative. It is flexible enough to allow for adaptation within the commander's intent yet sufficiently clear to ensure that all effort focuses on a common understanding of the desired end state.

INCULCATE AN OFFENSIVE MINDSET

4-6. Planning is essential to the ability to seize, retain, and exploit the initiative. Planning helps commanders anticipate events and set in motion the actions that allow forces to act purposefully and effectively. Exercising initiative this way shapes the situation as events unfold. Planning is inherently proactive, and effective plans instill that spirit into operations. Planning ensures that forces are postured to retain the initiative and consistently able to seek opportunities to exploit that initiative. Plans account for the interdependent relationship among initiative, opportunity, and risk; successful plans combine the three to reduce or counter the effects of complexity using the commander's intent to foster individual initiative and freedom of action.

4-7. Effective planning also anticipates the inherent delay between decision and action, especially between the levels of war and echelons of command. Sound plans draw on the fundamentals of mission command to overcome this effect, fostering initiative within the commander's intent to act appropriately and decisively when orders no longer sufficiently address the changing situation. This ensures commanders act promptly as they encounter opportunities or accept prudent risk to create opportunities when they lack clear direction. In such situations, prompt action requires detailed foresight and preparation.

4-8. Planning is especially important in situations in which experience is lacking; in such situations, creative and adaptive planning is the only viable substitute for experience. With sufficient experience in a given situation, commanders intuitively know what to expect, what goals are feasible, and what actions to take. In situations where experience is lacking, planning enables a systematic approach to problem solving that helps to formulate practical solutions to complex situations.

ANTICIPATE FUTURE EVENTS

4-9. Planning involves projecting thoughts forward in time and space to influence events before they occur. Rather than responding to events as they unfold, proactive planning anticipates these events. Proactive planning contemplates and evaluates potential decisions and actions in advance; it involves visualizing consequences of possible courses of action to determine whether they will contribute to achieving the desired end state. Proactive planning reduces the effects of complexity during execution.

4-10. Newton's third law of motion states that *for every action, there is an equal and opposite reaction*; thus, in a fundamentally complex environment, planning is essential to anticipating the most likely reactions to friendly action. Proactive planning entails anticipating results of friendly action and resulting reactions to those activities. Planning integrates these individual actions (tasks) together into likely sequences (operations) and examines the possible implications (results) of these sequences in time and space. These actions and sequences are linked through planning along lines of effort, which focus the outcomes toward objectives that help to shape the conditions of the operational environment.

BALANCE RESOURCES, CAPABILITIES, AND ACTIVITIES

4-11. During persistent conflict where operations will be increasingly multilateral and involve a diverse array of actors and stakeholders, requirements will often outpace available resources and capabilities necessary to reestablish conditions of peace and stability. Planning involves focusing efforts toward accomplishing the mission while carefully balancing resources, capabilities, and activities across multiple lines of effort.

4-12. Planning ensures that limited resources and capabilities are weighted according to priority of effort. While commanders typically focus resources on the decisive operation, they also provide sufficient resources to capitalize on unforeseen opportunities and to provide impetus for other efforts. The numerous tasks involved in a stability operation require specific capabilities that are often just as limited in availability. An effective plan judiciously applies these capabilities where and when they are most needed. Commanders synchronize the activities in time and space to create the greatest effect, one that achieves broad success in one line of effort while reinforcing progress in the others.

SHAPE A POSITIVE FUTURE

4-13. Planning is based on the principle that by intervening in events in the present, the results of friendly actions can shape a better future. If there was no way to influence the future, if military forces perceived that the natural course of events would lead to a satisfactory outcome, or if military forces believed they could achieve desired results purely by reacting to the situation, there would be no reason to plan. There may be cases in which these conditions apply, but these cases are rare.

4-14. Planning alone does not guarantee success. It does not ensure friendly actions will quantifiably improve the situation. Planning takes on value when performed properly. Commanders must use methods appropriate to the situation, the planned operation, and the roles and capabilities of actors involved. Performed properly and focused toward a common goal, planning proves a valuable activity that greatly improves performance and prudently applies time and effort. Performed haphazardly and without proper focus and effort, planning becomes time-consuming, ineffective, process-focused, and irrelevant. Proper, thoughtful, and informed planning is the only sure means to achieve lasting success and instill positive change in the operational environment.

RECOGNIZE TIME HORIZONS

4-15. All planning is based on imperfect knowledge and involves assumptions about the future that are fundamentally uncertain in nature. Regardless of the quality of the information available or the depth of understanding, operational limits affect the commander's ability to plan. The more certain the future, the easier it is to plan.

4-16. The time horizon refers to how far into the future that plans attempt to shape events. Uncertainty increases with the length of the planning horizon and the rate of change in the environment. Planning attempts to anticipate and influence the future; the farther into the future that plans reach, the more time commanders have for preparation. However, the farther into the future that plans reach, the wider the range of possibilities, and the more uncertain the forecast. A fundamental tension thus exists between the desire to plan in detail and the lack of certainty in future events. The farther the plans reach into the future to facilitate preparation and coordination, the less certain events may be, and the less relevant detailed preparations become.

UNDERSTAND THE PITFALLS

4-17. Planning can often be a time-consuming and frustrating endeavor. Familiarity with the requisite processes and steps typically speeds the planning effort, and repetition only serves to imbue it with an inherent efficiency. Collaborative planning in a stability operation, especially among the many diverse participants, presents unique challenges and opportunities. The challenges of various systems, cultures, and personalities involved can quickly derail effective planning; these challenges may create significant pitfalls to developing a coherent, integrated plan.

4-18. The first pitfall consists of *attempting to forecast and dictate events too far into the future*. This may result from the natural desire to believe a plan can control the future. People naturally tend to develop plans based on the assumption that the events will progress on a logical, linear path to the future. Their plans often underestimate the scope of changes in direction that may occur, especially in operations that occur among populations, where predictability is elusive at best. Even the most effective plans cannot anticipate the unexpected. Often, events overcome plans much sooner than anticipated; effective plans include sufficient branches and sequels to account for the nonlinear nature of events.

4-19. The second pitfall consists of *trying to plan in too much detail*. While sound plans must include detail, planning in more detail than needed only consumes limited time and resources. This pitfall often stems from the natural desire to leave as little as possible to chance. In general, the less certain the situation, the less detail included in the plan. However, people naturally respond to uncertainty by planning in greater detail to try to account for every possibility. This attempt to plan in greater detail under conditions of uncertainty can generate even more anxiety, which in turn leads to even more detailed planning. The result may become an extremely detailed plan that does not survive the friction of the situation and that constricts effective action.

4-20. The third pitfall consists of *using planning as a scripting process that tries to prescribe the course of events with precision*. When planners fail to recognize the limits of foresight and control, the plan can become a coercive and overly regulatory mechanism that restricts initiative and flexibility. The focus for subordinates becomes meeting the requirements of the plan rather than deciding and acting effectively.

4-21. The fourth pitfall is the danger of *institutionalizing rigid planning methods* that lead to inflexible or overly structured thinking. This tends to make planning rigidly process-focused and produce plans that overly emphasize detailed procedures. Planning provides a disciplined framework for approaching and solving complex problems. The danger is in taking that discipline to the extreme. This especially proves dangerous in the collaborative environments typical of stability operations, where the mix of different planning cultures and processes can stymie progress. Stakeholders may want to follow a rigid, institutionalized planning method or, in some situations, not use any planning methodology whatsoever. In a collaborative environment, it is imperative to streamline the planning effort, providing economy of effort and coordination among several people working on the same problem.

PLANNING FOUNDATIONS

4-22. Planning is an essential part of command and control. It helps commanders to decide and act more effectively in an uncertain and complex environment. As such, planning is one of the principal tools commanders use to exercise command and control. Planning involves elements of both art and science, combining analysis and calculation with intuition, inspiration, and creativity. Effective planning demonstrates imagination rather than an overreliance on mechanics. Fundamentally, planning struggles to reconcile the tension between the desire for preparation with the need for flexibility in recognition of the uncertainty of war.

4-23. Effective planning is founded on the bedrock of the commander's collective wisdom, experience, intellect, and intuition. The commander drives planning, providing sound advice, definitive direction, and seasoned leadership. In setting the tone for planning, the commander provides—

- Understanding.
- The commander's intent and planning guidance.
- A concept of operations.

UNDERSTANDING

4-24. Understanding is fundamental to planning. Without understanding, commanders cannot establish the situation's context. Analyzing the situation and the operational variables provides the critical information necessary to develop understanding and frame complex problems. To develop a truer understanding of the operational environment, commanders circulate throughout their operational areas as often as possible, talking to Soldiers performing their duties, making observations, and communicating with the local populace and other actors operating in the area. These commanders will better sense the local situation. Their intuition may cause them to detect trouble or opportunity long before the staff might. This deepens commanders' understanding. It allows them to anticipate potential opportunities and threats, information gaps, and capability shortfalls. Understanding becomes the basis of the commander's visualization.

4-25. Effective planning requires a broad understanding of the operational environment at all levels. It also requires practical creativity and the ability to visualize changes in the operational environment. Commanders need to project their visualization beyond the realm of physical combat. They must anticipate the operational environment's evolving military and nonmilitary conditions. Therefore, planning encompasses visualizing the synchronized arrangement and use of military and nonmilitary forces and capabilities to achieve the desired end state. This creativity requires the ability to discern the conditions required for success before committing forces to action.

4-26. Numerous factors determine the commander's depth of understanding. These include education, intellect, experience, and perception. Effective intelligence is essential to understanding; this is especially true in stability operations, when intelligence efforts focus on the local populace, the host-nation government, and the security apparatus of the state. Maintaining understanding is a dynamic ability, and situational understanding changes as the operation unfolds. Relevant information fuels understanding and fosters initiative. Greater understanding enables commanders and staffs to make quantifiably better decisions; it allows them to focus their intuition on visualizing the current and future conditions of the environment and describing them to subordinates.

4-27. Knowledge management is a key to understanding and exists to help commanders make informed, timely decisions despite the complexity inherent in stability operations. It enables effective collaboration by linking disparate organizations and the people across these organizations requiring knowledge. Knowledge management facilitates rapid adaptation in dynamic operations, focusing assessment and analysis to create knowledge from information. It bridges the gap between the information currently possessed and the relevant information required to make sound decisions. (FM 6-01.1 contains doctrine on knowledge management.)

4-28. Developing a knowledge management plan helps to—

- Address knowledge and information flow.
- Develop criteria for displaying the common operational picture.
- Access and filter information from external sources.
- Support developing situational awareness and situational understanding.
- Enable rapid, accurate retrieval of previously developed knowledge.
- Route products to the appropriate individuals in a readily understood format.
- Keep commanders, civilian leaders, and staffs from being overwhelmed by information.

4-29. In operations conducted among the people, understanding is informed by sustained engagement of the host-nation population. This is the essence of leader and Soldier engagement, the face-to-face interaction of military personnel with the local populace of the host nation. Such interaction not only informs understanding, it is fundamental to shaping the perceptions of the people among whom military forces operate. (See chapter 2 for a detailed discussion of leader and Soldier engagement.)

COMMANDER'S INTENT AND PLANNING GUIDANCE

4-30. Commanders summarize their visualization in their initial commander's intent statement. The initial commander's intent aims to facilitate planning while focusing the overall operations process. Commanders personally develop this commander's intent statement. It succinctly describes the commander's visualization of the entire operation; it clearly states what the commander wants to accomplish. The initial commander's intent links the operation's purpose with the conditions that define the desired end state. The commander's intent statement usually evolves as planning progresses and more information becomes available.

4-31. The initial commander's intent focuses the staff during the operations process. The staff uses this statement to develop and refine courses of action that contribute to establishing conditions that define the end state. Planning involves developing lines of effort that link the execution of tactical tasks to end state conditions. A clear initial commander's intent statement is essential to this effort.

4-32. Commanders also provide planning guidance with their commander's intent statement. Planning guidance conveys the essence of the commander's visualization. Guidance may be broad or detailed, depending on the situation. Effective planning guidance is essentially an initial concept of operations that includes priorities for each warfighting function. It reflects how the commander sees the operation unfolding. It broadly describes when, where, and how the commander intends to leverage combat power to accomplish the mission within the higher commander's intent.

4-33. Commanders use their experience and judgment to add depth and clarity to their planning guidance. They ensure staffs understand the broad outline of their visualization while allowing the latitude to explore different options. This guidance forms the basis for a detailed concept of operations without dictating specifics of the final plan. As with their commander's intent, commanders may modify planning guidance based on staff and subordinate input and changing conditions.

CONCEPT OF OPERATIONS

4-34. Every operation begins with a concept of operations that guides its conduct. In almost all cases, a commander's concept of operations includes the other instruments of national power present in the operational area working with the military toward a common end state. Commanders frame their concept by answering several fundamental questions:

- What is the force trying to accomplish (ends)?
- What conditions, when established, constitute the desired end state (ends)?
- How will the force achieve the end state (ways)?
- What sequence of actions is most likely to attain these conditions (ways)?
- What resources are required, and how can they be applied to accomplish that sequence of actions (means)?
- What risks are associated with that sequence of actions, and how can they be mitigated (risk)?

4-35. The concept of operations expands on the commander's intent by describing how the commander visualizes the force accomplishing the mission. It details the principal tasks necessary to accomplish the mission, the subordinate units responsible for those tasks, and how the tasks complement one another. The concept of operations promotes general understanding by explicitly stating the decisive operation—the task that directly accomplishes the mission, the units that will execute it, and the shaping and sustaining operations required to ensure the success of the decisive operation. The concept of operations also describes the status of the force at the end of the operation. (FM 5-0 discusses the concept of operations in detail.)

4-36. Conflict is fundamentally a human endeavor. Often, violence, uncertainty, chance, and friction characterize conflict. Land operations are inherently tied to the human dimension; they cannot be reduced to a simple formula or checklist. Planning is essential to the commander's ability to integrate diverse capabilities, including those related to the human dimension. It also helps commanders synchronize military actions with actions of other instruments of national power. Planning provides the conceptual framework for ordering thought when visualizing and describing operations. As a creative engine, planning drives commanders' ability to seize, retain, and exploit initiative.

DESIGNING STABILITY OPERATIONS

4-37. The elements of operational design are essential to identifying tasks and objectives that tie tactical missions to achieving the desired end state. They help refine and focus the concept of operations that forms the basis for developing a detailed plan or order. During execution, commanders and staffs consider the design elements as they assess the situation. They adjust current and future operations and plans as the operation unfolds.

4-38. Stability operations, more so than offensive and defensive operations, present a unique challenge. Where combat typically focuses on the defeat of an enemy force, stability focuses on the people. With an extended time horizon, people often gauge success over the course of several years. Such operations typically include significant offensive and defensive components. These components set the appropriate conditions to enable the success of concurrent stability tasks. These operations may set conditions as the operation progresses toward reestablishing the conditions of a stable, lasting peace necessary to plant the seeds of effective governance and economic development.

4-39. Planning for stability draws on all elements of operational design. However, certain elements are more relevant than others are, and some in particular are essential to successful stability operations. (See FM 3-0 for a detailed discussion of the operational art.)

END STATE AND CONDITIONS

4-40. Generally, the end state is represented by the broadly expressed conditions that will exist when an operation ends. The end state is thus an image of the operational environment consistent with the commander's visualization of the operation. In a stability operation, the end state is achieved through the integrated, collective activities of all the instruments of national power, not by any single instrument applied in isolation. Clearly describing the end state requires appreciating the nature of the operational environment and assessing its friendly, enemy, adversary, and neutral aspects. Ultimately, the end state shapes the operation's character. Commanders include it in their planning guidance and commander's intent. A clearly defined end state promotes unity of effort, facilitates integration and synchronization, and helps mitigate risk.

4-41. Commanders explicitly describe the end state and its defining conditions for every operation. Otherwise, the necessary integration between tactical tasks and the conditions that define the end state are not achieved. This is even more critical in stability operations, where military and nonmilitary tasks must be integrated and synchronized to achieve an end state formulated through collaborative planning. Therefore, every operation focuses on a clearly defined, decisive, and attainable end state. However, that end state may evolve over the course of an operation, as strategic and operational guidance is refined, the conditions of operational environment change, and understanding increases. Hence, all commanders continuously monitor operations and assess their progress against measures of effectiveness and the end state conditions. These conditions form the basis for decisions that ensure operations progress consistently toward the desired end state.

4-42. Military operations typically focus on attaining the military end state. However, the efforts of military forces also contribute to establishing nonmilitary conditions. Sometimes that is their focus. This is most apparent in stability operations, when integrating military and nonmilitary capabilities is essential to success. Achieving the desired end state in a stability operation requires deliberately coordinating and synchronizing military and civilian efforts. These efforts focus on a shared understanding of the conditions that support a stable, lasting peace. Due to the interrelated nature of the primary stability tasks, these efforts are fundamentally complementary and contribute toward shaping an enduring end state.

4-43. To achieve the desired end state, stability operations capitalize on coordination, cooperation, integration, and synchronization among military and nonmilitary organizations. These civil-military efforts aim to strengthen legitimate governance, restore rule of law, support economic and infrastructure development, reform institutions to achieve sustainable peace and security, foster a sense of national unity, and create the conditions that enable the host-nation government to reassume civic responsibilities.

OPERATIONAL APPROACH

4-44. The operational approach conceptualizes the commander's visualization of the surest technique for establishing the conditions that define the desired end state. Some operations are conducted among the people, where military interaction with the local populace is inherent to the mission. In those operations, the most effective operational approach achieves decisive results through combinations of stability and defeat mechanisms. While the stability mechanisms leverage the constructive capabilities inherent to combat power, the defeat mechanisms allow the commander to focus the coercive capabilities of the force to provide security and public order and safety for the local populace.

4-45. The conditions of the operational environment ultimately determine the operational approach. During planning, as commanders and staffs frame the problem, they determine the appropriate combination of stability and defeat mechanisms necessary to resolve the situation. This begins the process that ends with an integrated, synchronized plan for an operation that achieves the desired end state. At times, military forces intervene in an unstable situation where the security environment is actively violent in nature. In these cases, military forces may initially use defeat mechanisms to alter the conditions sufficiently to protect the civil populace. In a relatively benign environment where military forces primarily assist or facilitate civil efforts, the stability mechanisms will dominate.

Stability Mechanisms

4-46. Commanders use stability mechanisms to visualize how to employ the stability element of full spectrum operations. A *stability mechanism* is the primary method through which friendly forces affect civilians in order to attain conditions that support establishing a lasting, stable peace (FM 3-0). Combinations of the stability mechanisms produce complementary and reinforcing effects that help to shape the human dimension of the operational environment more effectively and efficiently than a single mechanism applied in isolation. The four stability mechanisms are compel, control, influence, and support.

4-47. Compel involves maintaining the threat—or actual use—of lethal force to establish control and dominance, effect behavioral change, or enforce cessation of hostilities, peace agreements, or other arrangements. Compliance and legitimacy interrelate. While legitimacy is vital to achieving host-nation compliance, compliance itself depends on how local populace perceives the force's ability to exercise force to accomplish the mission. The appropriate and discriminate use of force often forms a central component to success in stability operations; it closely ties to legitimacy. Depending on the circumstances, the threat or use of force can reinforce or complement efforts to stabilize a situation, gain consent, and ensure compliance with mandates and agreements. The misuse of force—or even the perceived threat of the misuse of force—can adversely affect the legitimacy of the mission or the military instrument of national power.

4-48. Control involves establishing public order and safety; securing borders, routes, sensitive sites, population centers, and individuals; and physically occupying key terrain and facilities. As a stability mechanism, control closely relates to the primary stability task, *establish civil control.* However, control is also fundamental to effective, enduring security. When combined with the stability mechanism compel, it is inherent to the activities that comprise disarmament, demobilization, and reintegration, as well as broader security sector reform programs. (Chapter 6 discusses security sector reform in detail.) Without effective control, efforts to establish civil order—including efforts to establish both civil security and control over an area and its population—will not succeed. Establishing control requires time, patience, and coordinated, cooperative efforts across the operational area.

4-49. Influence involves altering the opinions and attitudes of the host-nation population through information engagement, presence, and conduct. It applies nonlethal capabilities to complement and reinforce the compelling and controlling effects of stability mechanisms. Influence aims to affect behavioral change through nonlethal means. It is more a result of public perception than a measure of operational success. It reflects the ability of forces to operate successfully among the people of the host nation, interacting with them consistently and positively while accomplishing the mission. Here, consistency of actions and messages is vital. Influence requires legitimacy. Military forces earn the trust and confidence of the people through the constructive capabilities inherent to combat power, not through lethal or coercive means. Positive influence is absolutely necessary to achieve lasting control and compliance. It contributes to success across the lines of effort and engenders support among the people. Once attained, influence is best maintained by consistently exhibiting respect for, and operating within, the cultural and societal norms of the local populace.

4-50. Support involves establishing, reinforcing, or setting the conditions necessary for the other instruments of national power to function effectively; coordinating and cooperating closely with host-nation civilian agencies; and assisting aid organizations as necessary to secure humanitarian access to vulnerable populations. Support is vital to a comprehensive approach to stability operations. The military instrument of national power brings unique expeditionary and campaign capabilities to stability operations. These capabilities enable the force to quickly address the immediate needs of the host nation and local populace. In extreme circumstances, support may require committing considerable resources for a protracted period. However, easing the burden of support on military forces requires enabling civilian agencies and organizations to fulfill their respective roles. This is typically achieved by combining the effects of the stability mechanisms compel, control, and influence to reestablish security and control; restoring essential civil services to the local populace; and helping to secure humanitarian access necessary for aid organizations to function effectively.

Defeat Mechanisms

4-51. Defeat mechanisms primarily apply in combat operations against an active enemy force. They are defined in terms of the broad operational and tactical effects they produce—physical or psychological. Commanders translate these effects into tactical tasks, formulating the most effective method to defeat enemy aims. Physical defeat deprives enemy forces of the ability to achieve those aims; psychological defeat deprives them of the will to do so. Military forces prove most successful when applying deliberate combinations of defeat mechanisms. As with stability mechanisms, this produces complementary and reinforcing effects not attainable with a single mechanism. The four defeat mechanisms are—

- **Destroy**. It involves identifying the most effective way to eliminate enemy capabilities; it may be attained by sequentially applying combat power over time or with a single, decisive attack.
- **Dislocate**. It involves compelling the enemy to expose forces by reacting to a specific action; it requires enemy commanders to either accept neutralization of part of their force or risk its destruction while repositioning.
- **Disintegrate**. It involves exploiting the effects of dislocation and destruction to shatter the enemy's coherence; it typically follows destruction and dislocation, coupled with the loss of capabilities that enemy commanders use to develop and maintain situational understanding.

- **Isolate**. It involves limiting the enemy's ability to conduct operations effectively by marginalizing critical capabilities or limiting the enemy's ability to influence events; it exposes the enemy to continued degradation through the massed effects of other defeat mechanisms.

Combining Stability and Defeat Mechanisms

4-52. Stability and defeat mechanisms complement planning by providing focus in framing complex problems; they offer the conceptual means to solve them. By combining the mechanisms in a stability operation, commanders can effectively address the human dimension of the problem while acting to reduce the security threat. Therefore, one element of the force can focus on reestablishing security and control while another element can address the immediate humanitarian needs of the populace. This is essential in operations conducted among the people where success is often gauged by the effectiveness of long-term reconstruction and development efforts. Thus, early and deliberate combinations of the stability and defeat mechanisms are vital to success, especially in environments where actors may face active opposition.

LINES OF EFFORT

4-53. A line of effort links multiple tasks and missions to focus efforts toward establishing the conditions that define the desired end state. Lines of effort are essential in stability operations, where physical, positional references to an enemy or adversary are less relevant. In these operations, where the human dimension typically becomes the focus of the force, lines of effort often work best to link tasks, effects, conditions, and the end state. Lines of effort are essential to helping commanders visualize how military capabilities can support the other instruments of national power. They prove particularly valuable where unity of command is elusive, if not impractical, and when used to achieve unity of effort in operations involving multinational forces and civilian agencies and organizations.

4-54. Commanders use lines of effort to describe how they envision their operations creating the more intangible end state conditions inherent in stability operations. These lines of effort show how individual actions relate to one other and to achieving the desired end state. In these situations, lines of effort combine the complementary, long-term effects of stability tasks with the cyclic, short-term events typical of offensive or defensive tasks. Commanders at all levels use lines of effort to develop missions and tasks, identify complementary and reinforcing actions, and allocate resources appropriately. Commanders may designate actions on one line of effort as the decisive operation and others as shaping operations. They synchronize and sequence related actions across multiple lines of effort; recognizing these relationships helps them to assess progress toward achieving the end state.

4-55. Commanders typically visualize stability operations along lines of effort. At the corps and division levels, commanders may consider linking primary stability tasks to their corresponding Department of State post-conflict stability sectors. These stability tasks link military actions with the broader interagency effort across the levels of war. Figure 4-1 on page 4-17 provides an example. (Chapter 2 discusses the stability sectors in detail.) A full complement of lines of effort may also include lines focused on offensive and defensive activities, as well as a line that addresses the information element of combat power. Tasks along the information line of effort typically produce effects across multiple lines of effort.

4-56. Together, the stability sectors and the five primary stability tasks provide a framework for identifying the individual tasks that exert the greatest influence on the operational environment where stability operations are the major focus. They help to identify the breadth and depth of relevant civil-military tasks and emphasize the relationships among them. The stability sectors form the basis for the collaborative interagency planning and dialog that leads to developing lines of effort that synchronize the actions of all instruments of national power.

4-57. However, at the brigade level and below, the primary stability tasks and corresponding stability sectors are often too broad to focus effort appropriately; at lower tactical echelons, lines of effort are best designed using core or directed mission-essential task lists. (Chapter 3 includes additional detail on mission-essential stability tasks.) Lines of effort may focus on specific aspects of the local situation, such as the activities of host-nation security forces, local development projects, and essential services restoration. For example, efforts to restore those services are often shaped using lines of effort based on the memory aid, SWEAT-MSO (sewage, water, electricity, academics, trash, medical, safety, and other considerations) while addressing the need to provide emergency food aid and shelter. Figure 4-2 on page 4-18 provides the infrastructure reconnaissance and survey model used to integrate and synchronize tactical actions, delineate roles and responsibilities, and focus the civil-military efforts in pursuit of related objectives. This integrates efforts to reestablish local civil services with similar, related actions to establish a safe, secure environment. (See FM 3-34.170 for detailed discussion on infrastructure reconnaissance.)

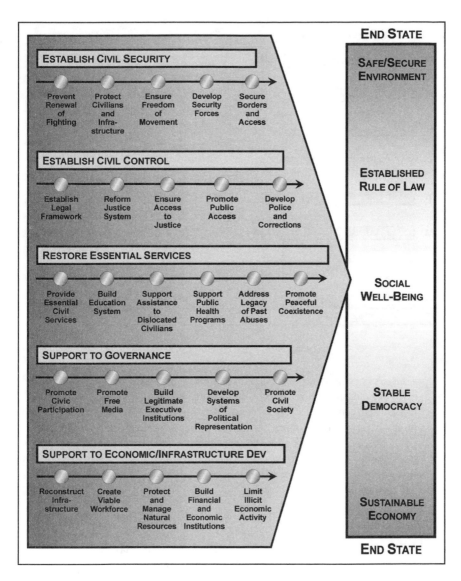

Figure 4-1. Example of stability lines of effort

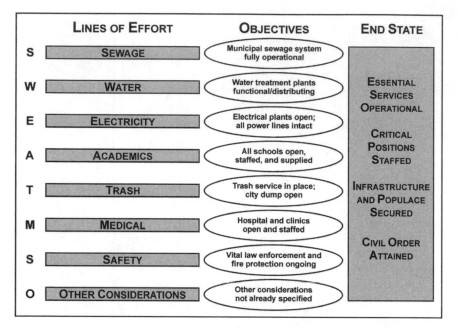

Figure 4-2. Using SWEAT-MSO

4-58. As operations progress, commanders may modify lines of effort after assessing conditions and collaborating with other actors in the operational area. Lines of effort typically remain focused on integrating the effects of military operations with those of other instruments of national power to support a broader, comprehensive approach to stability operations. Each operation, however, differs. Commanders develop and modify lines of effort to keep operations focused on achieving the end state, even as the situation evolves.

DECISIVE POINTS

4-59. During stability operations, decisive points may be less tangible and more closely associated with important events and conditions, and typically relate to the human dimension of the problem. A *decisive point* is a geographic place, specific key event, critical factor, or function that, when acted upon, allows commanders to gain a marked advantage over an adversary or contribute materially to achieving success (JP 3-0). Examples include—

- Securing national borders.
- Repairing a vital water treatment facility.

- Obtaining the political support from key tribal leaders for a transitional authority.
- Establishing a training academy for national security forces.
- Securing a major election site.
- Quantifiably reducing crime.

4-60. None of these examples is purely physical. Nonetheless, any may be vital to establishing conditions for transitioning to civil authority. In stability operations, commanders identify the decisive points that most directly influence the end state conditions. Decisive points that enable commanders to seize, retain, or exploit the initiative are crucial. Controlling them is essential to mission accomplishment. Ceding control of a decisive point may exhaust friendly momentum, force early culmination, or expose the force to undue risk. Decisive points shape the design of operations. They help commanders select clearly decisive, attainable objectives that directly contribute to establishing the end state.

4-61. The essential stability tasks offer an efficient means for commanders to identify those tasks most closely associated with decisive points. Success in stability operations depends on the commander's ability to identify the tasks essential to mission success and to prioritize and sequence the performance of those tasks with available combat power. These tasks include the essential tasks required to establish the end state conditions that define success. These tasks are linked to the end state through decisive points. Therefore, identifying essential tasks and tying them directly to decisive points and objectives most effectively identifies conditions that define the desired end state. (See chapter 3 for a discussion of the essential stability tasks.)

FORCE TAILORING AND TASK-ORGANIZING

4-62. *Force tailoring* is the process of determining the right mix of forces and the sequence of their deployment in support of a joint force commander (FM 3-0). During stability operations, it involves selecting the right force structure from available units within a combatant command or from the Army force pool. The selected forces are then sequenced into the operational area as part of force projection. Joint force commanders request and receive forces for each phase of an operation, both for combat and stability tasks, adjusting the quantity and Service component of forces to match the weight of effort required.

4-63. Army Service component commanders tailor their forces to meet specific land force requirements for stability operations as determined by the joint force commander. They also recommend types of forces for stability operations and a deployment sequence to meet those requirements.

Force tailoring is continuous: as new forces rotate into the operational area, forces with excess capabilities return to the supporting combatant and Army Service component commands.

4-64. *Task-organizing* is the act of designing an operating force, support staff, or logistic package of specific size and composition to meet a unique task or mission. Characteristics to examine when task-organizing the force include, but are not limited to: training, experience, equipage, sustainability, operating environment, enemy threat, and mobility. For Army forces, it includes allocating available assets to subordinate commanders and establishing their command and support relationships (FM 3-0). Task-organizing occurs within a previously tailored force package as commanders organize groups of units for specific stability missions or modify their staff accordingly. It continues as commanders reorganize units for subsequent missions. The ability of Army forces to task-organize gives them extraordinary agility. It lets operational and tactical commanders configure their units to best use available resources. It also allows Army forces to match unit capabilities rapidly to the priority assigned to offensive, defensive, and stability or tasks.

ASSESSMENT

4-65. Assessment is vital to the success of any operation. The commander and staff continuously assess the current situation, gauging progress against the desired end state for the operation. Based on that assessment, the commander directs adjustments as required, ensuring that the operation remains focused toward establishing the conditions that represent the end state. Assessment is a critical activity intended to inform situational understanding. It does this while providing a running comparison of the actual situation in the operational area to the forecasted conditions described in the concept of operations, mission, and commander's intent. Broadly, assessment is a continuous activity that encompasses three discrete tasks:

- Gauging the strengths, weaknesses, and vulnerabilities of enemies and adversaries.
- Monitoring the situation while measuring the progress of the operation against the desired end state.
- Evaluating the progress of the operation against measures of performance and measures of effectiveness.

4-66. Three measurement tools assist the commander and staff with the assessments function: measures of performance, measures of effectiveness, and indicators. Measures of performance assess proper completion of assigned tasks. Measures of effectiveness assess progress toward changing the state of the operational environment envisioned in the commander's intent. Indicators are subordinate measures that provide insight into measures of effectiveness and measures of performance.

4-67. A *measure of performance* is a criterion used to assess friendly actions that is tied to measuring task accomplishment (JP 3-0). At the most basic level, every Soldier assigned a task maintains a formal or informal checklist to track task completion. The items on that checklist are measures of performance. At battalion level and above, command posts monitor measures of performance for assigned tasks. Examples of measures of performance include the construction of a training facility for host-nation security forces or an increased border presence by friendly forces.

4-68. A *measure of effectiveness* is a criterion used to assess changes in system behavior, capability, or operational environment that is tied to measuring the attainment of an end state, achievement of an objective, or creation of an effect (JP 3-0). They focus on the results or consequences of task execution and provide information that guides decisions to take additional or alternate actions. Examples of measures of effectiveness include reduced insurgent activity, reduced inflation rates, and improvements in agricultural production.

4-69. An indicator is an item of information that provides insight into a measure of effectiveness or measure of performance. Indicators use available information to inform a specific measure of performance or measure of effectiveness. A single indicator can inform multiple measures of performance and measures of effectiveness. Valid indicators are measurable, collectable, and relevant to a specific time. Examples of indicators include bushels of apples sold in a specific market in the past month, number of escalation of force incidents along a given route in the past 90 days, and number of bridges repaired in a province.

4-70. Stability operations are often lengthy endeavors, and progress may be gauged over the course of months or years. Responsiveness is a particularly important consideration for selecting measurement tools in this type of environment. In this context, responsiveness is the speed with which a desired change can be detected by a measurement tool. In practice, responsiveness varies greatly among potential measures of effectiveness. It is critical to select measures of effectiveness and supporting indicators that are as responsive as possible during the conduct of stability operations.

4-71. Continuous assessment is a key to seizing, retaining, and exploiting the initiative. It provides a constant flow of vital information on the current situation that allows the commander and staff to quickly act on unanticipated changes, take prudent risks, and create opportunities for future success. (See appendix D for an overview of interagency conflict assessment.)

TRANSITIONS

4-72. Transitions mark a change of focus between phases or between the ongoing operation and execution of a branch or sequel. The shift in relative priority between the elements of full spectrum operations—such as from offense to stability—also involves a transition. Transitions require planning and preparation well before their execution. Potential transitions are identified during planning and accounted for throughout execution; assessment ensures that progress toward such transitions is measured and appropriate actions are taken to prepare for and execute them. The force is vulnerable during transitions, and commanders establish clear conditions for their execution. Transitions may create unexpected opportunities; they may also make forces vulnerable to enemy threats or unanticipated changes to the situation.

4-73. An unexpected change in conditions may require commanders to direct an abrupt transition between phases. In such cases, the overall composition of the force remains unchanged despite sudden changes in mission, task organization, and rules of engagement. Typically, task organization evolves to meet changing conditions; however, transition planning must also account for changes in the mission. Commanders attuned to sudden changes can better adapt their forces to dynamic conditions. They continuously assess the situation and task-organize and cycle their forces to retain the initiative. They strive to achieve changes in emphasis without incurring an operational pause.

4-74. Stability operations include transitions of authority and control among military forces, civilian agencies and organizations, and the host nation. Each transition involves inherent risk. That risk is amplified when multiple transitions must be managed simultaneously or when the force must conduct a series of transitions quickly. Planning anticipates these transitions, and careful preparation and diligent execution ensures they occur without incident. Transitions are identified as decisive points on lines of effort; they typically mark a significant shift in effort and signify the gradual return to civilian oversight and control of the host nation.

Chapter 5

Transitional Military Authority

Because of the ideological aspect of the struggle and because the United States acted as a member of a coalition of Allies, U.S. military leaders sometimes had to add to their traditional roles as soldiers those of the statesman and the politician. They were beset by the problems of resolving conflicting national interests and of reconciling political idealism and military exigency. On another level—in feeding hungry populations, in tackling intricate financial and economic problems, and in protecting the cultural heritage of a rich and ancient civilization—they had to exercise skills that are also normally considered civilian rather than military.

Harry L. Coles and Albert K. Weinberg
Civil Affairs: Soldiers Become Governors

AUTHORITY AND COMMAND RESPONSIBILITY

5-1. Under extreme circumstances, where the host-nation government has failed completely or an enemy regime has been deposed, the intervening authority has a legal and moral responsibility to install a transitional military authority on the behalf of the population. When military forces have invaded and are occupying enemy territory, such an authority is established by the occupying force pursuant to international law, including The Hague and Geneva Conventions. Such authority is limited in scope by international law. In other circumstances, transitional military authority may be established pursuant to a United Nations Security Council resolution or a similar international legal authority, which will also describe the limits of that authority. Furthermore, when occupying enemy territory, authority additional to that provided by traditional sources of international law, such as The Hague and Geneva Conventions, may be provided by United Nations Security Council resolutions or similar authority. Commanders should only take action with regard to transitional military authority after close and careful consultation with the legal advisor.

5-2. Transitional military authorities are installed to act on the behalf of the population and, in the case of occupation of enemy territory, to secure the occupying force. The United Nations Security Council resolution or similar authority may prescribe specific or additional roles of the transitional military authority. In cases other than the occupation of enemy territory, the international community generally will lead this effort through an intergovernmental organization such as the United Nations. The occupation of enemy territory may result in one nation or a coalition of nations providing the transitional military authority.

5-3. A transitional military authority may draw assistance from experienced civilian agencies and organizations. These agencies and organizations have the expertise to establish a system of government that fosters the gradual transition to a legitimate host-nation authority. Sometimes, however, sufficient civilian expertise is not present or conditions of the operational environment do not support introducing such civilian expertise. Military forces may then be required to lead this effort until they stabilize the security situation and can safely transition responsibility for governance to civil authority and control.

5-4. Effective transitional military authority enhances security and facilitates ongoing operations while fulfilling the legal obligations of occupying forces under international law. This authority enhances stability by promoting the safety and security of both military forces and the local populace, reducing active or passive sabotage, and maintaining public order. It helps ongoing operations by building host-nation capability and capacity to perform government functions and relieving maneuver forces of the responsibility of civil administration. Until the military authority can safely transition to civil authority and control, activities of the transitional military authority are performed with civilian personnel assistance and participation. These civilians may come from the host-nation, the United States Government (USG), or other agencies or organizations. This cooperation facilitates the transition while ensuring that all activities complement and reinforce efforts to establish conditions necessary to achieve success.

5-5. A transitional military authority exercises functions of civil administration. These functions include providing for the safety, security, and well-being of the populace; reestablishing and maintaining public order; and restoring essential services. Such functions—and the tasks that support them—evolve from the essential tasks described in the essential stability task matrix and are reflected in the five primary stability tasks. (See chapter 3 for a discussion of essential stability tasks.) Establishing transitional military authority may require military forces to execute tasks typically performed by the host-nation government. These tasks may be provided for under international law, including applicable treaties—such as The Hague and Geneva Conventions—and United Nations Security Council resolutions.

COMMAND RESPONSIBILITY FOR TRANSITIONAL MILITARY AUTHORITY

5-6. The exercise of transitional military authority is a command responsibility, exercised in accordance with international law. To ensure that understanding and cultural awareness inform planning and the conduct of transitional military authority, commanders at all levels maintain open, continuous dialog. They also collaborate among the echelons of command and various agencies, organizations, and institutions that share in efforts to restore legitimate governance to the host nation.

5-7. The authority to implement transitional military authority resides with the President and is exercised through the Secretary of Defense and the joint force commander. Broad policy formulation and initial planning for transitional military authority is conducted under the direction of the Joint Chiefs of Staff. However, the joint force commander, key staff, and subordinate Service component and allied commanders also participate to a lesser degree.

ESTABLISHING TRANSITIONAL MILITARY AUTHORITY

5-8. A *transitional military authority* **is a temporary military government exercising the functions of civil administration in the absence of a legitimate civil authority**. It restores and maintains public order, ensures the safety and security of the local populace, and provides essential civil services. Transitional military authority is not limited to the occupation of enemy territory. During operations outside the United States and its territories, necessity may also require establishing transitional military authority in various situations, including—

- An allied or neutral territory liberated from enemy forces.
- A technically neutral or allied territory proven to be hostile.
- Ungoverned areas.

5-9. The time during which a transitional military authority exercises authority varies based on the requirements of both the military operation and international law. To establish transitional military authority, commanders may require from the host-nation population a level of obedience commensurate with military necessity. Such obedience provides security of military forces, maintenance of law and order, and proper administration of the operational area. Commanders can reward civil obedience by reducing infringement on the individual liberties of the local populace.

5-10. The degree of control exercised by a transitional military authority varies greatly due to several factors, including—

- The legal authorities of the military commander under international law.
- The relationship that previously existed between the USG and the host-nation government.
- Existing attitudes and the level of cooperation of the host nation's national, regional, and local leaders, and the local populace.
- Ongoing and projected military operations.
- The presence of hostile or enemy forces.
- The level of civil obedience.

5-11. As conditions in the territory subject to transitional military authority stabilize, the degree of control exercised by a military authority can decrease. Authority and control can transfer either to the legitimate sovereign or to another civil authority.

ORGANIZING FOR TRANSITIONAL MILITARY AUTHORITY

5-12. The joint force commander is responsible for the detailed planning and operations of the transitional military authority under the general guidelines received from the President, Secretary of Defense, and Joint Chiefs of Staff. The structure and organization of the transitional military authority depend on—

- International law, including any applicable United Nations Security Council resolutions or similar authorities.
- The mission of the military force.
- The organization, capabilities, and capacities of deployed forces.
- The military and political conditions of the operational area.
- The nature, structure, and organization of the existing or former host-nation government.
- The physical, political, economic, and cultural geography of the host nation.

EXISTING LAWS, CUSTOMS, AND BOUNDARIES

5-13. The laws of the territory subject to transitional military authority may not be changed, except to the extent permitted by The Hague and Geneva Conventions. Commanders must consult closely and carefully with their legal advisors before attempting to change any local laws.

5-14. In general, the military authority should not impose the customs of another nation on an occupied territory. Implementing changes or reforms inconsistent with local customs may foster active or passive resistance, adding friction to an already complex effort. Commanders and their legal advisors must recognize that laws and customs often vary between political divisions of a country, such as between provinces or municipalities. Commanders need to identify issues related to ethnic and minority groups so policies of the transitional military authority do not inadvertently oppress such groups.

5-15. Local boundaries and political divisions may not be redrawn except to the extent permitted by international law. Unit boundaries should normally reflect these boundaries as closely as possible. Periodically, however, unit boundaries should shift to avoid inadvertently creating sanctuaries for adversaries. Existing police jurisdictional boundaries and lines should be examined to determine if their location contributes to setting the conditions for successful stability operations. Established precincts, zones, districts, regions, counties, parishes, or other mechanisms that delineate police authority can assist in command and control, decisionmaking, and employment of military forces. Police jurisdictional boundaries may reflect dominant or sensitive cultural realities or fault lines that exist in a community. Some police boundaries may also exist to ensure that police capability is commensurate or appropriate to the criminal conditions of an area.

FORMS OF TRANSITIONAL MILITARY AUTHORITY

5-16. In general, transitional military authorities are either operational or territorial. An operational military authority expands in authority as operations continue. In the territorial form of transitional military authority, a separate organization is established under the direct command of the joint force commander or an authorized subordinate.

Operational Military Authority

5-17. The responsibilities and geographic area over which a transitional military authority exercises civil administration may expand as operations continue. Commanders oversee civil functions of government in their respective operational areas. This includes ensuring the safety, security, and well-being of the local populace, and providing humanitarian assistance. Under operational military authority, the existing chain of command retains the responsibility for authority and is supported by the staff structure at that echelon.

5-18. Concentrating authority and responsibility in the commander helps ensure that activities related to civil administration are integrated consistently with ongoing operations. These activities include relations between the military force and civilians. By ensuring the integrity of unity of command in an operational area, commanders can mitigate much of the friction associated with operations in and among the local populace. As the situation permits, the responsibility for civil administration transfers to host-nation or other civil authority to help it return to full self-governance. Using host-nation civilian advisory groups helps accelerate this transfer of authority.

5-19. The advantages of operational military authority, however, are tempered by the rate of military activities. Generally, the higher the tempo within the operational area, the less the commander is able to address the requirements of transitional military authority. In areas where the tempo of operations and civil situation are consistently dynamic, civil administration policies may change frequently. Finally, operational headquarters are not always assigned operational areas corresponding to known political subdivisions. Even after hostilities, conformance of these areas to political boundaries may prove impossible, however desirable.

Territorial Military Authority

5-20. In territorial military authority, a separate organization is established to exercise the functions of civil administration. It may be under the direct command of the joint force commander or an authorized subordinate or may report directly to the Secretary of Defense or the President. The military governor may command subordinate military governors assigned to political subdivisions throughout the territory of the host nation. Generally, the territorial military authority represents a separate chain of command from operational forces.

5-21. A territorial military authority typically uses military manpower and expertise more effectively and economically than an operational military authority. Established after the operational area is stabilized, a territorial military authority may ensure improved continuity of policy and administration and better facilitate selecting and assigning specially trained military personnel. A territorial military authority operates under the provisions of unity of effort, representing the fundamental principles for unified action.

5-22. However, the existence of a separate chain of command within an operational area or a political subdivision presents unique challenges to the territorial military authority. Activities of the territorial military authority must be carefully coordinated with those of operational military forces. These activities must not interfere with ongoing operations or expose the operational force to undue risk. To ensure unity of effort, the territorial military authority and the operational forces must maintain close communications, cooperation, and coordination.

5-23. In practice, the exact form of authority should be adapted to suit the political and military situation in the operational area. A territorial military authority may draw certain features from an operational form, or vice versa. As operations progress, the character of the military authority may evolve according to the situation, mirroring the effort to build host-nation capacity. In certain cases, one type of military authority may dominate in one region of the host nation, while another type is better suited for another region.

LOCAL GOVERNMENT OFFICIALS AND DEPARTMENTS

5-24. Successfully implementing transitional military authority often depends on how the host-nation government and its civilians participate and contribute. The transitional military authority thoroughly assesses the capability of the remaining host-nation government officials. This assessment determines if those officials can support and contribute to transitional military authority. The long-term success of the operation may depend on this assessment. If permitted by international law, offices that are unnecessary or detrimental to the transitional military authority may close temporarily, and officials who refuse to serve the best interests of the transitional military authority may be suspended. However, such officials may be retained in an advisory capacity at the discretion of the military commander. In such cases, they should continue to receive compensation for their services.

5-25. Generally, if a transitional military authority needs to be established, high-ranking political officials of the former government will not continue to hold office. Such officials may include heads of the host-nation government, cabinet ministers, and other political elites. To the extent permitted by international law, the transitional military authority may be required to perform certain duties that would otherwise fall to individuals in these positions.

5-26. Typically, mere membership in unfriendly organizations or political groups is not by itself considered sufficient grounds for removal from office. However, officials who have served as active leaders of such organizations or political groups may need to leave office. Similarly, officials who prove unreliable or corrupt must leave office through legal action or through an open, transparent administrative process. The willful failure of retained officials to perform their duties satisfactorily is a serious offense against the transitional military authority.

5-27. The commander's decisions about whether or not to retain leaders of the local government will likely vary. In some areas, full local participation may be the norm, while in other areas entire departments and bureaus of the local government may need to close. Where practical, the transitional military authority should retain subordinate officials and employees of the local government. These officials can continue to properly discharge their duties under the direction and supervision of appropriately trained military personnel. Under certain circumstances, military forces may protect officials who continue to serve in, or are appointed to, local public service. Hostile elements may pose a threat to these individuals, putting their safety at risk.

5-28. In some areas, the local populace may have had very limited participation in government due to centralized power in an authoritarian regime or a dominating foreign power. Elitist groups may also have focused regional, provincial, or municipal power under their control, negating the participation of the local populace. In such cases, civilian officials of the former government may flee. Even if they remain, it may be impractical or unsafe for them to continue in office. For this reason, building new partner capability—training local nationals to assume certain government positions—must often precede long-term efforts in capacity building.

5-29. When a local official is removed or unavailable, the transitional military authority should seek a fully qualified, trained, and experienced replacement. When selecting officials, the military authority should consider their reliability, willingness to cooperate with the transitional military authority, and status in the community. The transitional military authority does not make permanent appointments, however. If a suitable candidate is not available, a representative of the transitional military authority should perform the duties of the position until an appropriate replacement can assume the duties.

5-30. Commanders at all echelons must avoid any commitments to, or negotiations with, local political elements without the approval of higher authority. Military personnel should refrain from developing or maintaining unofficial relationships with local officials and host-nation personnel.

Soldiers must refuse personal favors or gifts offered by government officials or the local populace unless authorized by higher authority.

GUIDELINES FOR TRANSITIONAL MILITARY AUTHORITY

5-31. For military forces, the successful completion of the mission is paramount. As long as operations continue, the commander must exercise the necessary control and take appropriate measures with host-nation personnel and the local populace to ensure mission success. The policies and practices adopted for transitional military authority can reduce the possibility that civilians interfere with ongoing operations.

5-32. To ensure operations continue unimpeded by civilians, transitional military authority focuses on ensuring the safety and security of civilians, restoring and maintaining law and order, building host-nation capability and capacity in key areas of government, and reestablishing living conditions to a normal, customary state. This effort is facilitated by thoroughly integrating civil affairs planning and capabilities into the operations process and maintaining positive interaction between military forces and the local people.

5-33. Commanders develop codes of behavior that avoid violation of, or insult to, local customs and practices. Foreign area officers, civil affairs and military intelligence personnel, and chaplains provide relevant information and intelligence on the local populace, specific aspects of culture, and general customs and behaviors. Civil affairs personnel and chaplains provide host-nation religious information that may restrict military use or targeting of religiously consecrated buildings or locations. Commanders may direct trained personnel, in coordination with chaplain support, to act as negotiators or mediators between opposing groups within the local populace. (See FM 27-10 for doctrine on customary and treaty law during land operations.)

TREATMENT OF THE POPULATION

5-34. Fair treatment of the local populace can help reduce the chance that it will be hostile to U.S. forces and increase the chance for obtaining its cooperation. The proper and just treatment of civilians helps military forces establish and maintain security; prevent lawlessness; promote order; and secure local labor, services, and supplies. Such treatment promotes a positive impression of the military force; the United States; and other government agencies, organizations, and institutions engaged in unified action. It strengthens the legitimacy of the operation and the transitional military authority in the eyes of the populace, bordering nations, and other members of the international community.

5-35. Nonetheless, a policy of proper and just treatment does not prevent the imposition of restrictive or punitive measures necessary to secure the objectives of the transitional military authority. In particular, such measures may be needed in an area where the population is actively and aggressively hostile.

5-36. The military's policies for treating any population vary depending on several factors. These factors include characteristics of the population, such as their attitude toward the governing forces, the degree of technical-industrial development, socioeconomic conditions, the political system, and local history and culture. Another determining factor is the policies of the United States with respect to the host-nation government. The commander must become familiar with host-nation customs, institutions, and attitudes and implement transitional military authority accordingly.

5-37. When determining policies for treating the local populace, commanders consider other factors:

- Generally, less restrictive measures are appropriate for civilians of friendly or nonhostile states. More restrictive measures generally are needed with civilians of hostile states.
- Depending on the culture, the local populace may perceive certain actions as characteristic of an illegitimate or weak military government. On the other hand, certain actions, though permissible under international law, may aggravate an already complex civil situation or reduce the effectiveness of the force in imposing civil control.
- Force may be used to subdue those who resist the transitional military authority or to prevent the escape of prisoners or detainees suspected of crimes. Force is limited to what is necessary and must be consistent with international law. Legal advisors should be consulted when formulating policies for the use of force and the treatment of prisoners, detainees, and other persons.

5-38. Military commanders are inherently empowered to take all prudent and proportional measures necessary to protect their forces. However, during stability operations, the nature of the threat can often inhibit the ability of friendly forces to differentiate between hostile acts, hostile intent, and normal daily activity among civilians. For this reason, military commanders and forces must retain the authority to detain civilians and an acceptable framework under which to confine, intern, and eventually release them to the operational environment. This authority has the most legitimacy when sanctioned by international mandate or when bestowed or conveyed from the local or regional government power. The initial or baseline authority granted to military forces to use force and detain civilians will ultimately determine the status of the persons they detain. The status of detained persons will further determine the manner in which they are processed, the degree of due process they are afforded, and whether their offense is military or criminal in nature.

ECONOMIC STABILIZATION AND RECOVERY

5-39. Transitional military authority generally focuses on security, the restoration and maintenance of law and order, and the immediate humanitarian needs of the local populace. In certain circumstances, military forces may need to act with regard to economic conditions to promote security and law and order. However, international law generally limits the authority of a transitional military authority in this area. Specific sources of international law directed at the activities of the transitional military authority, such as United Nations Security Council resolutions, may provide additional authority. Commanders must routinely consult legal advisors in this complex area.

5-40. When international law and the governing mandate permits a transitional military authority to engage in economic stabilization and recovery activities, two immediate goals generally exist for the economic sector. The first goal aims to use all available goods and services as efficiently as possible to meet the essential needs of the local populace. The second aims to revive the economy at the local level to reduce dependence on external support. It does this by stimulating production capability and workforce capacity. Typically, the authority achieves this goal by quickly identifying local sources of supply and services to support military operations. This infuses critical monetary resources into the local economy to stimulate further growth, investment, and development.

5-41. When international law permits the transitional military authority to engage in economic stabilization and recovery efforts, commanders have a task. They must keep in mind that actions taken to stimulate economic recovery at the local level must be closely tied to efforts to stabilize the national economy. Therefore, the transitional military authority must immediately draw on the expertise and advice of civilian agencies (such as the Department of the Treasury) and organizations (such as the International Monetary Fund) to contend with macroeconomic challenges. Issues such as stabilizing monetary policy, controlling inflation, and reestablishing a national currency generally exceed expertise resident in the transitional military authority. This lack of expertise underscores the necessity of introducing appropriate civilian expertise as soon as practical or puts the success of broader economic recovery programs at risk from the outset of operations.

5-42. Stimulating the economy at the microeconomic level is known to facilitate economic recovery, especially in areas suffering from market failure or collapse. The transitional military authority may apply micro-economics principles to influence local prices, supply and demand, or the availability of labor. For example, the transitional military authority can offer small-scale grants and low- or fixed-interest loans to encourage en-trepreneurial investment and host-nation enterprise creation. These prac-tices enable impoverished people to invest in projects that generate in-come and, in many cases, begin to build wealth and exit poverty. At the local level, this stimulation is essential to economic recovery; it sets the cornerstone for recovery and development on a national scale.

5-43. Economic assessments are critical to the success of recovery pro-grams. The transitional military authority must understand the economic conditions in the operational area, the factors that affect stabilization and growth, and the cultural nuances that influence how the market sector performs. Developing a shared understanding of the economic situation spurs market integration, helps to identify key needs and opportunities, increases private sector participation, and improves social and economic cohesion throughout the host nation.

5-44. An equitable distribution of necessities—such as food, water, shel-ter, and medicine—supports economic stability. To this end, it may be necessary to establish and enforce temporary controls over certain aspects of the local economy. These controls may be designed to affect the prices of goods and services, wage rates and labor practices, black market activ-ity, hoarding of goods, banking practices, imports or exports, and produc-tion rates within industry. However, these controls may also have adverse effects that can lead to renewed violence. These adverse effects may con-sist of causing potential shortages of goods and services, impeding eco-nomic progress, and causing corruption, conflict over limited resources, and social tension Commanders must weigh the decision to implement economic controls very carefully. In doing so, they should seek guidance from higher echelons and from personnel and organizations with appro-priate expertise. They may discover alternatives available that achieve the same results with fewer negative consequences. They determine how well the private sector can identify profitable lines of investment and enter-prise creation quickly, stimulate market-led economic recovery, and pro-vide reasonably priced consumable goods and services to the population. (See FM 3-05.40 for doctrine on populace and resources control.)

5-45. When permitted by international law, the transitional military au-thority may stimulate the economy to help the local industry develop, but it must do so with the end state of sustainable, private-sector activity in mind. This may include agriculture, manufacturing, mining, forestry, and any number of service trades. The transitional military authority may support the production in a specific operational area. Industries may require some form of initial subsidization to spur productivity as well as assistance with management. In potentially hostile areas, the transitional military authority may provide or train personnel for skilled positions (to replace people who have fled or are not cooperative or dependable). Detailed infrastructure assessments help to locate useable production facilities and identify damaged or inoperable facilities for reconstruction planning.

PUBLIC HEALTH

5-46. Establishing the public health policy is a primary concern of the transitional military authority for security, public safety, and humanitarian reasons. Sustained operations cannot exist without healthy military forces. Without a healthy, viable force, the military cannot provide for the health and well-being of the people adequately. To protect the health of the force, the transitional military authority may need to take measures to safeguard, and if necessary, improve, the health of the local populace. Generally, the force lacks the health service support capacity to provide sustained medical care for civilians. However, with appropriate resources and security, the transitional military authority may open and secure humanitarian access to the local populace. It may also take steps such as establishing temporary clinics, training local health professionals, and augmenting existing medical facilities.

5-47. The transitional military authority should take steps to secure the public health infrastructure. Such steps can enable functioning hospitals and clinics to remain open so local medical personnel can continue to serve civilians. The transitional military authority can also repair critical transportation infrastructure to ensure continued delivery of medical supplies and accessibility for emergency patient transport. The transitional military authority should ensure the continued functioning of essential services infrastructure so that adequate power, water, and sanitation are available to support health care facilities. Public health policy should also focus on burying or cremating remains; disposing of sewage, garbage, and refuse properly; purifying local water supplies; inspecting food supplies; and controlling insects and disease. Preventive medicine specialists, working with civil affairs personnel, provide the capability to exercise public health policy.

OTHER CONSIDERATIONS

5-48. During stability operations, leaders and Soldiers become governors in a much broader sense, influencing events and circumstances normally outside the bounds of the military instrument of national power. By virtue of their responsibilities to the local populace, they become the executors of national and international policy. They are often required to reconcile long-standing disputes between opposing parties, entrusted with responsibilities more suited to civilian rather than military expertise. They are frequently called up to restore host-nation civil authority and institutions, to facilitate the transition toward a desired political end state that supports national and international order. The burdens of governance upon a transitional military authority require culturally astute leaders and Soldiers capable of adapting to nuances of religion, ethnicity, and a number of other considerations essential to success.

Respect for Religious Customs and Organizations

5-49. The depth to which religious and political factors interact in other societies drives the motivations and perceptions of the local populace. The religious conventions and beliefs of a society may significantly influence the political dimension of conflict. Depending upon how that influence is leveraged often determines whether conflict and instability give way to peaceful outcomes. International law mandates that the religious convictions and practices of members of the local populace be respected. The military force should, consistent with security requirements, respect the religious celebrations and the legitimate activities of religious leaders. Places of religious worship should remain open unless they pose a specific security or health risk to the military force or the local populace.

Archives and Records

5-50. Archives and records, current and historical, of all branches of the former government should be secured and preserved. These documents are of immediate and continuing use to the military force as a source of valuable intelligence and other information. They are of even greater importance to the transitional military authority by providing invaluable information in running the government. Therefore, the military force must seize, secure, and protect archives and records.

Mail

5-51. Large quantities of mail and other documents are often found in post offices or at other points of central communications. These also represent an important source of intelligence and other information. The transitional military authority should seize, secure, and protect such materials until the forces can process and deliver them.

Shrines and Art

5-52. Except in cases where military operations or military necessity prevents it, the force protects and preserves all historical and cultural monuments and works, religious shrines and objects of art, and any other national collections of artifacts or art.

Atrocities

5-53. Under certain circumstances, the transitional military authority may be required to contend with the aftermath atrocities, including war crimes, crimes against humanity, and genocide. To the greatest extent possible, the transitional military authority should assist in establishing commissions and with identifying, processing, and memorializing remains of victims. These are especially sensitive matters and must be carried out with appropriate sensitivity and respect for local culture and customs.

Corruption

5-54. The transitional military authority will likely contend with corruption in certain sectors of the host nation. Appropriate anticorruption measures may need to be implemented to counter the influence of corrupt officials in host-nation institutions. Dismissing these officials, however, must be weighed against their prestige and influence. Transparent, legitimate processes are fundamental to effective anticorruption programs.

Vetting

5-55. Successful capacity building relies on dependable vetting processes to screen potential civil servants from the host nation. These processes help commanders select qualified, competent officials while reducing the threat of security risks. Vetting processes should include the participation of local inhabitants to ensure transparency, cultural sensitivity, and legitimacy. Commanders should monitor these processes closely to prevent the exclusion of specific religious, ethnic, or tribal groups.

COURTS AND CLAIMS

5-56. The ordinary courts in areas under control of the transitional military authority generally continue to function during a military occupation. They may only be suspended if judges abstain from fulfilling their duties, the courts are corrupt or unfairly constituted, or the administration of the local jurisdiction has collapsed. In such cases, the transitional military authority may establish its own courts.

5-57. The penal laws of the occupied territory remain in force during the occupation. However, the transitional military authority may suspend them during an occupation if they constitute a threat to security or an obstacle to the application of the Geneva Conventions.

5-58. During an occupation, the transitional military authority may enact special decrees and penal provisions essential for it to—

- Fulfill its obligations under The Hague and Geneva Conventions.
- Maintain orderly administration of the occupied territory.
- Ensure the security of the occupying forces.

5-59. Penal provisions enacted by the transitional military authority during an occupation may not be enforced until they are made public to the population of the occupied territory in the national language of that territory. Such penal provisions may not be retroactive and the penalty must be proportionate to the offense. Courts may only apply those provisions of law that were applicable prior to the alleged offense and are in accordance with the general principles of law.

5-60. The transitional military authority may establish courts to hear cases on alleged violations of the special decrees and penal provisions enacted by the transitional military authority. It may also establish courts and administrative boards for other certain purposes. These might include considering the cases of detainees and reconsidering the refusals of requests by aliens to leave the occupied territory. For further information on courts, commissions, and military tribunals, see the *Manual for Military Commissions*.

5-61. During an occupation, the transitional military authority has certain requirements. It may not declare that the rights and actions of enemy nationals are extinguished, suspended, or unenforceable in a court of law. During an occupation, U.S. forces and the transitional military authority are not subject to local laws. Nor are they subject to the jurisdiction of the local civil or criminal courts of the occupied territory unless expressly agreed to by the transitional military authority or by the occupying power. Only U.S. military courts should try U.S. personnel subject to the Uniform Code of Military Justice. Promptly investigating, arbitrating, and settling local damage claims—to the extent permitted by U.S. law, regulation, and policy—can help to strengthen the credibility of the transitional military authority. (See AR 27-20 for regulatory guidance on claims.)

Chapter 6

Security Sector Reform

Establishing security involves domestic security, secure borders, and relatively accommodating neighbors. Of the three factors in achieving stabilization and reconstruction, domestic security is the most important and often the most difficult to achieve.

James Stephenson
Losing the Golden Hour: An Insider's View of Iraq's Reconstruction[1]

BACKGROUND

6-1. National defense and internal security are the traditional cornerstones of state sovereignty. Security is essential to legitimate governance and participation, effective rule of law, and sustained economic development. For a state recovering from the effects of armed conflict, natural disaster, or other events that threaten the integrity of the central government, an effective security sector fosters development, encourages foreign investment, and helps reduce poverty.

6-2. Establishing security in a country or region affected by persistent conflict requires a comprehensive assessment of the drivers of conflict in the host nation. It also requires applying all available capabilities to reduce or eliminate the drivers of conflict and create an environment of security and rule of law. In nonpermissive areas, security is the first priority and therefore must be established before other external actors can enter the operational area. Such areas typically require the initial use of military forces to achieve security and set the conditions that enable the success of those actors.

6-3. The security sector comprises the individuals and institutions responsible for the safety and security of the host nation and its people. Generally, this includes the military and any state-sponsored paramilitary

---

[1] © 2007 by James Stephenson. Reproduced with permission from Potomac Books, Incorporated.

forces; national and local police; the justice and corrections systems; coastal and border security forces; oversight bodies; militia; and private military and security companies employed by the state. The security sector represents the foundation of effective, legitimate governance and the potential of the state for enduring viability.

6-4. *Security sector reform* **is the set of policies, plans, programs, and activities that a government undertakes to improve the way it provides safety, security, and justice.** Security sector reform aims to provide an effective and legitimate public service that is transparent, accountable to civil authority, and responsive to the needs of the public. It may include integrated activities to support defense and armed forces reform; civilian management and oversight; justice, police, corrections, and intelligence reform; national security planning and strategy support; border management; disarmament, demobilization, and reintegration (DDR); and concurrent reduction of armed violence.

6-5. The *National Security Strategy* seeks to contribute to a world of legitimate, effectively governed states that provide for the needs of their citizens and conduct activities responsibly within the international system. Security sector reform (SSR) can reinforce diplomacy and defense while reducing long-term security threats by helping to build stable, prosperous, and peaceful societies. SSR facilitates security cooperation, capacity-building activities, stability operations, and engagement. Ultimately, SSR builds on the Nation's tradition of working in partnership with foreign governments and organizations to support peace, security, and effective governance.

6-6. SSR involves reestablishing or reforming institutions and key ministerial positions that maintain and provide oversight for the safety and security of the host nation and its people. Through unified action, those individuals and institutions assume an effective, legitimate, and accountable role; they provide external and internal security for their citizens under the civilian control of a legitimate state authority. Effective SSR enables a state to build its capacity to provide security and justice. SSR promotes stability, fosters reform processes, and enables economic development. The desired outcome of SSR programs is an effective and legitimate security sector firmly rooted within the rule of law.

6-7. SSR includes reform efforts targeting the individuals and institutions that provide a nation's security as well as promote and strengthen the rule of law. By recognizing the inherently interdependent aspects of the security sector and by integrating operational support with institutional reform and governance, SSR promotes effective, legitimate, transparent, and accountable security and justice. SSR captures the full range of security activities under the broad umbrella of a single, coherent framework. It spans from military and police training to weapons destruction and from community security to DDR of former combatants to security sector oversight and budgeting.

INTEGRATED SECURITY SECTOR REFORM

6-8. The departments and agencies of the United States Government (USG), including the Department of Defense (DOD), pursue an integrated SSR based on a whole of government approach. With the support of the host nation, military forces collaborate with interagency representatives and other civilian organizations to design and implement SSR strategies, plans, programs, and activities. The Department of State (DOS) leads and provides oversight for these efforts though its bureaus, offices, and overseas missions. The DOD provides coercive and constructive capability to support the establishment, to restructure or reform the armed forces and defense sector, and to assist and support activities of other USG agencies involved in SSR. Army forces participate in and support SSR activities as directed by the joint force commander.

ROLES AND RESPONSIBILITIES

6-9. To implement SSR programs, elements of the U.S. country team cooperate to design SSR strategies, plans, programs, and activities. These programs work in partnership with the appropriate USG departments and agencies as well as the chief of mission's authority in the country.

6-10. The DOS leads U.S. diplomatic initiatives and oversees program support to SSR through its bureaus, offices, and overseas missions. These efforts coordinate closely with DOS regional and functional bureaus holding substantive or lead roles for developing and executing SSR programs. Such programs can include the Bureau for International Narcotics and Law Enforcement Affairs, the Bureau of International Organizations, the Bureau of Diplomatic Security, and the Office of the Coordinator for Reconstruction and Stabilization in connection with its National Security Presidential Directive 44 responsibilities.

6-11. The primary role of the DOD in SSR is the reform, restructuring, or reestablishment of the armed forces and the defense sector. The regional offices assume the lead DOD role in setting regional and country priorities for SSR. The Joint Staff director of strategic plans and policy is responsible for coordinating SSR guidance with the geographic combatant commands. These commands plan and direct SSR activities within their areas of responsibility. The military departments and defense agencies normally conduct SSR activities and implement SSR programs for the DOD.

6-12. The primary role for the United States Agency for International Development (USAID) is to support the governance, conflict mitigation and response, and rule of law agenda. USAID does this through programs aimed at building civilian capacity to manage, oversee, and provide security and justice as well as through reintegration and reconciliation programs. USAID regional bureaus as well as a number of functional offices may have substantive or lead roles to develop and execute SSR and rule of law programs. These functional offices include the Office of Conflict Management and Mitigation, the Office of Transition Initiatives, and the Office of Military Affairs.

6-13. In addition to DOS, DOD, and USAID, other USG departments and agencies provide important capabilities for executing SSR programs. In particular, the Departments of Justice, Homeland Security, Energy, and the Treasury may have substantive or lead roles in developing and executing SSR and rule of law. This whole of government approach to SSR is a cooperative activity. USG agencies and military forces, intergovernmental and nongovernmental organizations, multinational partners, and civil authorities conduct this activity. Through unified action, SSR actors integrate and synchronize reform activities to achieve unity of effort across all agencies, organizations, institutions, and forces contributing to SSR. Success requires a shared understanding of the desired end state and supporting conditions. This understanding develops as the actors collaborate and is expanded upon through open and continuous dialog. Unified action in a collaborative environment ensures more than unity of effort; it reinforces the broader effort to integrate SSR into the overall reconstruction and stabilization strategy for the host nation.

6-14. SSR programs nested within an integrated approach are complex undertakings that require time and patience. Managing expectations and setting realistic goals for SSR programs are essential to sustaining such programs. Many reforms require an adjusted frame of reference that responds to changes in the operational environment, local culture, and existing political conditions.

6-15. All SSR programs proceed from the understanding that good governance—the effective, equitable, responsive, transparent, and accountable management of civil services and resources—and the rule of law are essential to establishing an effective security sector. Effective, enduring security sector governance requires legitimate oversight and control of security policy and practices. Security sector governance expands the concept of civilian oversight and control to include administration, management, and policy formulation.

ELEMENTS OF THE SECURITY SECTOR

6-16. The security sector consists of both uniformed forces—police and military—and civilian agencies and organizations operating at various levels within the operational environment. Elements of the security sector are interdependent; the activities of one element significantly affect other elements. (See figure 6-1.) The four core elements of the security sector consist of—

- State security providers.
- Government security management and oversight bodies.
- Civil society and other nonstate actors.
- Nonstate security sector providers.

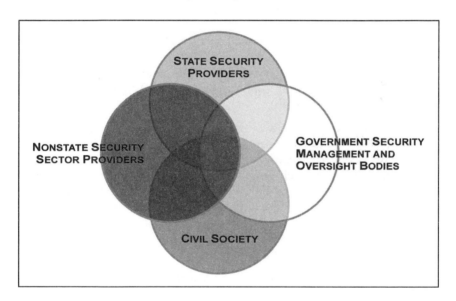

Figure 6-1. Elements of the security sector

6-17. State security providers are those bodies authorized by the state to use or support the use of force. They include the active armed forces, civilian agencies, executive protection services, formed police units, military and civilian intelligence services, coast guards, border guards, customs services, reserves or local security units (civil defense units), national guards, government militias, and other paramilitary organizations.

6-18. Government security management and oversight bodies are those bodies, both formal and informal, authorized by the state to manage and oversee the activities and governance of armed and public security forces and agencies. They may include (but are not limited to) the executive branch and ministries of defense, interior, justice, and foreign affairs; judicial branch, national security coordination and advisory bodies; the legislative branch and its committees; traditional and customary authorities; the ministry of finance and other financial management bodies; civilian review boards and compliance commissions; and local government structures. The latter includes governors, municipal councils, auditing bodies, civilian review boards, and public complaints commissions.

6-19. The third core element of the security sector consists of the civil society and other nonstate actors. The society consists of professional organizations, policy analysis organizations (think tanks and universities), advocacy organizations, human rights commissions and ombudsmen, informal and traditional justice systems, nongovernmental organizations, media, and other nonstate actors. In addition to monitoring security actor performance, civil society articulates the public demand for safety and security. In some cases, particularly where a host-nation government's capacity may be limited, civil society and other nonstate actors fill the security void by providing some degree of security and justice to local communities or constituents.

6-20. Nonstate security sector providers are nonstate providers of justice and security. These providers encompass a broad range of actors with widely varying degrees of legal status and legitimacy. Unaccountable nonstate actors or illicit power structures may engender human rights abuses. Sometimes, they facilitate inappropriate links between the private and public security sector and political parties, state agencies, paramilitary organizations, and organized crime. Conversely, local actors, such as informal or traditional justice systems, may provide a stabilizing influence during and after conflict.

6-21. Although normally focused on a specific state or area, SSR activities occur in a broader regional context. Within that context, cultural sensitivities, political concerns, or apprehensions of neighboring states can become obstacles to reform. This makes SSR inherently complex in execution. Effective SSR requires a broad understanding of the security environment and an appreciation for the time commitment required to achieve long-term success.

THE MILITARY ROLE IN SECURITY SECTOR REFORM

6-22. SSR can occur at any point across the spectrum of conflict, in conditions ranging from general peace to the aftermath of major combat operations. No matter the conditions, SSR activities focus on the stability of the host nation to ensure conditions do not foment crisis and conflict.

Within full spectrum operations, SSR is an aspect of stability operations. SSR includes tasks, functions, and activities from each of the primary task areas. It concentrates on generating the necessary capacity of the state and societal institutions to support responsible governance and the rule of law.

6-23. In general, military forces play a primary role in SSR activities affecting host-nation defense institutions and armed forces. Within the other elements of the security sector, military forces are typically limited to a role supporting the efforts of other SSR actors. However, military forces may assume a more active role in SSR activities affecting the nonmilitary elements of the security sector. Ultimately, conditions of the operational environment determine the role of military forces.

6-24. When the operational environment is characterized as nonpermissive, military forces can expect to lead reform efforts. When conditions permit, other SSR actors assume primary responsibility for their roles, allowing military forces to relinquish the lead. Initially, the presence of nonmilitary SSR partners may be limited, requiring military forces to undertake tasks normally performed by other interagency and civilian partners. Even when nonmilitary SSR actors are present, the nature of the environment may require military forces to support those actors extensively as they undertake their respective aspects of SSR. Many civilian agencies and law enforcement forces require a permissive or semipermissive environment before assuming responsibility for their respective elements. In certain situations, the military establishes security and control over an area so other elements of the security sector can become active. In these situations, the military role is essential to establishing the conditions that enable subsequent SSR efforts by civilian partners.

6-25. When the operational environment is more permissive and suitable to introduce nonmilitary SSR partners, reform efforts can focus on all SSR activities. These activities include the transition from external to host-nation responsibility for security and public safety. Under these conditions, SSR activities may also transition to new host-nation institutions, groups, and governance frameworks as part of the peace process. As the transition proceeds, military primacy recedes. Other civilian agencies and organizations come to the forefront. They apply their expertise to their respective areas of the security sector and leave the military to focus on the host-nation defense sector and forces. Often the situation requires disarming, demobilizing, and reintegrating personnel associated with armed forces or belligerent groups before and as part of SSR. Military forces can expect to assume a primary role in disarmament. As the situation and conditions of the operational environment allow, military forces begin establishing and training host-nation forces within a comprehensive reform program. As the host-nation forces train and validate their capabilities, they begin to conduct operations and to assume responsibility for security. Finally, the supporting, external military forces reduce their level of operations and supervision, and civil authorities assume full responsibility for security sector functions.

6-26. During peacetime military engagement, military forces may conduct SSR activities as part of the theater security cooperation plan. The military element of SSR during peacetime military engagement helps reform established host-nation defense institutions and processes as well as security force assistance activities aimed at promoting SSR objectives in host-nation forces. During peacetime military engagement, the chief of mission carries out SSR. The military role in SSR is normally limited to helping reform host-nation defense activities and security force assistance to the host-nation armed forces. These efforts may impact other, nonmilitary aspects of SSR. The military element of the security sector closely coordinates with the other elements, consistent with a collaborative, comprehensive approach.

SECURITY SECTOR REFORM AND HOST-NATION AUTONOMY

6-27. Stability operations seek to enhance the legitimacy of host-nation governance while leveraging efforts to reform the security sector. The host-nation institutions, laws, and processes, however developmental, should play a central role when formulating and implementing SSR programs and processes. External influences frequently shape SSR policy formulation and implementation, especially when the host-nation government functions poorly. Nonetheless, SSR planners carefully uphold the host nation's sovereignty by integrating its government into reform planning and execution.

6-28. Comprehensive peace agreements may be helpful where a national constitution is not in place or is not practiced. National security strategies or policies, national defense acts, and national justice codes illustrate host-nation guidelines that can help to add structure to the reform effort. Also important are host-nation groups in charge of specific responsibilities, such as government reform agencies, national reconciliation commissions, and national DDR bodies.

6-29. Participants in SSR help develop the program using their own policy guidance and policy implementation mechanisms. For example, United Nations (UN) Security Council resolutions define the mandates of UN peacekeepers and UN-integrated missions. National policy guidance; national justice systems; and relevant national legislation, treaties, and agreements—both bilateral and multilateral—provide a framework for host-nation and military forces. U.S. security assistance, in particular, must proceed within the framework of legislated provisions governing the delivery of foreign assistance by U.S. agencies, both military and civilian. While SSR integrates these influences, ultimately, it reflects the host-nation institutions, laws, and processes.

SECURITY SECTOR REFORM PLANNING

6-30. Sustainable SSR depends on thorough planning and assessment. Working within a collaborative environment, the various actors consider the unique capabilities and contributions of each participant. The ensuing plan aims for a practical pace of reform and accounts for the political and cultural context of the situation. The plan accounts for available resources and capabilities while balancing the human capacity to deliver change against a realistic timeline. The SSR plan reflects host-nation culture, sensitivities, and historical conceptions of security. It does not seek to implement a Western paradigm for the security sector, understanding that a Western model may not be appropriate. As with the broader campaign plan, the SSR plan seeks to resolve the underlying sources of conflict while preventing new or escalating future security crises.

6-31. The level of host-nation development—especially as it pertains to poverty and economic opportunity—is an important consideration in SSR planning. High levels of poverty and endemic corruption significantly challenge SSR efforts. These factors—both at the individual and institutional levels—are typically evidenced by inadequate government revenues and a chronically under-resourced public sector. SSR programs are tailored to challenges that such environments pose. These programs confront endemic corruption in the public sector and accommodate limited host-nation public administration and public management capacities. External resourcing and external fiscal management for elements of the host-nation security sector, including its military institutions, may be necessary until sufficient host-nation capacity exists to sustain SSR activities.

6-32. Ideally, the SSR plan is informed and guided by host-nation security strategy and defense policy. However, in states without established, legitimate government institutions able to develop mature strategy and policy, SSR planning draws on a broad review of international security strategy and defense policy before implementing a plan. This review, which accounts for the nuances of host-nation culture, ensures the SSR plan reflects the needs of the country. It also ensures the end state is a security apparatus appropriate for the needs of the state and its people.

PRINCIPLES OF SECURITY SECTOR REFORM

6-33. Effective SSR requires unity of effort and shared vision among the agencies, organizations, institutions, and forces contributing to the reform process—a comprehensive approach. SSR is a cooperative activity, conducted with the other agencies of the USG, intergovernmental organizations, nongovernmental organizations, multinational partners, and the host nation. Integrated programs that consider relationships among organizations, sectors, and actors increase the likelihood of success, minimize unforeseen developments, and ensure the most effective use of resources. Six principles guide SSR:

- Support host-nation ownership.
- Incorporate principles of good governance and respect for human rights.
- Balance operational support with institutional reform.
- Link security and justice.
- Foster transparency.
- Do no harm.

Support Host-Nation Ownership

6-34. The principles, policies, laws, and structures that form an SSR program are rooted in the host nation's history, culture, legal framework, and institutions. Notably, the needs, priorities, and circumstances driving SSR differ substantially from one country to another. Assistance is designed to support local civil authorities, processes, and priorities to ensure the sustainability of SSR. As a result, SSR programs generally should be conceived as lengthy in nature.

6-35. Ultimate responsibility for SSR rests with the host nation. Commanders clearly must respect the views and interpretations of the host nation regarding what it perceives the security architecture should look like. The host nation bases its perception on threats and its broader security needs. SSR programs nest within existing host-nation social, political, and economic institutions and structures. Commitment and constructive engagement by the host nation's leaders ensures that institutions, capabilities, and forces developed under SSR will be enduring, appropriate to the needs of the host nation, and trusted by the host-nation government and its population.

Incorporate Principles of Good Governance and Respect for Human Rights

6-36. Accountability, transparency, public participation, and legitimacy are integral features of security force development. Technical assistance not only aims to build operational capability but also to strengthen adherence to democratic principles and build respect for human rights. Security forces—whether military, police, or intelligence services—carry out their core functions in accordance with these principles. This is especially important in rebuilding countries where the legacy of abuse by the military may have eroded public confidence.

Balance Operational Support with Institutional Reform

6-37. Incentives, processes, resources, and structures are placed so that externally supported reforms, resources, and capacities are sustained after the assistance effort ends. Building training platforms and providing material assistance without parallel efforts to help develop the infrastructure, personnel, and administrative support systems ultimately undermines the ability of host-nation forces to perform their security functions. Equal emphasis is placed on how recipients of security force assistance efforts are managed, monitored, deployed, sustained, and supported. Success and sustainability depend on developing the institutions and governance processes that support SSR as well as the human capacity to lead and manage the elements of that sector.

Link Security and Justice

6-38. Host-nation security policies and practices are nested in the rule of law. Rule of law cannot flourish in crime-ridden environments or where public order breaks down and citizens fear for their safety. Assistance efforts consider the diverse array of actors and institutions that compose the justice system. Police assistance undertaken without accompanying efforts to reform other parts of the justice system might result in increased arrests without the means to adjudicate individual cases or to support the incarceration or rehabilitation of convicted offenders. Similarly, focusing solely on reforming and rebuilding host-nation military forces while police services and justice system institutions languish can lead to the militarization of civil security. It also might encourage using military forces in roles inconsistent with existing frameworks for host-nation justice and rule of law.

Foster Transparency

6-39. Effective SSR programs are conducted as transparent and open as possible. Program design includes robust communications to foster awareness of reform efforts among host-nation officials and the population, neighboring countries, the donor community, and other actors.

Do No Harm

6-40. In complex environments, donor assistance can become a part of the conflict dynamic serving to either increase or reduce tension. As with any policy or program activity that involves changes to the status quo, actors ensure their efforts do not adversely affect the security sector or the wider political climate in unanticipated or unaddressed ways. Developing a thorough understanding of the system for which change is sought is a prerequisite for the success of any SSR-related activity. Actors complete a risk assessment prior to implementation and make adjustments as required during the conduct of SSR.

FOUNDATIONS OF SECURITY SECTOR REFORM

6-41. During SSR, participating military forces understand that the ultimate responsibility for reform rests with the host nation. SSR planning is based on the recognition that successful efforts require an extended commitment of time and resources. The military judiciously selects and uses forces to create a secure environment for an SSR program to progress unimpeded. The military may provide temporary capability and expertise, but long-term success in reform depends on how quickly and effectively it transitions to appropriate civilian agencies and the host nation. The military participates in SSR under principles for stability operations.

6-42. The foundations of SSR are—

- **A concept of security developed by the host nation and ingrained in its culture.** The core values of a SSR program reflect the needs of the people and inculcate the principle of ownership.
- **A framework that encompasses all security sector participants and challenges.** A SSR program provides a framework to structure thinking concerning the diverse security challenges facing host nations and their populations. This inclusive framework is essential to better integrate SSR policies and greater civilian involvement and oversight. It is founded on understanding the security sector from the host nation's perspective.

- **Cooperation with and among civil authorities**. SSR approaches are developed in cooperation with civil authorities. SSR approaches have many sectors; they are based on a broad assessment of the security and justice needs of the people and the state. Strategies reflect a comprehensive plan that encompasses all participants in the security sector.
- **Human rights**. A SSR program is based on democratic norms and underpinned by international human rights principles. SSR creates an environment characterized by freedom from fear by measurably reducing armed violence and crime. A SSR program enhances the institutional and human capacity for security policy to function effectively and for justice to be delivered equitably.
- **Clear policies, accountability, and professionalism**. SSR programs include well-defined policies that strengthen the governance of security institutions. Programs build professional host-nation security forces that are accountable to civil authorities and capable of executing their responsibilities. The security sector and supporting SSR activities adhere to basic principles of governance and broader public sector reform programs, including transparency and accountability.

CONSIDERATIONS FOR PLANNING

6-43. Coordinated interagency planning is required to ensure balanced development of the entire security sector. Imbalanced development can actually undermine the long-term success of SSR efforts. Integrated planning helps prioritize and sequence the activities of each contributing agency into a comprehensive SSR strategy. SSR planning must account for several interrelated factors that influence reform:

- Cultural awareness.
- Leadership capacity building.
- Public trust and confidence.
- Host-nation dependency.
- Perseverance.
- End state.

Interactions among the security sector and these factors complicate reform. Additionally, actions taken to reform one aspect of the security sector invariably affect reform activities in another. Effective assessment of these factors will drive the process and help define success.

Cultural Awareness

6-44. Regardless of the need to develop a host nation's security forces quickly, SSR requires considerable tolerance, cultural awareness, and an environment of mutual respect. In particular, actors working closely with host-nation forces must respect the security culture of the host nation. This culture is shaped by history, language, religion, and customs and must be understood. Cultural awareness and sensitivity are necessary to dispel the natural tensions that arise when external actors dictate the terms and conditions of SSR for the host nation. Responsiveness, flexibility, and adaptability to local culture help limit resentment and resistance to reform while generating local solutions to local problems. Local help fosters acceptance and strengthens the confidence of the citizens in reform.

Leadership Capacity Building

6-45. Challenges associated with developing capable, legitimate, and accountable security forces require capable leadership in the host-nation security sector at all levels. To establish the conditions for long-term success, SSR may help the host nation identify and begin training and advising security force leaders as early as possible. Such efforts must avoid undermining host-nation legitimacy while recognizing that assistance, advice, and education may be needed.

6-46. Programs focused on developing senior leaders, such as those conducted by the DOD Regional Centers for Security Studies, may prove helpful. Often the host nation can augment programs for officer training and staff college courses of participating forces and may even develop similar institutions. This participation ensures that future leaders gain the knowledge and skills to manage security forces effectively while meeting the broader responsibilities normally associated with leaders in the security sector.

Public Trust and Confidence

6-47. In rebuilding the institutions of a failed state, commanders must engender trust and confidence between the local populace and the security forces. As SSR proceeds, these security forces carry a progressively greater burden in ensuring public safety. Frequently, they do so in an environment characterized by crime and violence. This proves true in areas recovering from violent, predatory forces. Recovery requires a community-based response that uses the unique capabilities of the security forces and police. Operating in accordance with the laws of the host nation, the success of these forces will help to gain the trust and confidence of the local populace. Furthermore, increased public confidence engenders greater desire among the people to support the efforts of the security forces.

6-48. External participants in SSR must focus on enhancing the functionality of host-nation security forces while sustaining and strengthening the perception of legitimacy for civilians. Public confidence is further strengthened as host-nation forces support activities that foster civil participation. These activities, such as providing security for elections, associate the security forces with positive processes; this improves the credibility of host-nation security forces while providing visible signs of accountability and responsibility.

Host-Nation Dependency

6-49. During reform, the risk of building a culture of dependency is mitigated by adopting a training process. This process sequentially provides training and equipment to security forces, a dedicated advising capability, and an advisory presence. After initial training efforts, this reform helps host-nation security forces progress toward the transition of security responsibility. A robust transition plan supports the gradual and coherent easing of host-nation dependency, typically in the form of increased responsibility and accountability.

6-50. Depending on the security environment, external actors in SSR may need to protect new host-nation security forces from many direct and immediate threats during their development. While this requirement usually applies only during initial training, security forces remain at risk throughout their development during SSR; these threats may contribute to problems with discipline, dependability, and desertion. In extreme circumstances, protecting host-nation security forces may necessitate training outside the physical boundaries of the state.

Perseverance

6-51. SSR is a complex activity, and participants must demonstrate persistence and resilience in managing the dynamic interactions among the various factors affecting the reform program. Within the SSR processes, some failures are likely. Early identification of potential points of failure, such as corruption within the police force, allows for mitigating action.

End State

6-52. In stability operations, the external assistance force cannot impose success on the host nation. The host-nation government should emerge as the only legitimate authority. Within SSR, security forces are developed to enhance the legitimacy of the host-nation government. The resulting security forces must be—

- **Competent** from the ministerial level to the individual soldier and police officer, across all related fields of interest and functional specialties.
- **Capable** in size and effective enough to accomplish missions, remain sustainable over time, and maintain resources within state capabilities.
- **Committed** to the security and survival of the state, the preservation of the liberties and human rights of the citizens, and the peaceful transition of authority.
- **Confident** in the ability to secure the country; earning the confidence of the citizenry, the government, and the international community.

TRANSITION OF AUTHORITY

6-53. Transferring security responsibility from intervening to host-nation forces is done according to the tactical, operational, and strategic conditions identified during SSR planning. As forces establish suitable conditions, responsibility for security gradually transitions to the local, provincial, and national government. During transition, the presence of advisors is reduced, although some advisors may be retained to ensure the long-term sustainability of SSR. Transition planning must begin early and focus on timeline adherence.

6-54. During the transition of authority, a formal network of committees or consulting agencies validates the readiness and accountability of host-nation security forces. Progress toward transition is gauged through a process that confirms the performance and capabilities of host-nation security forces. Typically, forces gauge capabilities through test exercises similar to those used to validate the readiness of forces for contingency operations. These procedures prevent a premature transition of authority, which can lead to a loss of confidence and cause the populace to seek alternative means of security.

6-55. When the host nation emerges from an extended period of violent conflict characterized by widespread human rights violations, a rigorous vetting process should reestablish the legitimacy of reconstituted or rebuilt security forces. Such processes must be demonstrably neutral and free from political manipulation and may require external control or administration. When public records have been destroyed or lost, effective vetting may require detailed background investigations by trained interviewers to identify past human rights violators and to screen out unsuitable recruits from reconstituting security forces.

COMPREHENSIVE SECURITY SECTOR REFORM

6-56. Through unity of effort, execution of SSR unites all elements of the security sector. The activities of military forces may be focused on reforming the host-nation military forces, but those actions are only part of a broader, comprehensive effort to reform the entire security sector. Military forces may directly support related reform efforts or indirectly support the efforts as related, integrated activities.

6-57. Once the security environment is considered stable, other participating agencies, organizations, and institutions can safely begin operations in the operational area. Military forces gradually transfer appropriate responsibilities to other participants in the stability effort, one military force to another military or civilian group. These transitions allow the military force to focus their efforts on other stability tasks, many of which fall within the bounds of the broader effort to reform the security sector of the host nation.

CIVILIAN OVERSIGHT AND CONTROL

6-58. Establishing civilian oversight and control of the defense sector is critical to the success of any SSR program. Oversight and control mechanisms and processes ensure civilian control of the military, a fundamental tenet of effective governance. These processes and mechanisms also ensure that the various components of the defense sector are accountable to elected and appointed civilian leadership, both in the executive and legislative branches. That accountability is essential to establishing a sound foundation for defense budget planning and program implementation.

6-59. The primary agent of civilian oversight and control within the defense sector is the ministry of defense. The ministry of defense operates within some form of interagency or cabinet framework that establishes political links and accountability between the ministry and the executive branch. Other agencies involved in the defense sector may share oversight and control responsibilities, such as the cabinet-level leadership of intelligence agencies, executive protection forces, and border forces. In transitioning or post-conflict states, these institutions are frequently weak, dysfunctional, or altogether absent. SSR programs encompass restructuring, rebuilding, and, in some cases, creating entirely new institutions to provide oversight and control mechanisms for the defense sector.

6-60. The legislative branch plays an important role in oversight and control. The legislature typically determines the funding level of government activities while providing the statutory framework for planning and implementation. Constitutional frameworks may vest in the legislature a share in the appointment of senior government officials, or in the structuring, commissioning, and promoting of military personnel. In this context, building an effective partnership between the executive and legislative branches becomes an important enabler of effective SSR.

6-61. Most transitioning and post-conflict states clearly define and delineate the roles and responsibilities of military forces and law enforcement agencies as they provide internal security for the state. As the security apparatus of a state begins to fracture, the necessary distinctions between military and law enforcement roles and missions erode or disappear entirely. This situation frequently leads to inappropriate military involvement in political affairs. As a result, military forces may subsume justice and law enforcement functions although they lack the training or equipment. Restoring the distinction between military and law enforcement functions, as well as providing robust mechanisms to sustain that distinction, is fundamental to SSR.

6-62. The primary agent of civilian oversight and control over law enforcement agencies will likely be a separate ministry, such as the ministry of interior or of justice. As host-nation capacity for law enforcement increases, inherent power struggles may develop as police leaders strive for primacy in the management of social order. For this reason, it becomes imperative to facilitate forcing functions and forums that improve communications and coordination between disparate ministries that have responsibility for maintaining civil security. Often, the threshold delineating military and police primacy issues depends on the quantifiable level of violent activities in an area. This threshold serves as a quantifiable measure of effectiveness for military or civilian security sector efforts.

SECURITY FORCES STRUCTURE

6-63. An integrated approach is essential to building partner capacity in the security sector. While it is important to develop all essential capabilities, structures must be kept simple. In determining the optimal security forces structure, SSR accounts for the following:

- Political oversight and control in the form of capable ministries or Departments of Defense, Justice, and Interior. This aspect of SSR links the political direction of the state to the implementation of national interests and policies.

- National force headquarters that provides overall command and translates national interests and policies to the operational level for military, police, and other security forces. For the military element, this may be a joint structure.
- Appropriate legislation defining the role of the different security sector elements and forces and delineating oversight mechanisms in both the legislative and executive branches.
- Operational headquarters for both the military and law enforcement sectors. These may be regionally based, capability based, or a combination of the two.
- Staff disciplines at all levels, from strategic to tactical, for both military and law enforcement sectors.
- The ethnic and cultural factors that influence the security sector. SSR approaches must be able to accommodate significant cultural differences across societies and states.

6-64. The size, structure, and capabilities of tactical organizations, whether in the law enforcement or the military sector, depend on various considerations. Tactical forces must meet all the operational functions identified when assessing the security sector. This assessment informs SSR; an interagency team completes the assessment, drawing on all of the functional specialties required for a successful program. The considerations and factors guiding the assessment include the following:

- Required capabilities and roles. This includes consideration of the requirement for different types of forces. These requirements stem from a thorough threat analysis that helps to identify functional capabilities and requirements.
- Historical lineage and traditions (their positive and negative influences) of previous host-nation security forces.
- A realistic consideration of available resources, including near- and long-term manpower.
- Legal and political requirements for peace settlements, mandates, host-nation tools of governance, bilateral agreements, and similar political documents, frameworks, or processes that shape the overall stability operation.

Equipment and Resources

6-65. An integrated and synchronized training plan provides guidelines for identifying and balancing resource requirements; accounts for resource planning and prioritization; and identifies budget, funding control, execution, and reporting requirements. It also addresses the funding, procurement, allocation, and distribution of resources necessary to reform host-nation security forces. This is a broad task with the military advising and assisting the host nation and other actors in the stability operation. Training plans address not only how to use the equipment and resources, but also how to maintain them. Likewise, equipment procurement includes sustainment plans that provide life cycle management for materiel systems.

Infrastructure and Essential Services

6-66. The initial SSR assessment identifies requirements to support the entire program, including the reform of host-nation security forces. These requirements are incorporated into the broad plan for SSR, and resources are allocated against them. Typically, these requirements consist of the basic infrastructure and services necessary to support training and operational requirements. While commanders try to use existing infrastructure, they may need to acquire resources to improve or expand that infrastructure to support the reform effort.

Geographical Force Dispositions

6-67. Several factors influence the geographical distribution of restructured security forces. These factors include regional requirements, force role and capabilities, geography and climate, and existing infrastructure. Other considerations include differing cultural regions, local and regional associations, and historical lines of authority.

Accession and Training Policies

6-68. SSR planning includes policies for accession and training host-nation security sector personnel. These policies are developed with, and as a complement to, the broad program for DDR. The accession effort includes a thorough, transparent vetting of all prospective recruits by an external agency that has credibility with all participants in SSR; vetting is conducted in consultation with civil authorities.

REQUIREMENTS FOR FORCE DEVELOPMENT

6-69. The initial SSR assessment identifies the nature and type of forces to be developed and their respective capabilities. While these capabilities reflect host-nation aspirations, they also represent a detailed capability requirements analysis. This ensures a qualitative, as well as quantitative, foundation for the development program that accounts for future contributions by the host nation. All efforts to build capable forces are balanced with support to the institutional systems, processes, and managers that support them.

Military Forces

6-70. Military forces are developed primarily to counter external threats. The design of these forces develops from the analysis of those threats and the specific capabilities required to counter them. Other key military missions include providing humanitarian assistance, and in special cases, countering certain types of internal military threats. External organizations executing SSR and the individuals assigned to them are selected for their specific abilities to train and advise the developing force. For example, military police should help develop military police forces. This provides for appropriate development of expertise while facilitating the advising process.

Justice and Law Enforcement Forces

6-71. An effective and accountable justice system and supporting law enforcement (especially police) forces are central to a legitimate security framework. Although the military may be involved initially in developing the justice and law enforcement forces, this task should be assumed by other agencies as soon as possible. Qualified, professional justice sector and police trainers support an improved advising process and ensure sustainable development with appropriate civilian oversight. Their expertise ensures an appropriate delineation of roles and responsibilities between military forces and law enforcement sectors. In policing, development of organizational substructure—supervision, process, policy, internal governance, planning, and budgeting—are vital to the long-term sustainability of reform efforts.

Other Security Forces

6-72. Requirements may arise for the development of other forces within the security sector. These requirements may include specialized security forces; presidential guards; a coast guard, border control, and customs services; or intelligence services. The host nation provides the specific requirements on which to develop these forces. Until such forces are developed and trained, other security forces assume responsibilities outside of their intended domain. In such cases, due caution ensures forces conduct operations in compliance with relevant host-nation constitutional and statutory provisions and consistent with international law and humanitarian guidelines. Such caution extends to how civilians perceive operations and the legitimacy of the forces supporting the operation; continuous assessment ensures that commanders remain aware of how their operations affect the local populace and the broader SSR program.

6-73. In general, the capabilities of the security forces reflect the roles for which they were designed and trained. There may be overlap, particularly in times of emergency or until all planned forces are developed and trained. Cooperation between military and police is emphasized from the outset, permitting both to maintain their appropriate and distinct constitutional roles in the security sector. SSR educates host-nation forces, civilian oversight agencies, and political leadership on the appropriate roles for each part of the security forces. Military forces should be restricted to their role as a force of last resort in the face of military threats. Their use may require several approaches within the constitutional rule of law when military support to civil authority is required.

6-74. Ultimately, force development clearly defines and institutionalizes the separation of roles and responsibilities between military forces and law enforcement agencies. Usually, their organization, training, and equipment reflect this distinction; their design clearly limits the amount and degree of force that law enforcement agencies can generate. For example, civilian police entities may adopt military-style command structures and systems but not their mobile organizational structure. Another separation exists in that police forces provide services to a particular local area, neighborhood, or community. Since they lack organization for a large-scale maneuver, they do not generally form like military forces.

INITIAL TRAINING AND EDUCATION

6-75. In areas of the world torn by conflict, disaster, poverty, or internal strife, host-nation security forces often possess only rudimentary proficiency and development. Initial training for security forces must focus primarily on developing basic skills appropriate to their roles. Host-nation security forces should not train for specialty skills until personnel exhibit sufficient competence and confidence with these basic core skills. Advanced technology or materiel, while representative of increased status among developing forces, often extends beyond the comprehension of local forces, creating an unnecessary training burden.

6-76. To foster development and ease transition, training exercise programs are progressive. They test all levels of command, gradually bringing together all the individuals and institutions representing the new security sector, from team-level organizations through senior ministerial personnel. Host-nation security forces also require a complementary education program that supplements training, ensures understanding of roles and responsibilities, and reinforces relationships across the security sector with the local populace. Education and training must encourage civilian oversight of the security forces and a culture of service to the host nation and its population.

DEVELOPING SECURITY FORCES

6-77. *Security force assistance* **is the unified action to generate, employ, and sustain local, host-nation, or regional security forces in support of a legitimate authority.** It is integral to successful stability operations and extends to all security forces: military, police, and border forces, and other paramilitary organizations. This applies to all levels of government within the host nation as well as other local and regional forces. Forces are developed to operate across the spectrum of conflict—combating internal threats such as insurgency, subversion, and lawlessness; defending against external threats; or serving as coalition partners in other areas. It is critical to develop the institutional infrastructure to sustain security force assistance gains; host-nation security forces must have the *capability* to perform required functions across the stability sectors. They must exist in sufficient numbers to have the *capacity* to perform these functions wherever and whenever required. Finally, they must have the *sustainability* to perform functions well into the future, long after external forces are no longer engaged. Successful security force assistance involves thorough and continuous assessment and includes the organizing, training, equipping, rebuilding, and advising of the forces involved.

6-78. Some security force assistance operations require **organizing** new institutions and units from the ministerial level to the smallest maneuver unit. Building infrastructure-related capability and capacity—such as personnel, logistics, and intelligence—is necessary for sustaining the new host-nation capacity. Developing host-nation tactical capabilities without the sustainment structure is inadequate. Host-nation organizations reflect their own unique requirements, interests, and capabilities; they should not simply mirror existing external institutions.

6-79. **Training** is conducted in institutions—such as training centers and academies—in units, and by individual personnel. It includes a broad range of subject matter including those issues that make security forces responsive to a civilian oversight and control.

6-80. **Equipping** is accomplished through several mechanisms including traditional security assistance, foreign military support, and donations. Equipment must be appropriate for host-nation sustainment—appropriate to the physical environment of the region and within reasonable appropriations for operations and maintenance—and property accountability procedures. Equipping police forces can be a dangerous and complex process, occurring at numerous, geographically disparate locations across an operational area.

6-81. In many cases, particularly after major combat operations, it may be necessary to **rebuild**—or build—infrastructure to support security forces. This typically includes facilities and materiel but may also include physical plants, information systems, communications infrastructure, transportation, personnel management processes, and other necessary infrastructure. Rebuilding police facilities often differs from rebuilding military compounds. Police stations must be approachable and accessible to the community they support to be legitimate and effective.

6-82. **Advising** host-nation units and institutions is key to the ultimate success of security force assistance. This benefits both the state and the supporting external organizations. To be effective, advising requires specially selected and trained personnel.

6-83. Military forces conduct security force assistance according to certain imperatives. Like the principles of war, these imperatives, if followed, give the operation the best chance for success:

- **Understand the operational environment**. An in-depth understanding of the operational environment including the available friendly host-nation forces, the opposing threats, and civil considerations—is critical to planning and conducting effective security force assistance operations.
- **Provide effective leadership**. Leadership, a critical aspect of any application of combat power, is especially important in the inherently dynamic and complex environments associated with security force assistance.
- **Build legitimacy**. Ultimately, security force assistance aims to develop security forces that contribute to the legitimate governance of the local populace.
- **Manage information**. Disseminating timely and protected relevant information, integrating it during planning, and leveraging that information appropriately during execution is critical to successful security force assistance. Effective and efficient information management supports decisionmaking throughout capacity building.
- **Ensure unity of effort**. The effort will include security force assistance and host-nation forces and may include large-scale conventional forces, as well. Additionally, other joint, interagency, intergovernmental, and multinational organizations involved in security force assistance need to be integrated into the overall effort.
- **Sustain the effort**. Sustainability consists of two major components: the ability to sustain the security force assistance ef-

fort throughout the operation and the ability of the host-nation security forces to sustain their operations independently.

6-84. As host-nation security forces gradually progress toward the transfer of authority, close relationships forged between host-nation forces and their partners prove essential to sustainable development and successful transition. Genuine relationships engender trust and confidence, enabling increased responsibility and a well-executed transition process. These relationships also foster a clear understanding of command responsibilities and authorities. Such an understanding ensures host-nation forces approach transition prepared to assume the full weight of their future role in the security sector. Success in developing host-nation forces often depends more on relationships and personalities at the unit level than any other factor. (FM 3-24 includes additional detail on developing host-nation security forces.)

6-85. Trainers and advisors play a significant role in transition. They offer a guiding influence for host-nation security forces before, during, and after the transfer of authority. Practical experience with development activities in SSR indicate that—

- Trainers and advisors provide a crucial link between host-nation forces and the forces, agencies, organizations, and institutions supporting the broader stability effort.
- Trainers and advisors must be capable of dealing with challenges inherent in working with poorly trained and equipped forces. To contend with these challenges, predeployment training focuses on the stresses and ambiguity associated with developing host-nation security forces.
- Continuity of personnel is essential to maintaining relationships on which the success of force development depends. Tour lengths for advisors must be long enough to develop these relationships and staggered enough to maintain continuity and expertise with the developing host-nation force. Continuity fosters understanding, which is essential to development.
- The nuances of language and dialect must be addressed, either through formal training or dedicated interpreters. If using interpreters, they must be capable of performing all of the activities conducted by embedded trainers and advisors.
- The organization, training, and equipping of trainers and advisors should be tailored to support the planned role for the host-nation force under development.
- Trainers and advisors at all levels should be linked through a collaborative network that facilitates information sharing across the security sector. This enables them to monitor the ac-

tions, challenges, and decisions among the host-nation forces under development while providing a means to alert one another should issues arise.

Developing Border Control Forces

6-86. To maintain its authority, the state must control access to its territory. External actors and host-nation military forces provide the necessary border security and control while trainers and advisors focus on training host-nation border control forces. These border security activities include managing land border areas, airspace, coastal and territorial waters, and exclusive economic zones. The control of border areas and crossings prevents smuggling, movement of irregular forces into host-nation territory, and uncontrolled flow of refugees. In a broad sense, border control also includes managing and regulating the flow of intangible goods through the information environment. This is common in electronic commerce and banking, where the state may levy duties and import and export fees on transactions conducted through the Internet.

6-87. Border guards often are involved in monitoring, detecting, and preventing crime in border areas, including illegal entry and the illicit trafficking of goods, services, and human capital. The activities of border guards correlate to those of customs in facilitating and securing legal trade, migration control, and antiterrorism efforts. Effective, accountable border guards encourage trade and economic activity, facilitating the ability of the state to generate revenue and investment.

6-88. In fragile states, ineffective border control and management systems can frustrate efforts to detect and prevent organized criminal and irregular activity. Such failures erode confidence, fuel conflict, and threaten security. This often results in increased trafficking in illegal arms, goods, and human capital. To avoid these conditions, initial development efforts include—

- Establishing a civil border service under the control of the host-nation government.
- Facilitating the efficient and regulated movement of goods and people. This helps to achieve an appropriate balance among security, commerce, and social normalization.
- Building capacity to detect and prevent illegal trafficking, organized crime, irregular force movements, terrorism, and other activities that threaten the security of border areas.
- Strengthening revenue-generating capacity, promoting integrity, and discouraging corruption.
- Integrating the activities of border control and customs.

- Establishing and coordinating cross-border protocols with adjoining states to enhance cooperation, trade, and social normalization.

Developing Intelligence and Security Services

6-89. Intelligence and security services provide advance warning, analysis, information, and insights concerning emerging and existing threats and trends that affect the security and economic stability of the state. In peacetime, their analysis and intelligence indirectly shape policy through the state's political leadership. They usually are organized under the central government and report directly to senior political leaders. During SSR, intelligence and security services often resist change and may actively attempt to subvert the reform effort. Participants in the reform program must acknowledge host-nation sensitivities and the potential lack of transparency, while recognizing the substantial commitment of time and resources required to develop intelligence and security services appropriate to the host nation. During the initial development of intelligence and security services, training and advising activities include—

- Strengthening the legitimacy of intelligence and security services through civilian oversight and control.
- Developing effective systems capable of providing strategic intelligence and measurable contributions to national security planning.
- Enhancing the professionalism and ethics of intelligence and security services personnel. This can include the disestablishment of illicit intelligence groups with specific political agendas or allegiances.
- Reducing functional redundancies among intelligence services and agencies.

JUSTICE REFORM

6-90. The host-nation justice system encompasses an array of formal and informal institutions and actors. These institutions can include the ministry of justice, law enforcement, law schools and bar associations, and legal advocacy organizations. The actors can include members of the judiciary, legislature, corrections, and prosecutor's office; public defenders; ombudsmen; regulatory bodies; and human rights and public interest groups. The legal framework includes the Constitution, laws, rules, and regulations. Peace agreements may also constitute part of the legal framework in post-conflict countries.

6-91. Justice systems differ significantly across national boundaries; there may also be multiple justice systems functioning in a country. To enhance host-nation legitimacy, justice reform should build upon the existing legal framework. This may include common law, civil law, criminal codes, and traditional or religious law, as well as international law. SSR planners do not impose their concepts of law, justice, and security on the host nation. The host nation's systems and values are central to its development of justice system reform.

Courts

6-92. A formal justice system may be complemented by informal customary or traditional justice systems unique to particular areas, cultures, or regions. Sometimes referred to as "nonstate justice systems," traditional justice systems frequently provide important alternatives to formal, codified systems and provide greater access to justice to remote or underserved populations. Traditional justice systems may enjoy high levels of legitimacy with host-nation populations and may possess unique advantages as a means of promoting SSR in a broader context. Conversely, nonstate systems may not adhere to international human rights law. At the very least, SSR planners gain a thorough knowledge of any alternative systems that may be operating in a particular host nation.

6-93. Transitioning and post-conflict states frequently confront significant unresolved justice concerns from past or ongoing conflicts. Those concerns may be especially widespread, involving large numbers of perpetrators and victims or have especially horrific violence accompanying intrastate conflict. In such cases, special venues and processes for conflict-related justice and reconciliation may be necessary. Such processes sometimes are incorporated in the comprehensive peace agreements that form the foundation of conflict transformation. SSR programs must recognize and account for the requirement for such approaches and ensure reform acknowledges, embraces, and facilitates such efforts by—

- Promoting access to justice and legal empowerment as a priority to rebuild legitimacy and generate a culture that supports the rule of law. It must increase citizens' awareness of their rights and their ability to use justice systems to build capacity to advocate for change.
- Rebuilding core functions, reconstructing the disrupted (and possibly dysfunctional) justice system, redefining the legal framework and institutional roles, and building partner capacity.
- Developing reconciliation mechanisms to promote public trust and create accountability for past abuses.

Law Enforcement

6-94. The creation of community-based police services, with clearly separated police and military roles, is essential to successful SSR. However, in many weak or fragile states, the police become an instrument of state security rather than a protective force for the local populace. In the absence of a functioning central government, unaccountable, corrupt, and abusive police forces may undermine authority and threaten, rather than protect, the population's safety and security. Instead of helping to establish the conditions for recovery, they further destabilize the environment. SSR efforts include demilitarization and professionalization of the police. Police often resist these efforts, especially when the security environment is unstable. Nevertheless, police services are the cornerstone of any justice system and a necessary component of a functioning society.

6-95. Law enforcement reform is nested within the larger justice system reform. The justice system consists of a number of interrelated steps—arrest, detention, corrections, prosecution, adjudication, corrections, and parole or rehabilitation. Functionality requires that all actors work together as a system. Law enforcement reform that outpaces the rest of the justice sector may result in more arrests with inadequate detention facilities and no means of adjudication.

6-96. Establishing police primacy for internal security is difficult when confronting a failed state; that challenge is compounded when no historical precedent for primacy exists. Police may need only selective reform, or they may require extensive reform that encompasses a long-term development effort. Ultimately, a police reform effort aims to build a professional police force that earns the trust and confidence of the local populace while strengthening the legitimacy of the host-nation government.

6-97. Following an intervention in a failed state, an effective police force may not exist. With the local security environment in disarray, international police trainers and advisors often cannot safely deploy into the area. Military forces may be required to take the lead in restoring and maintaining order until enough civilian police partners arrive to initiate that component of SSR. While conventional military forces may be capable of providing immediate security from armed threats, they are not effective trainers of policing skills. Nor are they appropriate providers of police services to local communities unless they act as an occupying force under the provisions of the law of land warfare. Formed police units trained in stability policing skills are appropriate to perform these functions. Initial planning for failed state interventions should plan to incorporate such forces at the earliest opportunity. Typically, military police assist in training and advising local police and establishing police stationing operations for local law enforcement forces; military police forces may also assist in training and advising corrections officers as part of capacity-building activities.

6-98. For effective skill-building efforts with host-nation police services, trainers and advisors—

- Assess police roles, responsibilities, structures, management, and practices.
- Understand the traditional role of police within the host nation's society. From that starting point, they develop a force that conforms to internationally accepted law. Changing the institutional mentality of the police force to one that secures and protects the population requires extensive effort, time, and resources.
- Support links across the justice system to ensure system wide functionality.
- Improve police training, including the police education system. In the aftermath of conflict, it is important to focus training on investigative processes, including the gathering, handling, and preserving evidence to support ongoing prosecutions.
- Enhance the ability of police services to plan and develop criminal intelligence analysis skills.
- Strengthen police accountability.
- Develop an integrated approach that complements the broader SSR program.

Corrections

6-99. Within fragile states, police often arrest and detain prisoners without charge or trial, often for extended periods; overcrowded and poorly managed prisons are the norm. Typically, the abuse and torture of inmates characterize these prisons. In addition, they present serious health and hygiene issues for the local populace. In these circumstances, military forces must take immediate action to quickly reform and develop the corrections system. Issues considered during the initial development of the corrections system include—

- Ensuring respect for the human rights and dignity of detainees.
- Reducing pretrial detention to manageable levels.
- Improving health, hygiene, and social services in prisons.
- Increasing civilian oversight of the corrections system.
- Promoting rehabilitation and reintegration of detainees.

- Developing an approach integrated with judicial reform.

THE ROLE OF INTERGOVERNMENTAL ORGANIZATIONS IN SECURITY SECTOR REFORM

6-100. Since the end of the Cold War, intergovernmental organizations have emerged as prominent actors in SSR efforts worldwide. The most prominently recognized among these is the UN. Its broad membership, international reach, and inherent legitimacy ensure generally unfettered access to any corner of the world. However, intergovernmental organizations often focus on regional or other specific interests. These organizations can include the North Atlantic Treaty Organization (known as NATO) and the African Union, and subregional organizations such as the Economic Community of West African States. Intergovernmental organizations exhibit significant qualitative differences; however, their ability to engage meaningfully in operations must be weighed against their expertise, personnel, and equipment. Intergovernmental organizations take active roles in SSR and represent partners that can provide legitimacy to the SSR effort while helping to marshal support for that effort from key subregional, regional, and international states. Regional and subregional intergovernmental organizations have emerged as important players in SSR efforts in recent years, providing vital support worldwide. Such organizations play a critical role in mobilizing multinational partners to support SSR and may provide an important source of legitimacy for the SSR effort.

6-101. The UN brings high levels of legitimacy, unique capabilities provided by a broad mix of member states, and a capacity for sustaining large missions over long periods. It deploys many agencies capable of supporting SSR efforts across all three elements of the security sector. UN-integrated missions—under the direction of a special representative to the United Nations Secretary General —encourage multiple actors across UN agency and functional mission lines to cooperate to support SSR activities. The integrated mission leverages this cooperative spirit—the essence of the comprehensive approach—to help build unity of effort among a diverse array of external and host-nation actors.

DISARMAMENT, DEMOBILIZATION, AND REINTEGRATION

6-102. DDR efforts aim to increase the stability of the security environment by disarming and demobilizing armed forces and by helping return former combatants to civilian life. The complex DDR process has dimensions that include culture, politics, security, humanity, and socioeconomics. DDR can potentially provide incentives for commanders and combatants to enter negotiations, facilitate political reconciliation, dissolve belligerent force structures, and present opportunities for former combatants and other DDR beneficiaries to return to their communities. A successful DDR program helps establish sustainable peace. A failed DDR effort can stall SSR, disrupt peace processes, and socially and economically destabilize communities. Such failure can potentially lead to a renewal of conflict.

6-103.   The immediate goal of DDR is to appropriately scope the armed forces to the security requirements of the host nation. Typically, a DDR program transitions from disarmament and demobilization to reintegration. Disarmament and demobilization refers to the act of releasing or disbanding an armed unit and the collection and control of weapons and weapons systems. Reintegration helps former combatants return to civilian life through benefit packages and strategies that help them become socially and economically embedded in their communities.

DISARMAMENT

6-104.   *Disarmament* **is the collection, documentation, control, and disposal of small arms, ammunition, explosives, and light and heavy weapons of former combatants, belligerents, and the local populace.** Disarmament also includes the development of responsible arms management programs. Ideally, disarmament is a voluntary process carried out as part of a broader peace process to which all parties accede. Disarmament functions best with high levels of trust between those being disarmed and the forces overseeing disarmament. Some groups may hesitate to offer trust and cooperation or even refuse to participate in disarmament efforts. In these circumstances, disarmament may occur in two stages: a voluntary disarmament process followed by measures that are more coercive. The latter will address individuals or small groups refusing to participate voluntarily. In this second stage, disarmament of combatant factions can become a contentious and potentially very destabilizing step of DDR. Military forces manage DDR carefully to avoid disarmament stimulating renewed violence.

DEMOBILIZATION

6-105.   *Demobilization* is the process of transitioning a conflict or wartime military establishment and defense-based civilian economy to a peacetime configuration while maintaining national security and economic vitality (JP 4-05). Within the context of DDR, demobilization involves the formal and controlled discharge of active combatants from armed forces or other armed groups. The second stage of DDR, demobilization, includes identifying and gathering former combatants for processing and predischarge orientation. This extends from the processing of individual combatants in temporary centers to the massing of troops in camps designated for this purpose (cantonment sites, encampments, assembly areas, or barracks). In many societies, women and children are active participants in violent conflict. During demobilization, separate facilities are necessary for adults and children. Additionally, child soldiers require specific services including health, education, food, assistance with livelihood development, and reintegration into communities.

6-106. SSR programs must adequately address demobilization to avoid reemerging violence from combatant groups or organized criminals. Demobilization involves deliberately dismantling combatant chains of command and belligerent group loyalties, replacing those with more appropriate group affiliations and restoring their identity as part of the national population. The *demilitarization* of combatant groups and individuals enables the eventual development of value systems, attitudes, and social practices that help them reintegrate into civil society. Former combatants and belligerents traumatized by violent conflict may require extended counseling prior to reintegrating into the local populace. This is especially important when dealing with child soldiers.

REINTEGRATION

6-107. **Reintegration is the process through which former combatants, belligerents, and dislocated civilians receive amnesty, reenter civil society, gain sustainable employment, and become contributing members of the local populace.** It encompasses the reinsertion of individual former fighters and dislocated civilians into host-nation communities, villages, and social groups. Reintegration is a social and economic recovery process focused on the local community; it complements other community-based programs that spur job training, employment services, and economic recovery. It includes programs to impart marketable skills to demobilized armed forces and groups, belligerents, and dislocated civilians; relocation assistance to support their resettlement in civilian communities; basic and vocational education; and assistance in finding employment in local economies. It accounts for the specific needs of women and children associated with armed forces and groups, as well as those of civilians forced to flee their homes after violent conflict or disaster. Reintegration also addresses the willingness of civilian communities to accept former fighters into their midst; amnesty and reconciliation are key components to successful reintegration. In this context, reintegration cannot be divorced from justice and reconciliation programs that are part of the broader transition process. Successful reintegration programs tend to be long term and costly, requiring the participation of multiple external and host-nation SSR actors.

6-108. Reintegration is part of the general development of a country. It leads to restoration of a national identity and a sense of citizenship and civil responsibility. Programs that genuinely reintegrate former combatants and belligerents make significant contributions economically, socially, and politically to the reconstruction of fragile states. Only through successful reintegration can a nation avoid renewed violence and instability. Reintegration inherently includes reinsertion. However, the repatriation and resettlement of personnel associated with armed forces and belligerent groups involve broader political and diplomatic issues. These issues extend beyond the role of military forces but may also be integral to the reintegration process:

- **Reinsertion** is the assistance offered to former combatants, belligerents, and dislocated civilians prior to the long-term process of reintegration. Reinsertion is a form of transitional assistance intended to provide for the basic needs of reintegrating individuals and their families; this assistance includes transitional safety allowances, food, clothes, shelter, medical services, short-term education, training, employment, and tools. While reintegration represents enduring social and economic development, reinsertion comprises short-term material and financial assistance programs intended to meet immediate needs.

- **Repatriation** is the return of individuals to their country of citizenship.

- **Resettlement** is the relocation of refugees to a third country, which is neither the country of citizenship nor the country into which the refugee has fled. Resettlement to a third country is granted by accord of the country of resettlement. It is based on a number of criteria, including legal and physical protection needs, lack of local integration opportunities, medical needs, family reunification needs, and threat of violence and torture.

6-109. Military forces may establish and operate internment facilities or reintegration centers to ensure the continuity of detainee programs. Such centers established in detention centers and reintegration efforts conclude at the points of release back into society. The local populace must widely recognize, understand, and accept these and other programs that facilitate reintegration. This is achieved through effective information engagement, utilizing leader and Soldier engagement to leverage the interaction between military forces and the local populace. Former combatants will participate in reintegration when their behavior shows some level of due process involvement links to their corrective behavior modification.

IMPORTANCE OF DISARMAMENT, DEMOBILIZATION, AND REINTEGRATION TO STABILITY

6-110. The DDR program is a critical component of peace and restoration processes and is accounted for in initial planning. Often, the terms of this program are negotiated in ceasefire or peace accords. DDR focus on the immediate management of people previously associated with armed forces and belligerent groups. DDR set the foundation for safeguarding and sustaining the communities in which these individuals live as contributing, law-abiding citizens. The DDR program is a central contributor to long-term peace, security, and development.

6-111. DDR dictate, and are dictated by, a variety of priority areas in planning for full spectrum operations and SSR. The promise of DDR to formerly competing fighting forces often plays a crucial role in achieving a peace agreement. DDR planning directly ties to SSR, determining the potential size and scope of military, police, and other security structures. In addition, reintegration of former combatants back into their communities sets the foundation for—and determines the success of—long-term peace building and development programs.

6-112. The success of DDR depends on integrating strategies and planning across all the sectors. For example, the employment opportunities extended to disarmed and demobilized former combatants result from an effectively governed, viable economy with an active market sector. If the DDR program expires without providing alternative economic opportunities to the former combatants, the likelihood of a return to violence substantially increases. DDR closely coordinate with reform efforts in all sectors to ensure an integrated approach that synchronizes activities toward a common end state. For additional information on DDR, see the Department of State's *Lessons-Learned: Disarmament, Demobilization, and Reintegration (DDR) in Reconstruction and Stabilization Operations*.

PLANNING AND EXECUTING DISARMAMENT, DEMOBILIZATION, AND REINTEGRATION

6-113. Planning for a successful DDR program requires an understanding of both the situation on the ground and the goals, political will, and resources in which actors and other donor organizations are willing to support. Effective DDR planning relies on analysis of possible DDR beneficiaries, power dynamics, and local society as well as the nature of the conflict and ongoing peace processes. Assessments are performed while consulting the local populace and with personnel from participating agencies who understand and know about the host nation. Military forces and other actors may enter the DDR process at many different stages; therefore, assessment is a continuous process used to guide decisionmaking throughout the DDR program.

6-114. Governmental and nongovernmental organizations from the international community and the host nation cooperate to plan and execute DDR programs. External and host-nation military forces and police working together in a peace support role may facilitate DDR. Conflict termination, represented by a negotiated or imposed settlement, provides the basis for DDR to proceed. Former combatants must develop confidence in DDR and the organizations charged with implementing it. To build this confidence, the DDR program focuses on restoring the society, the government, and the economy at all levels. This leads to the host nation taking responsibility for DDR processes.

6-115. Generally, the military does not lead the planning and execution of the DDR program. However, military forces must be integrated in the planning of DDR from its inception and may be involved more directly in the disarmament and demobilization stages. Military forces and police, whether from external sources or the host nation, are fundamental to the broad success of the program, providing security for DDR processes. Successful DDR programs use many approaches designed for specific security environments. Each program reflects the unique aspects of the situation, culture, and character of the state.

6-116. The best interests of children and their protection from violence and abuse are overarching principles during DDR. In operations involving the welfare of children, the entire process emphasizes integration and inherently is a community process. To the greatest extent possible, children associated with armed groups should be immediately released and reintegrated into civil society. Cash payments to demobilized minors are harmful and should therefore be avoided. Juvenile justice considerations, which may involve restorative as well as retributive actions, are central to any DDR program involving child soldiers. International DDR approaches must comply with *The Principles and Guidelines on Children Associated with Armed Forces or Armed Groups*, also known as The Paris Principles. The staff judge advocate is the staff principle responsible for providing command guidance on any situations pertaining to child combatants.

Appendix A

Interagency, Intergovernmental, and Nongovernmental Organizations in Stability Operations

BACKGROUND

A-1. Stability operations include a wide array of actors with various experiences, resources, mandates, and capabilities. This requires forging a comprehensive approach with a shared understanding and appreciation for the intended end state. This approach is both the overall goal and the greatest challenge to mission accomplishment. Many actors cannot be compelled to work within a coalition, nor do they have any incentive to do so. Therefore, military forces must build strong relationships through cooperation and coordination. This appendix provides a limited overview of certain interagency, intergovernmental, and nongovernmental organizations that U.S. forces can expect to operate alongside during stability operations.

INTERAGENCY ORGANIZATIONS

A-2. Military forces conduct stability operations under the authority of the President of the United States, in accordance with treaties, conventions, and executive and other agreements; statutory laws; and Federal and agency regulations. These operations are conceived and implemented through an interagency process under the general direction and supervision of the National Security Council and its staff. Normally, specific agencies such as the Department of State (DOS), Department of Defense (DOD), and Central Intelligence Agency (CIA) are designated as having the lead in the interagency working groups. These groups do the bulk of the day-to-day work involved in implementing policy. (See appendix B for a discussion of the Interagency Management System.)

NATIONAL SECURITY COUNCIL

A-3. The National Security Council (NSC) advises and assists the President in integrating all aspects of the national security policy—domestic, foreign, military, intelligence, and economic (in conjunction with the National Economic Council). The NSC system is the principal forum for considering national security issues requiring presidential decisions. The NSC system provides the foundation for interagency coordination in developing and implementing national security policy. It is the only level of the executive branch in which authoritative direction to the various departments can be given. The functions, membership, and responsibilities of the NSC were set forth in National Security Presidential Directive 1.

A-4. The members of the NSC include the President, the Vice President, the Secretary of State, and the Secretary of Defense. The Director of National Intelligence regularly attends NSC meetings as a cabinet officer. The Chairman of the Joint Chiefs of Staff attends NSC meetings and serves as a statutory advisor. Other regular NSC meeting attendees include the Secretary of Treasury, the assistant to the President for national security affairs (referred to as the national security advisor), the assistant to the President for economic policy, and the chief of staff to the President. Heads of executive departments and agencies and other senior officials, such as the United States permanent representative to the United Nations (UN), may be invited to attend meetings of the NSC on an ad hoc basis. The NSC staff tracks and directs the development and implementation of national security policies for the President.

DEPARTMENT OF STATE

A-5. The DOS is the United States Government (USG) agency responsible for planning and implementing the foreign policy of the United States. The DOS is headed by the Secretary of State, who is the ranking member of the President's cabinet and fourth in presidential succession. The Secretary of State is the President's principal advisor for conducting foreign affairs and formulating foreign policy. In its diplomatic role, the DOS is an important source of foreign affairs data, national security and economic information, and information on the policies and inner workings of countries. In its consular function, it provides notarial and citizenship services to American citizens abroad and assists in implementing U.S. immigration and naturalization laws.

Country Team

A-6. The *country team* is the senior, in-country, U.S. coordinating and supervising body, headed by the chief of the U.S. diplomatic mission, and composed of the senior member of each represented U.S. department or agency, as desired by the chief of the U.S. diplomatic mission (JP 3-07.4). The team composition varies widely depending on specific U.S. national interests, the desires of the ambassador, the situation in the country, and the number and level of presence of U.S. agencies. Figure A-1 shows possible members of the country team.

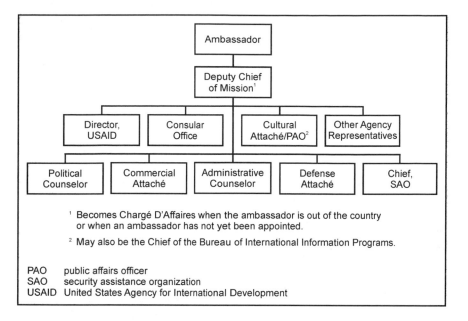

Figure A-1. Country team members

A-7. The country team facilitates interagency action on recommendations from the field and implements effective execution of U.S. programs and policies. It builds the foundation for rapid interagency consultation and action on recommendations from the field and effective execution of U.S. missions, programs, and policies. A country team is relatively small and may not be adequate for every need. A country team may not exist in every country, or it may be inoperative due to damage or casualties from a disaster. Country teams generally have received some crisis management training, but they usually are not prepared to plan in detail. The relationship with military chains of command is frequently ad hoc.

Senior Defense Official or Defense Attaché

A-8. The senior defense official or defense attaché serves as the defense attaché and chief of security assistance in the embassy. This official also acts as the in-country focal point for planning, coordinating, supporting, and executing U.S. defense activities in the host nation. These activities include theater security cooperation plans conducted under the oversight of the combatant commander. In addition, the senior defense official defense attaché—

- Serves as the principal embassy liaison with host-nation defense establishments and actively participates in national security and operational policy development and coordination.

- Represents the Secretary of Defense and the DOD components to host-nation counterparts and foreign diplomats accredited to the host nation.

- Presents coordinated DOD views on all defense matters to the chief of mission and acts as the single DOD point of contact to the chief of mission.

- Represents the Secretary of Defense and the appropriate combatant commanders for coordinating administrative and security matters for all DOD personnel not under the command of a U.S. military commander.

A-9. The defense attaché office, which consists of one or more defense or service attachés and support personnel, observes and reports on the country's military and political-military situation. This information can be valuable when planning and executing various missions in the country. These missions may include noncombatant evacuation operations and support to counterdrug and counterinsurgency. Defense attaché office personnel are active duty military attached to the embassy in a diplomatic status. The Defense Intelligence Agency rates and funds defense attachés. They may add to the daily embassy situation report and provide other written intelligence-related information. All military personnel, even those not assigned to the embassy or under direct control of the ambassador, should coordinate their activities through the senior defense representative (which may be the security assistance organization or the defense attaché, depending on the country.) Duties of the defense attaché office also include liaising with host-nation defense officials on military matters related to threat assessments, intelligence, and in-country capabilities. A smaller embassy may not have a defense attaché present; rather, it depends on a regional attaché accredited to the host nation but stationed elsewhere.

Security Assistance Organization

A-10. The security assistance organization (SAO) also maintains a liaison with the host-nation military forces. It is the most important military activity related to foreign internal defense under the ambassador's supervision. The SAO assists host-nation security forces by planning and administering military aspects of the security assistance program. It also helps the U.S. country team communicate host-nation assistance needs to policy and budget officials in the USG. In addition, the SAO oversees training and assistance teams temporarily assigned to the host nation. The SAO is prohibited from providing direct training assistance. Instead, training is provided through special teams and organizations assigned to limited tasks for specific periods, such as mobile training and technical assistance teams.

A-11. The SAO is a joint organization. Through the senior defense official or defense attaché, the chief of the U.S. diplomatic mission directs and supervises the SAO chief to accomplish the SAO's mission. The geographic combatant commander commands the SAO in matters that are not functions of the chief of the U.S. diplomatic mission. The director of the Defense Security Cooperation Agency prescribes policy for managing security assistance programs by the SAO.

A-12. In country, the SAO may be known by many names according to the number of persons assigned, the functions performed, or the desires of the host nation. Typical SAO designations include a joint military assistance group, a military liaison office, the military training mission, and the office of defense cooperation. In countries where the United States has no SAO, another member of the mission oversees security assistance. In many countries, security assistance functions are performed within the defense attaché office. The defense attaché may also serve as the SAO.

A-13. The United States tailors each SAO to the needs of its host nation; thus, no typical SAO exists. However, a large SAO normally has Army, Navy, and Air Force components. Each component must accomplish its Service portion of security assistance activities. A small SAO may have divisions by function but no separate Service components.

A-14. The primary functions of security assistance personnel are logistics management, fiscal management, training management, and contract administration of country security assistance programs. Security assistance personnel maintain a liaison with host-nation defense establishments. They operate with the host-nation military—primarily at the national level—to interpret U.S. policies, resolve problems in materiel delivery, and obtain technical assistance for defective materiel. They assess the capabilities of the host-nation military and determine additional materiel requirements.

A-15. The SAO provides host-nation governments with information necessary to make decisions about acquiring and using U.S. defense articles and services. (These services include training under the auspices of U.S. security assistance programs.) The SAO obtains information to evaluate the host-nation military's capability to employ and maintain the equipment requested. The SAO processes security assistance proposals of foreign governments. It also maintains communications with host-nation defense officials on military matters, such as the threat's and host-nation military capabilities.

A-16. Documents describing SAO responsibilities and functions include DODD 5105.65 and DODD 5132.3. The former establishes the responsibilities, functions, authorities, and relationships of the Defense Security Cooperation Agency as an agency of the DOD. The latter establishes DOD policy and assigns responsibilities pursuant to the Foreign Assistance Act of 1961, as amended, the Arms Export Control Act of 1976, as amended, and related statutory authorities, executive orders, and policies established by the Secretary of State relating security assistance.

Embassy Representatives

A-17. The chief of mission (the ambassador) has authority over all in-country USG elements except forces assigned to a combatant commander. The ambassador represents the President but takes policy guidance from the Secretary of State through regional bureaus. The ambassador integrates the programs and resources of all government agencies represented on the country team. As the President's representative in the host nation, the ambassador has extraordinary authority. This individual may tailor the country team as needed for any crisis that arises with few limits from written rules. The ambassador functions at both operational and tactical levels, where recommendations and considerations for crisis action planning are provided directly to the geographic combatant commander or senior military representative in the area.

A-18. The President gives the chief of mission immediate direction and control over USG personnel in country. This does not include personnel in another mission, assigned to an international organization, or assigned to a combatant command or its subordinate elements. The chief of mission ensures that all in-country USG activities serve U.S. interests as well as regional and international objectives. This individual promotes positive program direction by seeing that all activities are necessary, are efficiently and economically run, and are effectively interrelated.

A-19. The deputy chief of mission is the senior diplomatic official in the embassy below the rank of ambassador. This official has the diplomatic title of minister, minister-counselor, or counselor (depending on the size of the mission) and is usually a career foreign service officer. The deputy chief of mission or chief of staff (military equivalent) usually chairs the emergency action committee meetings and coordinates embassy staff. The deputy chief helps ensure that all U.S. in-country activities best serve national interests.

A-20. The U.S. defense representative is an additional title assigned to a military officer serving in a specifically designated position. This duty title may be assigned to either the defense attaché or the security assistance officer. This representative represents the Secretary of Defense, the Chairman of the Joint Chiefs of Staff, and the geographic combatant commander. This officer coordinates administrative, security, and logistic matters with USG officials for all DOD noncombatant command elements in the country in which the U.S. defense representative is assigned.

A-21. The chief of station is the senior intelligence advisor to the ambassador. The chief of station is an excellent source of information on the country and the current situation.

A-22. The administrative counselor, sometimes referred to as the management officer, oversees various activities at the embassy compound. These activities may include security at small posts; running the commissary, motor pool, and maintenance activities; and handling monetary aspects of embassy business, including foreign service national payroll, cash collection, and the budget. At a small post with no security officer assigned, the administration officer assumes the functions of the post security officer and has operational control of the Marine security guard detachment. The general services officer and information management officer work for the administration officer:

- The general services officer is responsible for buildings, grounds, construction, vehicles, and maintenance.
- The information management officer runs the post communications center; processes and tracks all classified pouch material; and oversees the computer system at the embassy. This officer is the point of contact for the post's communication capabilities.

A-23. The political counselor reports on political developments, negotiates with the host-nation government, and represents views and policies of the USG. This officer maintains regular contact with host-nation officials, political and labor leaders, and other influential citizens of the host nation, as well as other countries' diplomats. The political counselor makes major contributions to the overall intelligence picture.

A-24. The refugee coordinator works in a regional position to oversee USG assistance to refugees and other populations of concern. This coordinator works closely with the Bureau of Population, Refugees, and Migration at the DOS, United States Agency for International Development (USAID), international and local nongovernmental organizations (NGOs), and organizations such as United Nations Office of the High

Commissioner for Refugees and the International Committee of the Red Cross (ICRC).

A-25. The commercial attaché or economic officer analyzes, reports on, and advises superiors, DOS, and DOD personnel on economic matters in the host nation. This attaché also negotiates with the host nation on trade and financial issues.

A-26. Consular officers screen, process, and grant U.S. passports and visas. Other duties mandated by law include attending to the welfare of and maintaining a census of American citizens in the host nation. During noncombatant evacuation operations, the consular officer provides personnel to screen documents of all potential evacuees and instructs personnel in the evacuation control center.

A-27. The regional medical officer is qualified for general practice and can set up triage, trauma, and mass casualty operations. This officer may provide advice on indigenous diseases and proper prophylactic procedures for forces executing a noncombatant evacuation operation. These officers are only found in certain interagency coordination embassies where the support exists for them to carry out their duties.

A-28. The regional security officer (RSO) is a DOS diplomatic security agent responsible for the security functions of all U.S. embassies and consulates in a given country. This officer directs the Marine security guard detachment via the detachment commander. Similar to the regional medical officer, the RSO is found in all but the smallest embassies. The RSO oversees the following:

- **Post security officer**. Posts with no RSO have a post security officer. This officer has general security duties at a specific embassy (or consulate) and is usually the administration officer. The post security officer is supported by a designated RSO in a nearby country.
- **Mobile security division**. This division consists of DOS employees of the diplomatic security service who respond to crises in foreign countries. The mobile security division responds to increased threats or critical security needs at an embassy, provides additional security, and immediately responds to a security-related incident.
- **Local guard force**. Embassies enhance security by hiring civilian security guards to provide perimeter security.

A-29. The public affairs officer (PAO) is the ambassador's advisor concerning public affairs and overseer of U.S. cultural center operations. If the situation permits during an emergency, the PAO is responsible for all press releases and inquiries for information directed to the embassy. The PAO usually speaks at press conferences that the ambassador cannot attend. (See FM 46-1 for details on public affairs.)

A-30. A Marine security guard detachment has, on average, six Marines, with the maximum number assigned according to need. The Marine detachment commander is normally a member of the emergency action committee. This individual has responsibility to protect classified material, U.S. personnel, and USG property. Administrative control of detachment Marines is through their geographic combatant commander.

DEPARTMENT OF DEFENSE

A-31. The DOD coordinates with the DOS and other government agencies on many issues including—

- Bilateral and multilateral military relationships.
- Treaties involving DOD interests.
- Technology transfers.
- Armaments cooperation and control.
- Humanitarian assistance.
- Peace operations including those under the auspices of the UN.

A-32. Within an area of responsibility, the geographic combatant commander plans and implements theater and geographic military strategies that require interagency coordination. Coordination between the DOD and other government agencies may occur with a country team or within a combatant command. In some operations, a special representative of the President or special envoy of the UN Secretary General may be involved. Many USG organizations are regionally focused, such as the DOS in its regional bureaus and the USAID. In individual countries, the ambassador and country team supervise and direct the overall foreign assistance program.

A-33. A campaign plan is based on a joint force commander's intent and concept of operations. This plan presents a broad vision of the required aim or end state and how operations will be sequenced and synchronized to achieve objectives. A campaign plan is essential for laying out a clear, definable path linking the mission to the desired end state. Such a plan enables commanders to help political leaders visualize operational requirements for achieving objectives. Given the systematic military approach to problem solving, often the combatant commander formally or informally functions as the lead organizer of many operations. (JP 3-08 outlines how to develop and execute a campaign plan in the interagency arena.)

A-34. A political advisor is a foreign service officer from the DOS. Usually combatant commanders are augmented with a political advisor. Army component commanders in multinational operations and other operations may also be augmented with a political advisor. The political advisor provides diplomatic considerations and enables informal links with embassies in the area of responsibility to the DOS. The foreign policy advisor supplies information regarding DOS policy goals and objectives relevant to the geographic combatant commander's theater strategy. Other government agencies also may detail liaison personnel to operational-level staffs when requested to improve interagency coordination.

CENTRAL INTELLIGENCE AGENCY

A-35. The CIA coordinates the intelligence activities of other U.S. departments and agencies. It advises and recommends policy to the NSC on matters regarding intelligence activities of all government departments and agencies. It correlates and evaluates this intelligence and disseminates it in the government. The CIA also conducts special activities approved by the President. Executive Order 12333 directs that "no agency except the CIA (or the Armed Forces of the United States in time of war declared by Congress or during any period covered by a report from the President to the Congress under the War Powers Resolution ... may conduct any special activity unless the President determines that another agency is more likely to achieve a particular objective...."

UNITED STATES AGENCY FOR INTERNATIONAL DEVELOPMENT

A-36. USAID is an independent USG agency that answers to the President through the Secretary of State. It manages U.S. developmental, humanitarian, and civic assistance activities. USAID supervises and gives general direction on all nonmilitary assistance programs under the Foreign Assistance Act of 1961, Agricultural Trade Development and Assistance Act of 1954 (also known as "Food for Peace"), and related legislation. USAID also provides global technical leadership and technical assistance on development issues. It applies to multiple sectors that are critical for reconstruction and stabilization operations. Examples of these sectors include economic development, agriculture, health, democracy and governance, environment, humanitarian response, and conflict management and mitigation. This agency plans and implements programs to improve economic and social conditions overseas, to help countries improve governance, to build legitimate institutions and manage conflict, and to address global problems. The agency administers food assistance programs with the Department of Agriculture. Under arrangements made with USAID, U.S. affiliates of international voluntary agencies conduct most bilateral food assistance programs appropriated under Agricultural Trade Development and Assistance Act of 1954. USAID also administers development assistance programs with the U.S. Millennium Challenge Corporation. Although USAID is concerned primarily with development and civic assistance, many programs it administers, particularly in weak or fragile states, are security related. The agency representative in the host nation coordinates USAID managed assistance programs with other members of the country team, including the DOD representative. Coordination is also with all other assistance programs managed by USG departments or agencies active in the host nation. The USAID representatives in a host nation help coordinate U.S. foreign assistance with other multilateral, bilateral, and U.S. private assistance programs to that country.

A-37. USAID, through its Office of Foreign Disaster Assistance, leads U.S. humanitarian assistance efforts overseas. The Office of Foreign Disaster Assistance developed the disaster assistance response team to provide rapid response to foreign disasters. This team provides various trained specialists to assist U.S. embassies and USAID missions with short-term assistance. It is a major component of USG capability in foreign humanitarian crisis or complex emergencies. (See JP 3-08 for more information.)

A-38. The overseas USAID mission is part of the American embassy; it operates under chief of mission authority and guidance. Its size varies widely depending upon the size and complexity of the U.S. foreign assistance program to that host nation. A small USAID mission may consist of a single U.S. representative supported by several locally hired employees. A large mission may have 50 or more U.S. direct hire employees. These employees often receive support from 50 to 125 locally hired host nation, U.S., or third country contract employees. A medium to large USAID mission overseas usually has a USAID mission director, deputy director, program office, and various technical offices. The latter may include economic growth, democracy and governance, health and education, and other support offices. More than 70 developing countries have USAID missions, while over 100 countries have active USAID programs. USAID implements U.S. foreign assistance through agreements with implementing partners. Implementing partners may be host-nation entities or organizations, other USG departments or agencies, intergovernmental or nongovernmental organizations, contractors, or private sector entities. While the numbers of USAID staff in a country is usual small, it often has substantial reach and influence through its implementing partners.

INTERGOVERNMENTAL ORGANIZATIONS

A-39. Intergovernmental organizations possess area or global influence. Examples of intergovernmental organizations with global reach include the UN, its agencies, and the World Bank. These organizations have well-defined structures, roles, and responsibilities as well as the resources and expertise to lead and participate in complex operations. Regional examples include North Atlantic Treaty Organization (NATO), the African Union, the Organization of American States, the European Union, and the Organization for Security and Cooperation in Europe. Paragraphs A-40–A-52 discuss formal or informal ties between the United States and some of the larger intergovernmental organizations.

THE UNITED NATIONS

A-40. Coordination with the UN begins at the national level with the DOS, through the U.S. permanent representative to the UN. In some administrations, this individual has cabinet status. The U.S. representative is assisted at the U.S. mission to the UN by a staff of 100 foreign nationals, military, and civilian personnel. This staff includes a military assistant who coordinates appropriate military interests primarily with the United Nations Office for the Coordination of Humanitarian Affairs (OCHA), the UN Development Programme, and the United Nations Department for Peacekeeping Operations (UNDPKO).

A-41. The Foreign Assistance Act of 1961, the United Nations Participation Act of 1945, and Executive Order 10206 authorize various types of U.S. military support to the UN, either on a reimbursable or nonreimbursable basis. U.S. military operations to support the UN usually fall within Chapter VI or Chapter VII of the UN Charter. (See JP 3-08 for details regarding the UN Charter and Chapters VI and VII of that charter.)

A-42. The UN Security Council normally authorizes peace operations or conducts humanitarian assistance under the provisions of a resolution or mandate from the UN Security Council or the general assembly. As politicians and diplomats try to reach a compromise, they develop mandates. The compromises often challenge military commanders who translate these mandates into workable mission orders. Additionally, fast-changing events on the ground can quickly render a mandate obsolete. Commanders must quickly inform the chain of command of significant changes in the situation.

A-43. The UN headquarters coordinates peace operations and humanitarian assistance around the world. It maintains a strategic-operational-tactical structure equivalent to the armed forces for implementing UN Security Council resolutions. The UN organizational structure consists of the headquarters and the operational field elements. Strategic decision-making resides with the UN Security Council. The Secretariat provides strategic guidance between resolutions of the UN Security Council as well as exercises a measure of operational authority. Within an operational area, the special representative to the United Nations Secretary General (UNSG) at the integrated mission headquarters—normally based in the host-nation capital—provides operational-level command as well as a link to the tactical level. At the tactical level, the various heads of the sectors into which the host nation has been divided for mission implementation provide tactical counterparts for military commanders operating at that level.

A-44. The OCHA coordinates humanitarian operations. This office makes necessary arrangements for UN relief organizations to deliver assistance quickly and effectively. The UN emergency relief coordinator appoints humanitarian coordinators for natural disasters and complex emergencies. In complex emergencies, the emergency relief coordinator appoints a field-based humanitarian coordinator. This latter coordinator works under the authority of the special representative to the UNSG. Under certain circumstances, the UNSG may appoint a special representative to direct day-to-day operations. This representative reports to the UNSG directly and advises UNDPKO and OCHA at UN headquarters.

A-45. The OCHA is a part of the UN Secretariat. It coordinates UN assistance in humanitarian crises that exceed the capacity and mandate of any single humanitarian organization. The head of this office, the emergency relief coordinator, chairs the Interagency Standing Committee, thus uniting all major humanitarian actors inside and outside the UN system. This committee works to analyze a given crisis. It also ensures interagency decisionmaking when responding to complex emergencies and developing humanitarian policy. The UN country team led by the humanitarian coordinator coordinates the responses to specific crises at the country level for the UN system.

A-46. The UNDPKO is the operational arm of the UNSG for managing day-to-day peacekeeping operations. In this capacity, the department acts as the main channel of communications between UN headquarters and the field when a peacekeeping force is deployed.

A-47. The UN Development Programme is a separate agency that is part of the UN system. As indicated by its name, this agency focuses more on long-term development than emergencies. The in-country program representative is often the UN humanitarian coordinator, responsible to mobilize and manage the local UN humanitarian resources and provide direction for the field relief effort. If conflict erupts, a special representative to the UNSG—who has greater expertise in emergencies and negotiations—may replace the UN resident coordinator.

A-48. Normally, UN-sponsored operations employ a force under a single commander. The force commander is appointed by the UNSG with the consent of the UN Security Council. This commander reports to the special representative to the UNSG or to the UNSG directly. In any multinational operation, the U.S. commander retains command authority over all assigned U.S. forces. The U.S. chain of command flows from the President through the combatant commander. With presidential authorization, the multinational force commander may exercise operational control over U.S. units in specific operations authorized by the UN Security Council.

THE NORTH ATLANTIC TREATY ORGANIZATION

A-49. NATO is a good example of the interagency process on a regional level. NATO has been challenged by the demands for cooperation that characterize every regional effort and has endured for over 50 years. U.S. efforts within NATO are led and coordinated by the permanent representative. This representative is appointed by the President and has the rank and status of ambassador extraordinary and chief of mission (see the Rogers Act). Table A-1 lists the 26 members of NATO.

Table A-1. Members of NATO

Belgium	Bulgaria	Canada	Czech Republic
Denmark	Estonia	France	Germany
Greece	Hungary	Iceland	Italy
Latvia	Lithuania	Luxembourg	Netherlands
Norway	Poland	Portugal	Romania
Slovakia	Slovenia	Spain	Turkey
United Kingdom	United States		

A-50. Over the years, NATO has undergone changes in organization, orientation, and membership. Following the Cold War, the alliance was restructured to enable it to participate in peacekeeping and crisis management tasks. The alliance undertakes the tasks in cooperation with countries that are not members of the alliance and with other international organizations. NATO support to UN operations in the former Yugoslavia illustrates this cooperation.

A-51. In Kosovo, Operation Allied Force demonstrated for the first time NATO's ability to conduct offensive operations to force a noncompliant to assent to the alliance's collective will. The alliance has been actively involved in planning, preparing, and implementing peace operations, such as protection for humanitarian relief and support for UN monitoring of heavy weapons.

A-52. Beyond day-to-day operations, training exercises, and logistics authorized by statute, extraordinary use of military forces with NATO across the spectrum of conflict requires presidential approval. They may also be subject to congressional review, including those employments authorized and limited by the War Powers Resolution of 1973.

NONGOVERNMENTAL ORGANIZATIONS

A-53. NGOs do not operate within the military or governmental hierarchy or the chain of command. Therefore, any relationship between the armed forces and an NGO is best characterized as a professional or circumstantial association. Generally, coordination between military forces and NGOs is facilitated through the UN, USAID, or DOS. The military force ordinarily orchestrates this interaction with other agencies and organizations through the activities of a civil-military operations center (CMOC).

A-54. NGOs are frequently present and actively engaged in development activities when U.S. forces arrive. They often remain long after military forces have departed. Some NGOs are independent, diverse, flexible, grassroots-focused, primary relief providers. Others, however, provide a channel for funds and collaborate with other primary relief NGOs (usually local) to carry out the programs. These organizations often provide support to host-nation populations. NGOs assist over 250 million people annually. The funding received by NGOs comes from a multitude of sources, including governmental, international, and private organizations; that is, the NGOs act as independent implementing partners for funding agencies. Because they can respond quickly and effectively to crises, they can lessen the civil-military resources that commanders would otherwise have to devote to an operation. Despite differences that may exist between military forces and civilian agencies, certain objectives may be similar. Discovering common ground is essential to unity of effort. The commander's assessment of conditions and resources includes the activities and capabilities of NGOs and their role and mission within the operational area.

A-55. NGOs range from internationally based groups with global reach to local organizations focused on a specific area or state. They include groups with multimillion-dollar budgets and decades of global experience in development and humanitarian relief as well as newly created small organizations dedicated to a particular emergency or disaster. Most NGOs are not relief-oriented but carry out long-term development projects. The professionalism, capability, equipment, resources, and expertise vary greatly from one NGO to another. NGOs participate in diverse activities such as human rights, education, technical projects, relief activities, refugee assistance, public policy, and development programs. The connection between NGOs and the DOD is ad hoc, with no specific statutory link. Generally, military forces work through the UN, USAID, or the DOS to establish contacts with NGOs from the United States. While their focus remains grassroots and their connections informal, NGOs are major actors in many areas where military forces conduct stability operations. Such organizations affect many lives and control significant resources, making NGOs powerful in the relief, reconstruction, and development community. UN and USG agencies often use individual organizations to carry out specific relief functions.

A-56. Military forces are likely to encounter many NGOs in an operational area. In Somalia, there were 78 private organizations contributing relief support, and in the Rwanda crisis, over 100 relief organizations assisted the UN relief. Over 350 such agencies are registered with the USAID. The first line of security for most NGOs is their adherence to strict principles of impartiality, neutrality, and independence. Actions that blur the distinction between relief workers and military forces may be perceived as a threat to these principles. Such perceptions can increase the risk to civilian aid workers, both expatriates and nationals. However, NGOs may request certain types of military support from forces geographically co-located within an operational area. For example, command-approved chaplain support helps to build unity of effort and enhances relationships among diverse groups.

A-57. Their extensive involvement, local contacts, and experience make NGOs valuable sources of information about local and regional governments and civilian attitudes toward an operation. While some organizations seek the protection of the armed forces or the use of military aircraft to move relief supplies to overseas destinations, others may avoid a close affiliation with military forces, preferring autonomous operations. Their rationale may be fear of compromising their impartiality with the local populace or suspicion that military forces intend to take control of, influence, or even prevent their operations. Staffs should consult these organizations, along with the host-nation government (if applicable), to identify local issues and concerns the proposed public affairs guidance should reflect.

A-58. Public affairs planning includes identifying points of contact in NGOs operating in an affected area. Generally, the PAO refers media queries regarding NGO operations to an authorized NGO spokesperson. Military spokespersons should only comment on an NGO based on specific guidance received from that NGO or the UN. The office of the assistant Secretary of Defense (public affairs) or a regional organization (such as NATO) may also provide guidance in cooperation with the in-country headquarters of the organization.

A-59. The President may determine that it is in the national interest to task U.S. forces with missions that bring them into close contact with (if not support of) NGOs. All participants benefit when they closely coordinate their activities. Military forces seek to establish a climate of cooperation with NGOs. Missions to support NGOs are short term, usually necessitated by extraordinary events. In most situations, the NGOs need logistics, communications, and security capabilities. However, in such missions, the role of the armed forces is to enable—not perform—NGO tasks. Often U.S. military assistance has proven to be the critical difference that enabled success of an operation. Commanders understand that mutually beneficial arrangements between the armed forces and NGOs may determine the success of the military operation. (Appendix B of JP 3-08 describes many agencies that commanders may encounter in an operational area.)

OTHER ORGANIZATIONS

A-60. Other organizations that assist people in need include the International Red Cross and Red Crescent Movement, the CMOC, and various liaisons.

THE INTERNATIONAL RED CROSS AND RED CRESCENT MOVEMENT

A-61. The International Red Cross and Red Crescent Movement is a well-known global network of humanitarian actors. It consists of three independent elements: the ICRC, the National Societies, and the Federation. Five citizens of Switzerland founded the ICRC in 1863 as the "International Committee for Relief of Wounded." Voluntary contributions by governments provide the majority of ICRC funding, complemented by financing from national Red Cross and Red Crescent Societies and private sources.

A-62. The ICRC mission is, on the basis of the Geneva Conventions and protocols, to protect and assist victims of armed conflict and those affected by internal disturbances or tension. More specifically, this means to—

- Visit, interview, and transmit messages to, without witnesses, prisoners of war, and detained or interned civilians.
- Provide aid to the populations of occupied territories.

- Search for missing persons.
- Offer services for establishing hospital zones, localities, and security.
- Receive requests for aid from protected persons.
- Exercise its right of initiative to pursue the above tasks and to offer its services to the parties of internal disputes.

A-63. In its own country, a national Red Cross (such as the American Red Cross) or Red Crescent Society assists the public authorities in humanitarian matters. It primarily backs up the military medical services during conflict. The International Federation of Red Cross and Red Crescent Societies supports the humanitarian activities carried out by the national societies.

A-64. The ICRC is often described as a NGO, but it is not; it is also not an international or intergovernmental organization. The ICRC is an organization with a hybrid nature. As a private association organized under the Swiss Civil Code, its existence is not in itself mandated by governments. Yet its functions and activities—to provide protection and assistance to victims of conflict—are mandated by the international community of states and are founded in international law.

A-65. The terms *neutrality* and *independence* acquire a specific meaning when related to the activities of the ICRC. The ICRC applies almost exclusively to armed conflicts, disturbances, and tensions. It strictly avoids any involvement in hostilities or in controversies of a political, racial, religious, or ideological nature as an imperative for humanitarian action. This strict and specific neutrality that fosters and maintains universal trust also requires the ICRC to act openly and in good faith toward the nations and parties to the conflict. To discharge the mandate conferred by the Geneva Conventions and to take the humanitarian initiatives fundamental to its role as neutral intermediary, the ICRC must remain independent. Therefore, the ICRC adopts a special structure that allows it to resist political, economic, and other pressures and to maintain its credibility in the eyes of the governments and the public that support its activities.

A-66. In terms of civil-military relations, ICRC's humanitarian activities aim to protect human dignity and lives. ICRC humanitarian activities cannot be subordinated to political or military objectives. The ICRC must maintain a role independent of such influence or association. While consulting closely with international military missions deployed in the same operational area, it must create and maintain a specific humanitarian space. This space clearly distinguishes humanitarian action and political-military action.

CIVIL-MILITARY OPERATIONS CENTER

A-67. The CMOC is a standing capability formed by all civil affairs units. This capability provides the commander with the core personnel and equipment to form a CMOC organization. The CMOC serves as the U.S. forces' primary technique to interface among the local populace and institutions, humanitarian organizations, intergovernmental and nongovernmental organizations, multinational military forces, and other civilian agencies of the USG. The supported commander establishes the CMOC. The civil affairs staff officer or the supporting civil affairs unit may direct the CMOC. The size, structure, and location of the CMOC are situation dependent and may be augmented by the commander with other forces (such as military police, engineers, or Army Medical Department). Normally, the supported unit civil affairs staff officer conducts detailed civil affairs operations or civil-military operations analysis and planning and provides staff oversight of the supporting civil affairs unit. The supporting CMOC executes, assesses, and provides feedback relating to the effects of the operation. As a coordination center, the CMOC is neither a unit nor an organization.

A-68. If there is a host-nation government, it has the presumptive right to establish the mechanisms for civil-military coordination in the form commonly known as a humanitarian operations center. The structure of a humanitarian operations center can be formal or informal.

A-69. The CMOC may be the first, second, or even third coordinating mechanism, depending on the situation. Strong consideration should be given to co-locating CMOC functions with previously existing mechanisms, such as a humanitarian operations center, humanitarian assistance coordination center, or a civil-military cooperation center. (See table A-2 on page A-20.) Protection is always a concern for the commander considering where to locate the CMOC; while placing the CMOC "inside the wire" increases protection, it can also interfere with its ability to interact with NGOs and other actors. The commander must consider this difficulty when analyzing the situation according to the mission variables (mission, enemy, terrain and weather, troops and support available, time available, and civil considerations).

A-70. Coordination centers have various names and functions according to the mission and needs of the establishing commander. The CMOC is the type of coordination center employed at the direction of Army commanders. (JP 3-57 discusses these coordination centers in greater detail.)

Table A-2. Example of coordination centers

Coordinating Center	Description
Humanitarian Operations Center	This center is usually established by a host-nation government or UN. The HOC coordinates the overall relief strategy in large-scale foreign humanitarian assistance operations. It is responsible for policy making and coordinating, but does not exercise command and control. The HOC may submit requests for support to a commander through a CMOC. HOCs were established in the UN operations in Somalia and Rwanda.
Humanitarian Assistance Coordination Center	The supported combatant commander may establish a HACC to assist with interagency coordination and planning. The HACC provides the critical link between the combatant commander and other government agencies, intergovernmental organizations, and NGOs that may participate in a foreign humanitarian assistance operation. Normally, the HACC is a temporary body that operates during the early planning and coordination stages of the operation. Once the lead relief agency has established a CMOC or civilian humanitarian operations center, the role of the HACC diminishes, and its functions are accomplished through the normal organization of the combatant commander's staff.
Civil-Military Cooperation Center	Civil-military cooperation is a NATO doctrinal organization that roughly equates to the CMOC. Thus, when the NATO-led implementation force in Bosnia-Herzegovina established a center for coordination with the NGO community, it was known as the civil-military cooperation center rather than a CMOC, but it performed the same functions.

CMOC	civil-military operations center	NATO	North Atlantic Treaty Organization
HOC	humanitarian operations center	NGO	nongovernmental organization
HACC	humanitarian assistance coordination center	UN	United Nations

A-71. Participants in CMOC operations may include representatives of U.S. forces, interagency and multinational partners, the host-nation or foreign nation organizations (if outside the United States), intergovernmental organizations, the private sector, and NGOs. Mission requirements, command directives, operations security, workload, and accessibility to civilian agencies affect its actual organization. (Figure A-2 on page A-21 shows a notional CMOC organization.)

A-72. The officer in charge typically has both civilian- and military-related staff sections:

- The public affairs branch handles media inquiries to coordinate the release of information to the public with the PAO and to synchronize CMOC information with the unit's civil affairs staff section.
- The security branch manages the various aspects of security (physical, operations, personnel, and command and control) inherent to CMOC functions.
- Liaison officers or representatives are on-site CMOC contacts for both military and civilian agencies and organizations.
- The plans and operations section maintains current status of routes.

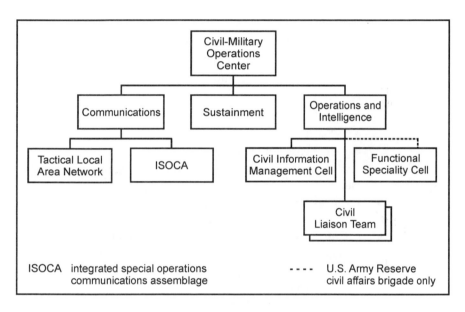

Figure A-2. Notional civil-military operations center (battalion and above)

A-73. The logistics section maintains a database of all points of contact and host-nation resources available for military or humanitarian purposes (facilities, transportation assets, goods, and services). Generally, this section also tracks costs incurred by military forces and other participating government agencies.

A-74. The number of CMOCs supporting a given operation varies according to mission requirements and the situation in the operational area. Commanders at any echelon may establish a CMOC. The decision to establish a CMOC stems from civil-military coordination requirements. The distance from the headquarters serving a particular geographic or tactical area can also influence the decision. A joint task force often establishes a CMOC; however, in operations where the joint force headquarters is located in one locale and units are spread throughout the operational area, subordinate Army commanders may establish their own CMOCs.

A-75. The CMOC will usually host daily meetings to identify requirements and determine available resources. CMOC personnel validate requests for additional resources and forward those to the appropriate joint force, Service, or agency representative for action. CMOC tasks may include—

- Facilitate civil-military coordination among those involved (see figure A-3 on page A-23):
  - Host nation (understood throughout).
  - Intergovernmental organizations.
  - International and regional organizations.
  - Other government agencies.
  - Military forces.
  - NGOs.
  - Private sector entities.
- Assist in facilitating transitions to civil authorities or the host nation.
- Receive, validate, coordinate, and monitor requests from NGOs for routine and emergency military support.
- Coordinate requests to NGOs for their support.
- Convene ad hoc mission planning groups to address complex military missions that support NGO requirements (such as convoy escort and management as well as security of refugee camps and feeding centers).
- Convene follow-on assessment groups.
- Provide situation reports regarding force operations, security, and other information for external actors.
- Chair meetings on NGO logistic prioritization issues and liaising with port and airfield control authorities.
- Help develop and organize a logistic distribution system to support provision of essential civil services (critical food, water, shelter, medical care, and basic sanitation).
- Provide information updates to support chemical, biological, radiological, and nuclear as well as other explosives hazard clearance and mine awareness activities.

- Provide input to update briefings, including incidents of crime, landmine strikes, militia activity, and general safety.

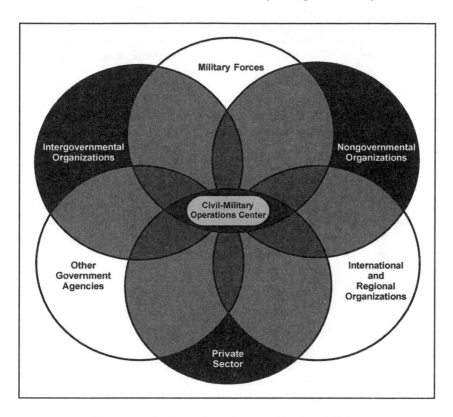

Figure A-3. Coordination within the CMOC

A-76. The PAO attends daily CMOC meetings. As an active member of the CMOC, the PAO ensures that member agencies agree on message and press releases and develop a group consensus in response to media queries. Although each agency's message need not be identical, agencies must not contradict each other.

LIAISON

A-77. Liaison maintains contact and communications between elements of military forces and other government and nongovernmental agencies and organizations to ensure understanding and unity of effort. Liaison is essential in stability operations because of the variety of external actors and the inherent coordination challenges.

A-78. Liaison officers are a focal point for communications instability operations. Liaison officers centralize direction and facilitate understanding while conducting operations with external agencies or forces. (See also appendix E of FM 6-0.) Multinational military and civilian partners need a clear understanding of the military planning process. This is best accomplished by direct liaison. Liaison officers normally work closely with the operations officer to seek and resolve interagency problems. Liaison teams establish authoritative representation of the commander, accurately interpret the commander's intent, and explain the capabilities of the force. Conversely, the teams interpret the commander's intent and capabilities of the nonmilitary organizations. Liaison teams provide input while developing courses of action for future operations. They also work to maximize current operations through proactive interaction with the departments, agencies, and organizations to which they are attached.

A-79. The professional abilities of the liaison officer determine a successful liaison. Additional factors that contribute to successful liaisons are—

- Knowledge of the doctrine, capabilities, procedures, and culture of partner organizations.
- Transportation.
- Foreign language ability.
- Regional orientation.
- Communication.
- Single point of contact in the headquarters.
- Support to humanitarian assistance missions by aligning functional skills and experience with the need for medical and logistics expertise.

A-80. Liaison teams are formed when a representational capability is required. Teams are tailored to the specific situation and may require communications assets controlled by the Chairman of the Joint Chiefs of Staff. Individual liaison officers are assigned when representation is not required and adequate communications with the joint task force staff are available.

COMMUNITIES OF PURPOSE

A-81. The ability to quickly form communities of purpose comprised of military forces, government agencies, and NGOs is essential to successful stability operations. A community of purpose is a group of people tasked or voluntarily agreeing to perform a specific task or objective. Often the life span of these communities is limited to the time required to perform the task or objective. Communities of purpose are valuable for teams and working groups. Usually they have a hierarchal structure and provide for some level of managed dialog and information sharing.

A-82. Collaboration within these communities may occur in real time—using forums such as a working group meetings, chat rooms, or conference calls—or be facilitated through other means, such as telephone calls, electronic mail, and instant messaging. Other tools that communities of purpose may use include desktop video teleconference collaboration tools, knowledge repositories, expertise locators, and "wikis." (A "wiki" is software that lets users create collaborative Internet sites. These sites are also referred to as "wikis.")

A-83. Key to an effective community of purpose is the ability to link expertise rapidly to solve a specific problem. An example of a community of purpose might be an improvised explosive device defeat community formed to identify the best way to counter a specific device type.

This page intentionally left blank.

Appendix B

Interagency Management System

Weak and failed states pose a serious security challenge for the United States and the international community. They can become breeding grounds for terrorism, weapons proliferation, trafficking in humans and narcotics, organized crime, and humanitarian catastrophes. Since the end of the Cold War, the United States has been involved in or contributed significant resources to more than 17 reconstruction and stabilization operations. And the challenge persists. RAND recently reported that in this same time period, the pace of U.S. military interventions has risen to about one every two years. If the U.S. Government is going to meet these threats, we must adapt our national security architecture.

John E. Herbst
Coordinator for Office of Reconstruction and Stabilization

BACKGROUND

B-1. The Department of State's Office of the Coordinator for Reconstruction and Stabilization (S/CRS) was established in July 2004. Designed as an interagency office, S/CRS was constituted primarily with staff from within the Department of State and complemented with staff from other departments. These included the Departments of Defense, Treasury, Justice, Homeland Security, and Labor; the United States Agency for International Development (USAID); the staff of the Director for National Intelligence, Central Intelligence Agency; and the Defense Intelligence Agency. S/CRS promotes unity of effort to leverage limited resources and avoid unnecessary duplication, with two primary tasks:

- Ensure that the entire United States Government (USG) is organized to plan for and manage USG responses to reconstruction and stabilization crises affecting national interests, to include balancing civilian and military activities.
- Build a staff of trained civilians to deploy to support these missions when called upon to respond.

RECONSTRUCTION AND STABILIZATION

B-2. On December 7, 2005, President Bush signed National Security Presidential Directive 44 (NSPD-44), directing the Secretary of State to coordinate and lead integrated USG efforts to prepare, plan for, and conduct reconstruction and stabilization activities. These activities depend on the conditions of the operational environment; they may be conducted with or without U.S. military engagement. NSPD-44 outlines the President's vision for promoting the security of the United States through improved coordination, planning, and implementation of reconstruction and stabilization activities. The directive requires the Secretaries of State and Defense to coordinate and synchronize civilian and military efforts to ensure integrated civilian and military planning. The DODD 3000.05 complements NSPD-44.

B-3. Since that time, S/CRS has led an interagency effort to implement NSPD-44. A major element of that effort has been the creation of the Interagency Management System, a new management structure for the conduct of whole of government reconstruction and stabilization operations.

INTERAGENCY MANAGEMENT SYSTEM ORGANIZATION

B-4. The Interagency Management System (IMS) for reconstruction and stabilization was approved by senior decisionmakers in March 2007, along with triggering mechanisms for planning operations. The IMS consists of three elements:

- Country reconstruction and stabilization group (CRSG). A Washington-based decisionmaking body equivalent to a policy coordinating committee with a planning and operations staff.
- Integration planning cell (IPC). A civilian planning cell deployed to the relevant geographic combatant command or multinational headquarters to integrate and synchronize civilian and military planning.
- Advance civilian team. A team consisting of one or more subordinate interagency management and coordination field advance civilian teams that deploy to support the chief of mission.

B-5. These structures are flexible in size and composition to meet the particular requirements of the situation and to integrate personnel from all relevant agencies. Recruitment of personnel may require flexible hiring authorities, training, and resources not presently available. Interagency or coalition partners may also be represented. Each team is designed to support and augment, not replace, existing structures in Washington, at the geographic combatant command, and in the field.

B-6. The IMS is designed to provide coordinated interagency policy and program management for complex crises. These crises include national security priorities that involve widespread instability, may require military participation, and where multiple U.S. agencies are involved in the response. It may be used in cases that do not require military operations. The IMS is designed to provide an interface and support improved coordination with multinational partners, international organizations, and host-nation governments. It is not intended to respond to the political and humanitarian crises that are regularly and effectively handled through the current Washington and field systems. When a significant crisis occurs or begins to emerge, senior government leaders may choose to convene the IMS.

B-7. The IMS clarifies roles, responsibilities, and processes for mobilizing and supporting interagency teams conducting reconstruction and stabilization operations. It assists Washington policymakers, chiefs of mission, and military commanders with managing these complex operations by ensuring coordination among all USG agencies at the strategic, operational, and tactical levels. The IMS facilitates and supports integrated planning processes for unified USG strategic and implementation plans. These plans include funding requests, joint interagency field deployments, and a joint civilian operations capability including shared communications and information management systems.

COUNTRY RECONSTRUCTION AND STABILIZATION GROUP

B-8. The CRSG serves as the central coordinating body for the USG effort. The group consists of a policy coordinating committee jointly chaired by the regional assistant secretary of state, the coordinator for reconstruction and stabilization, and the relevant National Security Council director. S/CRS primarily focuses on coordination and planning; policy development and management is led by the regional bureau and other traditional policy players. The CRSG is supported by a secretariat, complete with planning and operations staff.

B-9. The CRSG prepares the whole of government strategic plan for reconstruction and stabilization, including shared strategic goals, a concept of operations, the major essential tasks to undertake, and the resources required to achieve stability. It can build on earlier interagency situation-based planning. The CRSG prepares and forwards strategic guidance recommendations for decisions by senior government officials, ensuring appropriate guidance and direction for USG civilians in Washington and in the field.

B-10. Once the USG integrated strategic plan is approved, the CRSG facilitates preparation and integration of operations support, information management, partnership development, and resource mobilization. The group also works with the appropriate chief of mission to develop and update interagency implementation plans.

INTEGRATION PLANNING CELL

B-11. An IPC can be deployed to a geographic combatant command or to the headquarters of a multinational peacekeeping or other force. The CRSG may establish and deploy an IPC at the request of Department of Defense or a multinational headquarters, and by direction of the Secretary of State in consultation with the relevant regional assistant secretary.

B-12. The IPC helps to integrate and synchronize civilian and military planning processes and operations. It generally consists of interagency planners and regional and sectoral experts. The CRSG empowers the IPC to synchronize and coordinate USG planning within a geographic combatant command, United Nations peacekeeping operation, or a multilateral planning mission. This synchronization and coordination ensures integration and constant dialog among strategic, operational, and tactical echelons.

B-13. The IPC is a flexible interagency team with size and team composition adjustable depending on the requirements of a specific situation. The IPC helps the combatant commander integrate the interagency strategic and implementation plans with those of the joint force. The cell is critical to integration across echelons of command; it ties strategic efforts at the CRSG with the tactical efforts of the advance civilian team and field advance civilian teams.

ADVANCE CIVILIAN TEAM

B-14. To supplement an existing USG civilian presence or to establish such a presence where none currently exists, the CRSG may recommend that the Secretary of State deploy an advance civilian team. As a skills-specific team, it provides surge capacity to support chiefs of mission and country team efforts that develop, integrate, and execute reconstruction and stabilization plans. This team can operate with or without the involvement of military forces.

B-15. The advance civilian team coordinates with existing embassy structures and personnel to support implementation of the USG reconstruction and stabilization plan by the chief of mission. In the absence of an existing USG diplomatic presence, the designated chief of mission leads the advance civilian team with the additional task of establishing a more permanent USG presence. If necessary, this team can deploy several field advance civilian teams. These field teams provide the chief of mission with maximum capacity to implement reconstruction and stabilization programs at the provincial or local level. When required, field advance civilian teams integrate with military forces to maximize unity of effort.

WHOLE OF GOVERNMENT PLANNING

B-16. As a companion to the IMS, a framework for whole of government planning is necessary for addressing both immediate crisis response and long-term engagement scenarios. Whole of government planning builds from a foundation of conflict prevention planning common to security cooperation efforts. Proposals for initiating planning for specific countries are based on a set of established criteria integral to whole of government planning. Work continues on standardizing a whole of government planning framework.

TRIGGERING WHOLE OF GOVERNMENT PLANNING

B-17. In March 2007, the deputies committee approved a national-level document that defines the triggering mechanisms for whole of government planning for reconstruction and stabilization operations and conflict transformation. The triggering mechanisms describe a general decision structure for determining the whole of government planning for reconstruction and stabilization.

B-18. The triggering mechanisms for whole of government planning for reconstruction and stabilization describe the criteria and processes for tasking joint interagency planning (civilian and military). Planning generally takes two forms: long-term, situation-based planning and crisis action planning for immediate response. When necessary, whole of government planning may also be initiated for a specific country or region. Whole of government planning usually takes place within the context of the IMS; however, it may be initiated under other circumstances, as required.

PRINCIPLES OF USG PLANNING AND THE PRACTITIONER'S GUIDE

B-19. On May 13, 2008, the reconstruction and stabilization policy coordinating committee approved the *Principles of the USG Planning Framework for Reconstruction, Stabilization and Conflict Transformation,* known within the interagency as the "planning framework principles." These principles are the product of significant collaboration among eight USG departments and agencies and seven bureaus within the Department of State. The planning framework principles describe the key principles, decision points, and processes used when triggering whole of government planning for reconstruction and stabilization operations. It details the types of reconstruction and stabilization planning: specific steps in the planning process and the method of incorporating monitoring and evaluation into planning. The planning framework principles reflect the collective lessons learned gained from four years of planning efforts and exercises.

B-20. To translate these principles into a comprehensive guide for planners, a supporting planning framework practitioner's guide is under development. When complete, this guide will be subject to approval by the reconstruction and stabilization policy coordinating committee. The processes described in the planning framework principles and detailed in the draft guide will be used to complete contingency planning for a specified country beginning in October 2008. S/CRS will facilitate the country selection process for this effort.

CIVILIAN RESPONSE CORPS

B-21. The Civilian Response Corps (CRC) represents the USG civilian rapid response capability that enables the management and conduct of reconstruction and stabilization operations. The CRC consists of active, standby, and reserve components.

B-22. The CRC active component consists of Federal employees in the Department of State and throughout various civilian agencies. They work full time to support reconstruction and stabilization activities. This includes training and preparing to deploy immediately to a crisis location. Seventy-five percent of the active component is deployable at any given time for up to six months.

B-23. The CRC standby component consists of existing USG employees with a wide range of skill sets and expertise. Members of the standby component have full-time jobs with responsibilities that extend beyond reconstruction and stabilization. They are available for training and subsequent deployments of up to six months on 30 to 45 days notice. This component increases the number of skilled personnel available to meet specific mission requirements.

B-24. The CRC reserve component represents the third tier of rapid civilian responders in the USG. The reserve component can work reconstruction and stabilization projects for the Departments of State and Justice,

USAID, and other government agencies. When deployed, members of the reserve component provide management capacity to the embassy and technical assistance to the host-nation government. Using the reserve component offers two advantages over relying solely on contractors for additional response: faster response and greater accountability.

B-25. The reserve component provides immediate expertise in the field on a short-term basis. When activated, the reserve component would consist of U.S. citizens from outside Federal agencies.

TRAINING

B-26. To support NSPD-44 implementation, S/CRS established an interagency training working group to unite representatives from the Departments of State, Defense, Justice, Commerce, Treasury, Agriculture, Health and Human Services, and Homeland Security; USAID; and the U.S. Institute of Peace. This working group fosters collaboration among agencies. Together, these agencies develop individual and collective training to prepare personnel and organizations for reconstruction and stabilization operations. The training working group builds upon and leverages existing resources to connect multiple interagency training programs, including exercises.

B-27. S/CRS coordinates training in reconstruction and stabilization with the Department of State's Foreign Service Institute. It also offers courses in conflict transformation for USG personnel from the Department of State and other government agencies. S/CRS assists in designing courses for personnel deploying to provincial reconstruction teams. (See appendix F.) S/CRS also assists in developing courses for Joint Knowledge Online to promote interagency understanding.

B-28. CRC active and standby component personnel attend S/CRS courses. They attend additional training available through the military, other civilian agencies, international counterparts, and outside organizations.

INTERNATIONAL COLLABORATION

B-29. Building close working relationships with international partner nations and organizations enhances the effectiveness of reconstruction and stabilization operations. These organizations range from the United Nations and European Union to partner countries like the United Kingdom and Canada. National and multinational experiments and exercises improve civil-military cooperation among international partners while helping to enhance interoperability in practical application. S/CRS and interagency partners engage in ongoing cooperation with international partners worldwide.

B-30. The Department of State accomplishes missions using the range of tools of diplomacy; it works with a wide range of partners on a global scale. Broad application of the range of tools of diplomacy, development, and defense—including the capabilities of domestic agency partners—supports building and sustaining effective, legitimate states. These states will respond to the needs of their people, reduce the drivers of conflict, and enable responsible participation in the international community. NSPD-44 instructs USG agencies to work with international partners on early warning systems, planning, conflict prevention, and conflict response.

SUMMARY

B-31. S/CRS has led interagency partners through the development of three distinct yet tightly linked capabilities that can be customized in scale and scope. The emergence of interagency planning and response capability, along with the structures of the IMS, enable USG leaders to integrate the efforts of civilian agencies and, when necessary, military forces to achieve unified USG reconstruction and stabilization operations in an international context. A civilian reconstruction and stabilization capacity facilitates the development of unity of purpose across the USG and translates into unity of effort by the USG during execution. This capacity also relieved military forces of numerous reconstruction and stabilization activities best performed by civilian agencies and actors, thereby allowing greater focus on the primary mission for military forces. Ground forces rely on a robust civilian capacity for reconstruction and stabilization. Increased civilian capacity provides the USG with the ability to partner civilian and military efforts when necessary or deal with some crises without invoking military power.

Appendix C

USAID Principles for Reconstruction and Development

*The development community and the military commu-
nity will continue to move towards closer and increased
collaboration. It is critically important that the military
and development communities achieve a better understanding of each other's comparative advantages and
collaborate accordingly...while the military is the best
instrument to enter a conflict environment and provide
an immediate stabilizing force; civilian agencies are
better equipped to oversee actual reconstruction and
development work.*

Andrew S. Natsios
former Administrator of the U.S. Agency for
International Development[2]

BACKGROUND

C-1. The tragic events of 11 September 2001 ushered in a new development and security paradigm; the implications have been far-reaching,
extending through all branches of the United States Government (USG).
This new paradigm suggests that complex emergencies and fragile states
will increasingly impact U.S. national security interests. The United
States must engage failed states while understanding the potential corre-
lation between fragile states and terrorist-induced instability. Effective
engagement will increasingly require the use of the tools of diplomacy,
development, and defense in a collaborative fashion. The success of U.S.
military strategy and development assistance policy in these countries
have become mutually reinforcing. Development cannot effectively occur
without the security that armed force provides, and security will not be
sustained until local populaces see the promise of development as a viable alternative to violence to meet their needs. While involved in recon-

---

[2] © 2005 by Andrew S. Natsios. Reproduced with permission of
Parameters.

struction activities in Iraq and Afghanistan, the U.S. military has been called upon to manage substantially increased levels of U.S. bilateral foreign assistance. This assistance included official development assistance funding traditionally managed by the United States Agency for International Development (USAID). To use these resources effectively, commanders involved in stabilization and reconstruction activities need to understand and apply basic reconstruction and development principles. Such principles have evolved by the development community through years of experience.

PRINCIPLES OF RECONSTRUCTION AND DEVELOPMENT

C-2. USAID and the development community assist fragile states with finding solutions and resources to meet their requirements for sustained development and growth. To accomplish this, the development community relies on specific operating principles for stabilization, reconstruction, and development assistance. The principles have been tested through years of practical application and understanding the cultural and socioeconomic influences in the host nation. Understanding these generally accepted principles enables those involved in development, and in the development aspects of stabilization and reconstruction, to incorporate techniques and procedures effectively. Then those involved can help countries improve the economic and social conditions of their people. The USAID principles for reconstruction and development are ownership, capacity building, sustainability, selectivity, assessment, results, partnership, flexibility, and accountability.

C-3. Development officials improve the likelihood of success by applying the principles of reconstruction and development. Timely and adequate emphasis on these principles increases the opportunity for immediate success or, at a minimum, provides a means to adapt to the changing conditions. Development assistance officials assume risk in their programs when these principles are violated or ignored.

OWNERSHIP

C-4. The principle of ownership creates conditions of success by building on the leadership, participation, and commitment of the host nation and its people. Ownership implies relying on the host nation to establish and drive the development priorities. The host nation leads this unified effort with support from external donor organizations. Ownership begins with and is focused on the people. It is founded on community involvement. This is fundamental to success, since the host-nation government may not exist or may lack the legitimacy to assume full ownership for peaceful governing processes.

C-5. Donor organizations support and assist the reconstruction and development process as partners working with the host nation toward common objectives. The local populace should view development as belonging to them and not the donor community. Reconstruction and development projects and initiatives should first address the needs of the country, its communities, and its populace. The presence of outside assistance agencies can help build credibility, trust, and consensus in the local populace. Building host-nation or community ownership is a delicate and time-consuming process. It often requires a long-term commitment of personnel and resources.

C-6. When ownership exists and a community invests itself in a project, citizens will defend, maintain, and expand the project after donor organizations have left. Citizens will abandon what donor organizations leave behind if they perceive that the project fails to meet their needs or does not belong to them. The development community achieves positive results when it patiently engages national and local leaders in their own development rather than trying to impose development quickly and autocratically from the outside.

> ## Ownership
>
> U.S. policy in Afghanistan embodies the principle of ownership and focuses on encouraging Afghans to take government leadership positions. The selection of Hamid Karzai as President of Afghanistan is a good illustration. In December 2001, the four major Afghan factions met in Bonn, Germany, to select an interim leader. They subsequently chose Karzai to head the Afghan Transitional Authority. The significance of this model is that Karzai and his ministers are all Afghan-born. Karzai has additionally strived for ethnic balance; the interim cabinet comprehensively represented all the various political groups in Afghanistan, from Mujahidin and Northern Alliance factions to European and American members of the Afghan Diaspora.

C-7. It is important to have a national lead the country and to have nationals head the ministries for several reasons. Such leaders can—

- Foster national legitimacy.
- Eliminate language barriers.

- Develop ownership and responsibility for governance decisions.
- Understand and better navigate the national political landscape.
- Maximize national support of government policy.

CAPACITY BUILDING

C-8. The principle of capacity building involves the transfer of technical knowledge and skills to the local populace and institutions. Capacity building aims to strengthen national and local institutions, transfer technical skills, and promote effective policies and programs. Once met, these goals enable a long-term host-nation capacity to establish policies and provide competent sustained public services.

C-9. An important by-product of capacity building is that the country increases its ability to retain, absorb, and facilitate economic investment. The investments can come from donor assistance or from private sources of foreign direct investment. Ultimately, an improved governance and investment environment is a necessary condition for sustained economic growth in any country.

C-10. The development community recognizes that the right government policies underscore all successful development efforts. Simply put, a country with weak governance institutions and misguided policies will have a limited ability to lead its own economic and social development. For example, it is not enough to build universities and educate a country's population. This effort must be accompanied by direct opportunities that will allow university graduates to become future political and business leaders.

Capacity Building

In Afghanistan, USAID built individual teacher capacity using programs such as the radio-based teacher training program. This program targets teachers who reside in remote areas of the country. As of June 2005, some 65,000 teachers have been trained through broadcasts that strengthen their teaching skills and spread civic and educational messages. About 7,500 more teachers have been trained through face-to-face instruction, and 6,800 more were taught in an accelerated training program. As more teachers have been trained, more children have returned to school: Pri-

> mary school enrollment increased from a prewar total of one million (2001) to 4.8 million by December 2004.

SUSTAINABILITY

C-11. Development assistance agencies design programs with an impact that endures beyond the end of the project. The sustainability principle encompasses two premises: a nation's resources are finite, and development should ensure a balance among economic development, social development, and democracy and governance. The sustainability principle compels aid managers to consider whether the technology, institution, or service they are introducing will have a lasting effect on a society. In some cases, managers may pursue programs without long-term sustainability to establish stability. Nevertheless, program implementation affects potential long-term implications of the assistance. When implementing the program, commanders ultimately strive for attaining long-term sustainability, even when circumstances dictate short-term solutions to immediate conditions.

C-12. Sustainability is applicable in the military context. The military balances the need to execute immediate mission requirements quickly and the subsequent withdrawal of intervening forces with the obligation to develop sustainable host-nation security forces. These forces can protect the country against resurgent and future threats, both internal and external. Military forces cannot equate success with merely training and equipping host-nation forces. The best-trained military will languish and deteriorate without ongoing government support and funding. Sustainability demands that the government eventually start replacing external military assistance with domestic tax revenues to fund national military forces and other public services.

Sustainability

Civil servants of Iraq's Diyala Province gained confidence and the capability to track and implement resources for development through computer training. They received the training from the local provincial reconstruction team. Employees of the Diyala provincial government received hands-on computer literacy training, an important step in moving Diyala towards effective self-governance. Their lack of basic computer skills and technology slowed their capacity-building efforts. For example, budget execution, a slow and tedious process, was done using handwritten documents. Providing training to improve the skills of government servants was the first step in creating a more efficient office environment. This training sped up routine tasks that have been computerized for years in much of the world.

An additional step in bringing Diyala into the digital age was creating a sustainable computer infrastructure within the provincial government by providing a locally sustainable source of electricity to power the computers. Without attention to the second two elements, the computer training was not only likely to be a waste of time and money but could be counterproductive; It might have disrupted what may have been a slow but effective resource management and accounting system, leaving no adequate system in its place.

SELECTIVITY

C-13. The selectivity principle directs U.S. bilateral assistance organizations to invest scarce aid resources based on three criteria: humanitarian need, foreign policy interests of the United States, and the commitment of a country and its leadership to reform. To maximize effectiveness, donor organizations allocate resources where resources make a significant impact and where the recipient community demonstrates a commitment to development goals. The underlying idea is that resources are finite and are most effective when concentrated together in select situations. Any allocation of resources, whether in combat operations or infrastructure projects, must consider foreign policy interests, political circumstances, and ground-level needs and requirements.

Selectivity

In Afghanistan, the restored Kabul-to-Kandahar highway illustrates the selectivity principle. More than 35 percent of the country's population live within 50 miles of the highway. Restoring the highway was a high priority for the presidents of Afghanistan and the United States. They asked USAID to implement the project over a short time. The project was crucial to extending the influence of the new government. Since its completion, the highway has led to increased rates of economic development, fostered civil society development, and helped ensure unity and long-term security in the country. In addition, the road travels through several Taliban strongholds. Its upgrade has diminished the Taliban's ability to exert influence in this area. The highway was a development priority since it opened access to the cities and markets. It serves U.S. foreign policy interests by promoting economic development, country unity, and the commitment of the country's leadership while counteracting Taliban influence.

ASSESSMENT

C-14. A development assistance agency must complete a comprehensive assessment of local conditions before designing and implementing a program. Development agencies have the important task of conducting careful research, adapting best practices, and designing for local conditions. A serious concern for foreign aid programs is forcing too much money into local institutions that cannot responsibly spend the increased external funding. As a result, development agencies must consider several questions in their assessment:

- Do reconstruction plans conform to conditions on the ground?
- What are the best practices for each intervention?
- What is the society able to absorb?

C-15. Development agencies must work with entities such as provincial reconstruction teams to ensure proposed projects fit into national plans. A democratically elected government should provide essential and needed public services. Providing services builds public support to and perceived legitimacy of the government. To facilitate this, each ministry within the government must produce a strategy that fits into the overall national development plan to maximize limited resources. Donors ensure potential programs are included in the host nation's strategic plan and budgeted to fund their support for continuous resourcing and ultimate project effectiveness.

Assessment

USAID's collaboration with the provincial reconstruction teams (PRTs) in Afghanistan—which are joint civil-military organizations consisting of 70 to 80 personnel—illustrates the assessment principle. Productive development demands that an agency complete ground-level assessments before starting a project.

> USAID uses PRTs in select situations; the teams allow civilian personnel to complete field assessments in areas that are otherwise unstable. The instability may be from the presence of Taliban insurgents, regional warlords, drug-financed criminal organizations, or an atmosphere of general lawlessness. With support from PRTs, USAID has the ability to monitor critical reconstruction projects, complete needs assessments, and mobilize local partners.

C-16. Without a comprehensive field assessment, it is almost impossible to predict whether a project will have a measurable and definable effect. The principle of assessment is linked closely to the principle of developing results. Rapid assessment techniques are vital to helping reduce delays in aid project implementation.

RESULTS

C-17. The principle of results includes directing resources to achieve clearly defined, measurable, and strategically focused objectives. The principle of results draws on the assessment principle. This principle ensures that before a donor organization invests in a certain country, it first determines its strategic objectives or what impact the donor organization and the country hope to achieve.

C-18. The donor organization and host nation must consider how they can best attain the desired impact and what types of programs and resources will lead to the goal. Together they must determine specific benchmarks. The benchmarks indicate whether the two are accomplishing their strategic objectives and whether implemented programs are achieving the intended impact.

C-19. USAID incorporates the principle of results in its programs and operations worldwide. USAID believes that when an agency considers a program's impact from the beginning stages, the agency will have more clearly defined and strategically focused objectives. Since 1993, the notion of managing for results has emerged as an explicit core value of the agency. When deciding whether to implement a particular project, the agency applies a "results framework" that visually depicts the objectives to be achieved by USAID and through contributions from other donor organizations.

Results

USAID Iraq's Community Action Program works to promote grassroots democracy and better local governance via demand-driven community development. It ensures community buy-in by requiring communities to contribute between 15 and 25 percent of the value of each project. Community action groups certify that projects are completed successfully before final payments are authorized. The effort has worked in Kirkuk, where a PRT-backed initiative helped revitalize the local market. The shop had been a major outdoor public market, but was losing business as it degenerated in a mass of potholes and fetid, standing water that attracted bugs and rodents. USAID helped pave the road, install new sidewalks, and dig a drainage canal for excess water. The local community contributed more than $10,000 to the $60,000 project. For that investment, the market is now awash in fresh fruits and vegetables, meats, clothes, and people of all ethnicities and religions shopping at the tables and stalls.

PARTNERSHIP

C-20. The partnership principle holds that donor organizations should collaborate closely at all levels with partner entities, from local businesses and nongovernmental organizations to government ministries and other donors. Development agencies like USAID usually implement projects through a network of public and private partners that often include nongovernmental organizations and private contractors or private businesses. These partners can directly oversee an entire program, or a local entity like a university can implement a part of a program, such as a civic education initiative within a larger governance program. USAID uses a highly decentralized structure, where implementation and much program design takes place in missions located in the host nation. The USAID equivalent of "commanders" is its "mission directors." These directors have much greater autonomy than do their counterparts in the military and most other international aid agencies. USAID missions work in a linear, horizontal organizational structure. The structure links various voluntary partnerships, many different parts of civil society, and local and national governments through voluntary agreements and funding mechanism.

Partnership

From all across Iraq, people are traveling to the northern city of Erbil to learn about democracy, elections, civil society, and governance. The U.S. funded National Democratic Institute (NDI) has been teaching these courses to thousands of Iraqis. The group does not teach what policies to adopt. Instead, it teaches how to debate issues and reach agreements peacefully. For example, in Kirkuk, where ethnic tension is high, NDI gets representatives from the three main ethnic groups to talk about security, services, and education. "We walk through methods of negotiation," said the director. Despite the violence, Iraqis still want to learn. They go to Erbil then return to their communities to try and advocate for the issues important to them, such as services and education. The trainees back home organize in their apartment block or use the Internet and media to organize people around issues.

C-21. USAID first seeks a strong, local partner on the ground when considering a project. This partner must be able to manage the program effectively from design and assessment to implementation. The agency has developed a set of analytical tools to determine which potential partners have the highest likelihood of success.

FLEXIBILITY

C-22. Development assistance is laden with uncertainties and changing circumstances that require an agency to assess current conditions continuously and adjust its response appropriately. The principle of flexibility maintains that agencies must be adaptable to anticipate possible problems and to seize opportunities. Flexibility must be balanced against the premise that good development takes time and reconstruction efforts should be systematized and executed on a large scale.

Flexibility

The provincial reconstruction team's (PRT's) role in providing procedures for safe, secure potable water systems in Iraq illustrates the importance of being responsive and flexible. Most people in the Fallujah District of Al Anbar Province, Iraq receive drinking water from wells or directly from the Euphrates River, which is contaminated. This same district lacked reliable sources on power. However, in 2008, it received solar-powered water purification units to help prevent water-borne disease. This purification unit is a point distribution system that uses solar panels to generate electricity to power the pump. The pump draws source water through a series of filters and ultraviolet lights and into a holding tank for distribution. The people then draw water from a storage tank or directly from the unit; they do not require a water distribution network.

To ensure equitable placement of the units, the PRT worked closely with the Fallujah District Council. This council consisted of the municipal and tribal leadership of the major Fallujah subdistricts. The result is access to potable (drinking) water for the entire population. At the same time, the PRT avoided exacerbating ethnic tensions with preferential distribution of the units to certain groups or communities. The solar-powered water purification units provide crucial future capacity for preventing diseases that strike vulnerable population groups.

C-23. The fact that stability operations incorporate such an expansive agenda—encompassing everything from antiterrorism exercises to humanitarian assistance—underscores the need for military flexibility. Flexibility is an integral component of stability operations as political considerations guide stabilization efforts. Military forces and development agencies must remain constantly aware of the political environment and be prepared to change tactics accordingly.

ACCOUNTABILITY

C-24. The host nation, donor organizations, and the development community must design accountability and transparency into systems. By doing so, they build effective checks and balances to guard against corruption, while meeting the needs of the local populace. Donors should work to fight corruption in the countries where they operate. Within the USG, oversight bodies help guard against cost overruns, financial abuse, and contractor mismanagement. These oversight bodies can include the inspector general, independent auditors, the Government Accountability Office, and congressional investigative committees. Externally, development agencies should prevent corrupt local officials from preying on potential projects. These same agencies should ensure that development programs enhance effective governance structures and local accountability systems. Political institutions—especially in developing countries—are fragile, and if these countries lack a strong rule of law foundation, then the risk of corruption increases.

C-25. The accountability principle closely relates to stability operations as well. The local populace must view the military operation as legitimate while perceiving that their government has real authority. If corruption takes root, either on the side of the U.S. aid program or on the part of the host-nation government, then the entire principle of legitimacy is undermined.

C-26. Agencies such as USAID follow a standard set of accountability guidelines based on institutional experience. USAID limits prime contracting to major international firms but ensures that the international firm subcontracts with local firms and builds in several layers of oversight. It distributes smaller amounts of money to local organizations to avoid overwhelming underdeveloped systems. It disperses funds only after work on a project run by a new local organization is completed or as bills arrive. The agency seldom provides up-front money to untested implementing organizations. USAID provides significant financial system training to local groups to build their capacity to handle larger sums of monetary assistance. USAID compiles a list of corrupt organizations and bars them from receiving future funding. Finally, the agency chooses experienced organizations as primary fiduciary agents to facilitate timely and accountable completion of large-scale projects.

Accountability

The Kabul-to-Kandahar road project illustrates the first two factors in practice. USAID selected the prime contractor, which in turn subcontracted various pieces to local firms. For purposes of accountability, the agency built in several layers of oversight. First, the agency has an in-country engineering staff that performed quality assurance inspections of contractor work and that operated as watchdogs over the entire process. Second, USAID's inspector general consistently reviewed financial invoices and completed two general audits to ensure regularity and compliance. Third, the agency contracted with the U.S. Army Corps of Engineers to provide technical oversight over the contractor. The result was that the project finished to specification and on schedule.

SUMMARY

C-27. The nine principles of reconstruction and development formalize customary practices and operating procedures. The principles reflect key institutional principles that most aid agencies incorporate into the reconstruction framework. The principles are designed to ensure local ownership and sustainability of program results while building local capacity and thus eventual independence from outside assistance. They take advantage of the skills and resources others can bring to the effort by forging partnerships. Following these principles helps the host nation to adjust reconstruction and development activities to the dynamic political environment usually encountered in a violent conflict or post-conflict situation.

This page intentionally left blank.

Appendix D

Interagency Conflict Assessment Overview

BACKGROUND

D-1. Successful stability operations are predicated on identifying and reducing the causes of instability and reestablishing or building community and state capacity to diminish, manage, or prevent them from recurring in the future. The conflict assessment frameworks discussed in this appendix were developed collaboratively by the departments and agencies of the United States Government (USG) to identify the causes of instability, develop activities to diminish or mitigate them, and evaluate the effectiveness of the activities in fostering stability. This appendix presents these assessment frameworks for information purposes only. Army forces use doctrinal assessment tools to inform understanding, aid in planning, and shape execution. These frameworks will inform, but not replace, those doctrinal tools.

INTERAGENCY CONFLICT ASSESSMENT FRAMEWORK

D-2. Addressing the causes and consequences of weak and failed states has become an urgent priority for the USG. Conflict both contributes to and results from state fragility. To effectively prevent or resolve violent conflict, the USG needs tools and approaches that enable coordination of U.S. diplomatic, development and military efforts in support of local institutions and actors seeking to resolve their disputes peacefully.

D-3. A first step toward a more effective and coordinated response to help states prevent, mitigate, and recover from violent conflict is the development of shared understanding among USG agencies about the sources of violent conflict or civil strife. Achieving this shared understanding of the dynamics of a particular crisis requires both a joint interagency process for completing the assessment and a common conceptual framework to guide the collection and analysis of information. The interagency conflict assessment framework (ICAF) is a tool that enables an interagency team to assess conflict situations systemically and collaboratively; it supports USG interagency planning for conflict prevention, mitigation, and stabilization.

PURPOSE

D-4. The ICAF is intended to develop a commonly held understanding across relevant USG departments and agencies of the dynamics driving and mitigating violent conflict in a country. This understanding informs national policy and planning decisions. The ICAF may also include steps to establish a strategic baseline against which USG engagement can be evaluated. It is a process and a tool available for use by any USG agency to supplement interagency or military planning.

D-5. The principles of interagency conflict assessment outline the key concepts, processes, and products essential to completing an interagency assessment. The USG departments and agencies develop supplementary documents to provide a fuller treatment of the analytical framework, appropriate tools and data collection procedures, and set the composition and functions of an interagency conflict assessment team.

D-6. The ICAF draws on existing conflict assessment procedures used by USG departments and agencies as well as with some international and nongovernmental organizations. It is not intended to duplicate or replace existing independent analytical processes, such as those conducted within the intelligence community. Rather, the ICAF builds upon those and other analytical efforts to provide a common framework. It allows USG departments and agencies to leverage and share the knowledge gained from their own assessments and establish a common interagency perspective.

D-7. The ICAF is distinct from other forecasting tools that identify countries at risk of instability or collapse and that describe conditions leading to outbreaks of instability or violent conflict. The ICAF builds on this forecasting. It helps an interagency team to understand why such conditions may exist and how to best engage to transform them. To do so, the ICAF draws on social science expertise to describe a process that an interagency team uses to identify societal and situational dynamics shown to increase or decrease potential violent conflict. In addition, the ICAF provides a shared, strategic perspective of the conflict against which future progress can be measured. (See chapter 1 for a discussion of conflict transformation in stability operations.)

APPLYING THE INTERAGENCY CONFLICT ASSESSMENT FRAMEWORK

D-8. The ICAF is the first step in any interagency planning process, informing and clarifying USG goals. It also provides information concerning the design and adjustment of activities, implementation, or revision of programs, and resource allocation. Within the interagency planning process, the ICAF determines who initiates and participates in the assessment, the time and place for the assessment, the type and application of products needed, and the appropriate level of classification. When the ICAF is used, all of its analytical steps should be completed; however, the nature and scope of the information collected and assessed may be constrained by time, security classification, or access to the field.

D-9. The ICAF is a flexible, scalable interagency tool suitable for use in—

- Steady-state engagement and conflict prevention planning.
- USG reconstruction and stabilization contingency planning.
- USG reconstruction and stabilization crisis response planning.

Steady-State Engagement and Conflict Prevention Planning

D-10. In a steady-state or conflict prevention planning effort, sufficient time to allow for a full-scale assessment and a generally permissive operational environment are the norm. Such efforts may include—

- Preparing an embassy for National Defense Authorization Act funding.
- Answering requests by an embassy or combatant command for interagency assistance in understanding and planning for leveraging U.S. interests in fragile or at-risk countries.
- Assisting with the development of combatant command theater security cooperation plans.
- Developing country assistance strategies or mission strategic plans.
- Designing interagency prevention efforts for countries listed on state failure watch lists and early warning systems.

United States Government Reconstruction and Stabilization Contingency Planning

D-11. Contingency planning is based on a hypothetical future. Thus, the ICAF provides relevant background concerning existing dynamics that could trigger, exacerbate, or mitigate violent conflict. The ICAF is a robust element of contingency planning, providing critical information for situational analysis. A Washington, DC-based tabletop or an in-country verification assessment often proves useful when using the ICAF as part of this planning process.

United States Government Reconstruction and Stabilization Crisis Response Planning

D-12. The ICAF provides critical information for the initial step of interagency planning, which provides detailed situational analysis. The ICAF is updated as more information becomes available and better access is obtained to inform the policy formulation, strategy development, and interagency implementation planning steps of the framework. When used for crisis response, the ICAF might be a Washington-based tabletop assessment that could be completed in as little as one and one-half days or, with longer lead-times to the crisis, could take place over several weeks with conversations back and forth between Washington and any USG field presence.

ROLES AND RESPONSIBILITIES

D-13. The planning process within which the ICAF is used determines which agencies and individuals serve on the team and in what capacities they should serve. An established country team may use the ICAF to inform country assistance strategy development while a geographic combatant command might use the ICAF to bring an interagency perspective to theater security cooperation planning. In crisis response under the Interagency Management System, the ICAF normally is part of the strategic planning process led by the country reconstruction and stabilization group. (See appendix B for an overview of the Interagency Management System.) The ICAF may also be used with a key bilateral partner as part of collaborative planning. The agency or individual responsible for managing the overall planning process is also responsible for proposing the ICAF and requesting necessary agency participation.

D-14. As a rule, participants in an ICAF assessment include the broadest possible representation of USG departments and agencies with expertise or vested interest in a given situation. An ideal interagency field team would represent diverse skill sets and bring together the collective knowledge and experience of various USG departments and agencies. Participants might include relevant regional bureaus, sectoral experts, intelligence analysts, and social science or conflict specialists. When the ICAF is used to support planning, the team includes members of the strategic planning team. This team may be expanded as needed to include local stakeholders and international partner representatives.

D-15. To ensure the most comprehensive analysis, members of the interagency team must provide all relevant information retained by their department or agency, including the results of past assessments and related analyses. These representatives must retain reachback capability with their agencies to obtain further information to fill critical information gaps identified through the ICAF process.

ELEMENTS OF THE INTERAGENCY CONFLICT ASSESSMENT FRAMEWORK

D-16. The ICAF can be used by any USG department or agency at any planning level. Using the ICAF involves an iterative process with initial results refined as the USG engagement expands. For example, an assessment completed in Washington at the outset of a crisis might be expanded upon later by a more in-depth examination conducted in the host nation. The level of detail achieved from the assessment depends upon the conflict and type of USG engagement. The ICAF includes two major elements: conflict diagnosis and segue into planning.

Conflict Diagnosis

D-17. Conflict diagnosis allows the interagency team to deliver a product that describes the context, core grievances and resiliencies, drivers of conflict and mitigating factors, and opportunities for increasing or decreasing conflict. Figure D-1 on page D-6 illustrates the conceptual framework for conflict diagnosis. To identify the critical elements of the conflict dynamic, the interagency conflict assessment team follows a series of analytical steps:

- Establish context.
- Understand core grievances and sources of social and institutional resilience.
- Identify drivers of conflict and mitigating factors.
- Describe windows of vulnerability and windows of opportunity.

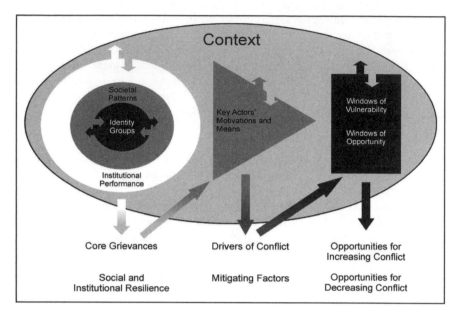

Figure D-1. Conflict diagnosis

Step 1: Establish Context

D-18. During the first step of conflict diagnosis, the team evaluates and outlines key contextual issues of the operational environment. Context does not cause conflict but describes the often long-standing conditions that are resistant to change. This context may create the conditions for conflict by reinforcing divisions between communities or contributing to pressures making violence appear as a more attractive means for advancing individual interests. Context can shape perceptions of identity groups and be used by key actors to manipulate and mobilize constituencies. The context may include environmental conditions, poverty, recent history of conflict, youth bulge, or a conflict-ridden region.

D-19. Each ICAF step begins with identifying and acknowledging the context from which the conflict evolved. This process, depicted in figure D-1, reflects the complex interaction between the context and each of the other elements of the ICAF.

Step 2: Understand Core Grievances and Sources of Social and Institutional Resilience

D-20. The team should understand, agree upon, and communicate the concepts of core grievance and sources of social and institutional resilience, and describe them within the specific situation being assessed. A core grievance is the perception, by various groups in a society, that their needs for physical security, livelihood, interests, or values are threatened by one or more other groups or social institutions. A source of social and institutional resilience is the perception by various groups in a society that social relationships, structures, or processes are in place, able to provide dispute resolution, and meet basic needs through nonviolent means.

D-21. During the second step of conflict diagnosis, the team must—

- Describe identity groups who perceive threats to their identity, security, or livelihood.
- Articulate how societal patterns reinforce perceived deprivation, blame, and intergroup cleavages as well as how those social patterns promote comity and peaceful resolution of disputes.
- Explain how positive or negative institutional performance contributes to or aggravates the resolution of conflict.

D-22. Identity groups are groups of people that identify with one another, often because of characteristics used by outsiders to describe them. These can include ethnicity, race, nationality, religion, political affiliation, age, gender, economic activity, or socioeconomic status. Identity groups are inclined to conflict when they perceive that other groups' interests, needs, and aspirations compete with and jeopardize their identity, security or other fundamental interests.

D-23. Societal patterns associated with conflict reinforce divisions between groups. These patterns can include elitism, exclusion, corruption, chronic state capacity deficits, and unmet expectations. Capacity deficits consist of systemic economic stagnation, scarcity of necessary resources, and ungoverned spaces. Unmet expectations may be a lack of a peace dividend, land tenure issues, disillusionment, and disenfranchisement. Impacts of societal patterns often include negative economic consequences for disadvantaged groups.

D-24. Institutional performance considers formal and informal social structures to determine the groups' performance level and if they contribute to or mitigate conflict and instability. Formal social structures consist of governments, legal systems, religious organizations, public schools, security forces, and economic institutions. Informal social structures include traditional dispute resolution bodies; families, clans or tribes; and armed groups. Assessing institutional performance involves distinguishing between outcomes and perceptions. Institutional outcomes are results that can be measured objectively; perceptions are the evaluative assessment of those outcomes. Understanding how outcomes are perceived by various groups within a society, especially in terms of effectiveness and legitimacy, is essential to conflict diagnosis.

Step 3: Identify Drivers of Conflict and Mitigating Factors

D-25. The team should understand and outline the drivers and mitigating factors of conflict and enumerate them within the specific situation being assessed. Drivers of conflict represent the active energy moving the conflict—the dynamic situation resulting from key actors' mobilization of social groups around core grievances. While core grievances can be understood as the potential energy of conflict, key actors translate that energy into drivers of conflict. Mitigating factors represent the dynamic situation resulting from key actors' mobilization of social groups around sources of social and institutional resilience. Mitigating factors can be understood as the energy produced when key actors mobilize the potential energy of social and institutional resilience.

D-26. During the third step of conflict diagnosis, the team identifies the key actors central to producing, perpetuating, or profoundly changing the societal patterns or issues of institutional performance identified previously. The team determines whether key actors are motivated to mobilize constituencies toward inflaming or mitigating violent conflict and what means are at their disposal. To perform the analysis required in this step, the team—

- Identifies the key actors:
  - Who: The people, organizations, or groups that, because of their leadership abilities or power—such as political position, moral authority, charisma, wealth, and weapons—affect societal patterns and institutional performance, can shape perceptions and actions, and mobilize people around core grievances or social and institutional resilience.
  - Where: Key actors in leadership positions in governing, social, or professional organizations or networks (either within or external to a state or territory). They include private businesses, religious organizations, government positions, informal and illicit power structures, media, and academic institutions.

- What and how: What motivates key actors to exert influence on each of the political, economic, social, and security systems within the host nation—such as commitment to a cause or a people, greed (money or notoriety), and religious beliefs—and how they exert that influence (leadership capacity, moral authority, personal charisma, access to resources or weapons, or networks).

- Determines key actors'—

  - Supporting and opposing constituencies and the core grievances or social or institutional resilience around which they are being mobilized.

  - Critical motivations, means, and resources.

D-27. Using this information, the team drafts brief narrative statements describing how and why key actors mobilize specific constituencies around core grievances and sources of social and institutional resilience. Each statement relating to core grievances becomes an entry in the list of drivers of conflict and each relating to sources of social and institutional resilience becomes an entry in the list of mitigating factors.

Step 4: Describe Windows of Vulnerability and Windows of Opportunity

D-28. In the final step of conflict diagnosis, the team—

- Identifies potential situations that could contribute to an increase in violent conflict.

- Identifies potential situations that might offer opportunities for mitigating violent conflict and promoting stability.

D-29. The team should specify opportunities for increasing and decreasing conflict and describe those expected within the specific situation being assessed. These are described as windows of vulnerability and windows of opportunity. Windows of vulnerability are potential situations that may trigger conflict escalation. They often result from large-scale responses to an increase of uncertainty during elections or following an assassination. They also result from an exclusion of parties from important events (such as negotiations or elections) or attempts to marginalize disenfranchised followers. Windows of vulnerability are moments when events threaten to rapidly and fundamentally alter the balance of political or economic power. Elections, devolution of power, and legislative changes are examples of possible windows of vulnerability. Key actors may seize, retain, and exploit the initiative during these moments to amplify the drivers of conflict. Windows of opportunity describe potential situations that may enable significant progress toward achieving stable peace. They may include situations where overarching identities assume prominence among disputing groups, natural disasters impact multiple identity groups, the response requires a unified response, or a key leader driving the conflict is killed. These windows are moments when over-arching identities become more important than subgroup identities, such as when a natural disaster impacts multiple groups and requires a unified response. These occasions may present opportunities to provide additional support for a conflict's mitigating factors.

D-30. The team completes conflict diagnosis by considering windows of vulnerability and windows of opportunity and prioritizing drivers of conflict and mitigating factors identified previously. The team uses the list of prioritized drivers and mitigating factors as the basis for its findings.

Segue into Planning

D-31. When the ICAF is used to support crisis response or contingency planning, the findings of the conflict diagnosis feed into the situational analysis and policy formulation steps of interagency, whole of government planning. When the ICAF is used to support steady-state engagement or conflict prevention planning, the team begins preplanning activities after completing conflict diagnosis. During the segue into these types of planning, the team maps existing diplomatic and program activities against the prioritized lists of drivers of conflict and mitigating factors. This mapping identifies gaps in current efforts as they relate to conflict dynamics. However, this is not intended as an evaluation of the overall impact or utility of any specific program or initiative. The team uses these findings as a basis for making recommendations to planners on potential entry points for USG activities.

D-32. When the ICAF is used to support steady-state engagement or conflict prevention planning, the following steps are used to facilitate the planning process:

- Step 1: Specify current USG activities (identify USG departments and agencies present in the country and the nature and scope of their efforts) by—
  - Identifying the impact of these efforts on drivers of conflict and mitigating factors.
  - Identifying efforts that target similar outcomes and coordination mechanisms in place.
- Step 2: Specify current efforts of non-USG actors, including bilateral agencies, multilateral agencies, nongovernmental organizations, and private sector and local entities by—
  - Identifying the impact of the efforts on the drivers of conflict and mitigating factors.

- Identifying efforts that target similar outcomes (including USG efforts) and coordinating mechanisms in place.
- Step 3: Identify drivers of conflict and mitigating factors not sufficiently addressed by existing efforts (gaps).
- Step 4: Specify challenges to addressing these gaps.
- Step 5: Describe risks associated with failing to address gaps (relate directly to windows of vulnerability).
- Step 6: Describe opportunities to address gaps (relate directly to windows of opportunity).

D-33. The team draws on the information generated from this effort to determine potential entry points for USG efforts. The description of these entry points explain how the dynamics outlined during conflict diagnosis may be susceptible to outside influence.

TACTICAL CONFLICT ASSESSMENT AND PLANNING FRAMEWORK

D-34. To increase the effectiveness of stability operations, the U.S. Agency for International Development created the tactical conflict assessment and planning framework (TCAPF). The TCAPF was designed to assist commanders and their staffs identify the causes of instability, develop activities to diminish or mitigate them, and evaluate the effectiveness of the activities in fostering stability at the tactical level (provincial or local). The TCAPF should be used to create local stabilization plans and provide data for the ICAF, which has a strategic and operational-level (country or regional) focus.

CONCEPTUAL FRAMEWORK

D-35. The TCAPF is based on the following four premises:

- Instability results when the factors fostering instability overwhelm the ability of the host nation to mitigate these factors.
- Assessment is necessary for targeted and strategic engagement.
- The population is the best source for identifying the causes of instability.
- Measures of effectiveness are the only true measure of success.

Instability

D-36. Instability results when the factors fostering instability overwhelm the ability of the host nation to mitigate these factors. (See figure D-2.)

To understand why there is instability or determine the risk of instability, the following factors must be understood:

- Grievances.
- Key actors' motivations and means.
- Windows of vulnerability.

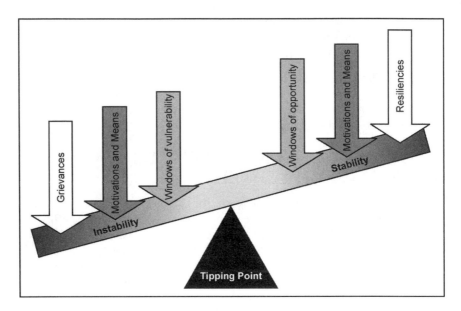

Figure D-2. Dynamics of instability

D-37. Grievances are factors that can foster instability. They are based on a groups' perception that other groups or institutions are threatening its interests. Examples include ethnic or religious tensions, political repression, population pressures, and competition over natural resources. Greed can also foster instability. Some groups and individuals gain power and wealth from instability. Drug lords and insurgents fall in this category.

D-38. Key actors' motivations and means are ways key actors transform grievances into widespread instability. Although there can be many grievances, they do not foster instability unless key actors with both the motivation and the means to translate these grievances into widespread instability emerge. Transforming grievances into widespread violence requires a dedicated leadership, organizational capacity, money, and weapons. If a group lacks these resources, it will not be able to foster widespread instability. Means and motivations are the critical variables that determine whether grievances become causes of instability.

D-39. Windows of vulnerability are situations that can trigger widespread instability. Even when grievances and means are present, widespread instability is unlikely unless a window of vulnerability exists that links grievances to means and motivations. Potential windows of vulnerability include an invasion, highly contested elections, natural disasters, the death of a key leader, and economic shocks.

D-40. Even if grievances, means, and vulnerabilities exist, instability is not inevitable. For each of these factors, there are parallel mitigating forces:

- Resiliencies.
- Key actors' motivations and means.
- Windows of opportunity.

D-41. Resiliencies are the processes, relationships, and institutions that can reduce the effects of grievances. Examples include community organizations, and accessible, legitimate judicial structures. Key actors' motivations and means are ways key actors leverage resiliencies to counter instability. Just as certain key actors have the motivation and means to create instability, other actors have the motivation and the means to rally people around nonviolent procedures to address grievances. An example could be a local imam advocating peaceful coexistence among opposing tribes. Windows of opportunity are situations or events that can strengthen resiliencies. For example, the tsunami that devastated the instable Indonesian province of Aceh provided an opportunity for rebels and government forces to work together peacefully. This led to a peace agreement and increased stability.

D-42. While understanding these factors is crucial to understanding stability, they do not exist in a vacuum. Therefore, their presence or absence must be understood within the context of a given environment. Context refers to longstanding conditions that do not change easily or quickly. Examples include geography, demography, natural resources, history, as well as regional and international factors. Contextual factors do not necessarily cause instability, but they can contribute to the grievances or provide the means that foster instability. For example, although poverty alone does not foster conflict, poverty linked to illegitimate government institutions, a growing gap between rich and poor, and access to a global arms market can combine to foster instability. Instability occurs when the causes of instability overwhelm societal or governmental ability to mitigate it.

Assessment

D-43. Assessment is necessary for targeted engagement. Since most stability operations occur in less developed countries, there will always be a long list of needs and wants, such as schools, roads, and health care, within an operational area. Given a chronic shortage of USG personnel and resources, effective stability operations require an ability to identify and prioritize local sources of instability and stability. They also require the prioritization of interventions based on their importance in diminishing those sources of instability or building on sources of stability. For example, if village elders want more water, but water is not fostering instability (because fighting between farmers and pastoralists over land is the cause), then digging a well will not stabilize the area. In some cases, wells have been dug based on the assumption that stability will result from fulfilling a local want. However, ensuring both farmers and pastoralists have access to water will help stabilize the area only if they were fighting over water. Understanding the causal relationship between needs, wants, and stability is crucial. In some cases, they are directly related; in others, they are not. Used correctly, the TCAPF, triangulated with data obtained from other sources, will help establish whether there is a causal relationship.

D-44. Understanding the difference between symptoms and causes is another key aspect of stability. Too often, interventions target the symptoms of instability rather than identifying and targeting the underlying causes. While there is always a strong temptation to achieve quick results, this often equates to satisfying a superficial request that does not reduce the underlying causes of instability and, in some cases, actually increases instability.

D-45. For example, an assessment identified a need to reopen a local school in Afghanistan. The prevailing logic held that addressing this need would increase support for the government while decreasing support for antigovernment forces. When international forces reopened the school, however, antigovernment forces coerced the school administrator to leave under threat of death, forcing the school to close. A subsequent investigation revealed that the local populace harbored antigovernment sentiments because host-nation police tasked with providing security for the school established a checkpoint nearby and demanded bribes for passage into the village. The local populace perceived the school, which drew the attention of corrupt host-nation police, as the source of their troubles. Rather than improve government support by reopening the school, the act instead caused resentment since it exposed the local populace to abuse from the police. This in turn resulted in increased support for antigovernment forces, which were perceived as protecting the interests of the local populace. While the assessment identified a need to reopen the school, the act did not address a cause of instability. At best, it addressed a possible symptom of instability and served only to bring the true cause of instability closer to the affected population.

The Population

D-46. The population is the best source for identifying the causes of instability. Since stability operations focus on the local populace, it is imperative to identify and prioritize what the population perceives as the causes of instability. To identify the causes of instability, the TCAPF uses the local populace to identify and prioritize the problems in the area. This is accomplished by asking four simple, standardized questions. (See paragraph D-49.)

Measures of Effectiveness

D-47. A measure of effectiveness is the only true gauge of success. Too often, the terms "output" and "effect" are used interchangeably among civilian agencies. However, they measure very different aspects of task performance. While "outputs" indicate task performance, "effects" measure the effectiveness of activities against a predetermined objective. Measures of effectiveness are crucial for determining the success or failure of stability tasks. (See chapter 4 for a detailed discussion of the relationship between among assessment, measures of performance, and measures of effectiveness.)

THE TACTICAL CONFLICT ASSESSMENT AND PLANNING FRAMEWORK PROCESS

D-48. The TCAPF consistently maintains focus on the local populace. Organizations using the TCAPF follow a continuous cycle of *see-understand-act-measure*. The TCAPF includes four distinct, but interrelated activities:

- Collection.
- Analysis.
- Design.
- Evaluation.

Collection

D-49. Collecting information on the causes of instability within an operational area is a two-step process. The first step uses the following four questions to draw critical information from the local populace:

- Has the population of the village changed in the last twelve months?
- What are the greatest problems facing the village?
- Who is trusted to resolve problems?
- What should be done first to help the village?

D-50. Has the population of the village changed in the last twelve months? Understanding population movement is crucial to understanding the operational environment. Population movement often provides a good indicator of changes in relative stability. People usually move when deprived of security or social well-being. The sudden arrival of dislocated civilians can produce a destabilizing effect if the operational area lacks sufficient capacity to absorb them or if there is local opposition to their presence.

D-51. What are the greatest problems facing the village? Providing the local populace with a means to express problems helps to prioritize and focus activities appropriately. The local populace is able to identify their own problem areas, thus avoiding mistaken assumptions by the intervening forces. This procedure does not solicit needs and wants, but empowers the people to take ownership of the overall process.

D-52. Who is trusted to resolve problems? Identifying the individuals or institutions most trusted to resolve local issues is critical to understanding perceptions and loyalties. Responses may include the host-nation government, a local warlord, international forces, a religious leader, or other authority figure. This question also provides an indication of the level of support for the host-nation government, a key component of stability. This often serves as a measure of effectiveness for stability tasks. It also identifies key informants who may assist with vetting or help to develop messages to support information engagement activities.

D-53. What should be done first to help the village? Encouraging the local populace to prioritize their problems helps to affirm ownership. Their responses form the basis for local projects and programs.

D-54. A central facet of the collection effort is determining the relationship between the symptoms and cause of the basic problem; understanding why a symptom exists is essential to addressing the cause. For example, an assessment completed in Afghanistan identified a lack of security as the main problem within a specific operational area. Analysis indicated this was due a shortage of host-nation security forces in the local area and an additional detachment of local police was assigned to the area. However, the assessment failed to identify the relationship between the symptom and cause of the problem. Thus, the implemented solution addressed the symptom, while the actual cause remained unaddressed. A subsequent assessment revealed that the local police were actually the cause of the insecurity: it was common practice for them to demand bribes from the local populace while discriminating against members of rival clans in the area. By addressing the symptom of the problem rather than the cause, the implemented solution actually exacerbated the problem instead of resolving it.

D-55. The second step of collection involves conducting targeted interviews with key local stakeholders, such traditional leaders, government officials, business leaders, and prominent citizens. These interviews serve two purposes. First, targeted interviews act as a control mechanism in the collection effort. If the answers provided by key stakeholders match the responses from the local populace, it is likely the individual understands the causes of instability and may be relied upon to support the assessment effort. However, if the answers do not match those of the local populace, that individual may be either an uninformed stakeholder or possibly part of the problem. Second, targeted interviews provide more detail on the causes of instability while helping determine how best to address those causes and measure progress toward that end.

D-56. Information obtained during collection is assembled in a formatted TCAPF spreadsheet. This allows the information to be easily grouped and quantified to identify and prioritize the most important concerns of the population.

Analysis

D-57. During analysis, the information gained through collection is compiled in a graphical display. (See figure D-3 on page D-18.) This display helps identify the main concerns of the population and serves as a reference point for targeted questioning. The TCAPF data is combined with input from other staff sections and other sources of information—such as intergovernmental organizations, nongovernmental organizations, and private sector entities. All this input is used to create a prioritized list of the causes of instability and sources of resiliency that guides the conduct of stability operations.

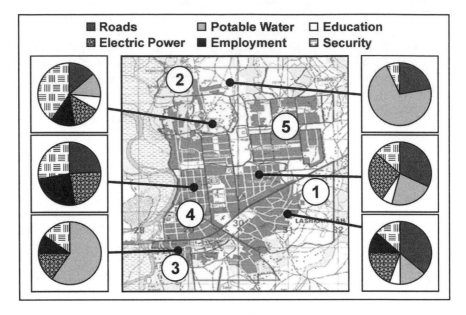

Figure D-3. Analyzing causes of instability

Design

D-58. The design effort is informed through analysis, the results of which are used to create a tactical stability matrix for each of the causes of instability. (See table D-1 on page D-19.) After identifying the causes of instability and sources of resiliency, a program of activities is designed to address them. Three key factors guide program design, which ensures program activities:

- Increase support for the host-nation government.
- Decrease support for antigovernment forces.
- Build host-nation capacity across each of the stability sectors.

D-59. The tactical stability matrix and program activities form the basis for planning within an operational area. The plan targets the least stable areas and ensures instability is contained. It is nested within the higher headquarters plan and details how specific stability tasks will be integrated and synchronized at the tactical level. The TCAPF data is collated at each echelon to develop or validate assessments performed by subordinate elements.

Table D-1. Tactical stability matrix

Grievance	Causes (Perceptions)	Causes (Systemic)	Objective	Impact Indicators	Monitoring Methods
Police abuse the situation	Police extort bribes Police do not serve the people Police are untrustworthy Police use the law to help themselves There is no control over the police	Police are not paid on time Police are not accountable Police are not representative of the local populace Local police are largely autonomous Police include many former militia members	Increase popular support for the police	Increased popular support More actionable intelligence to police from population Increased positive police interaction with the population Adequate police presence	TCAPF or public surveys Truck driver surveys Numerous illegal checkpoints Develop police intelligence on the local populace Increased, sustained police presence

Evaluation

D-60. The TCAPF provides a comprehensive means of evaluating success in addressing the sources of instability. Through measures of effectiveness, analysts gauge progress toward improving stability while diminishing the sources of instability. Measures of effectiveness are vital to evaluating the success of program activities in changing the state of the operational environment envisioned during the design effort.

D-61. While evaluation is critical to measuring the effectiveness of activities in fostering stability, it also helps to ensure the views of the population are tracked, compared, measured, and displayed over time. Since these results are objective, they cannot be altered by interviewer or analyst bias. This creates a continuous narrative that significantly increases situational awareness.

Best Practices and Lessons Learned

D-62. Capturing and implementing best practices and lessons learned is fundamental to adaptive organizations. This behavior is essential in stability operations, where the ability to learn and adapt is often the difference between success and failure. The TCAPF leverages this ability to overcome the dynamics of the human dimension, where uncertainty, chance, and friction are the norm. Examples of best practices and lessons learned gained through recent experience include the following:

- Activities and projects are products that foster a process to change behavior or perceptions. Indicators and measures of effectiveness identify whether change has occurred or is occurring.
- Perceptions of the local populace provide the best means to gauge the impact of program activities.
- Indicators provide insight into measures of effectiveness by revealing whether positive progress is being achieved by program activities. (See paragraph 4-69 for a discussion on the role of indicators in assessment.)
- "Good deeds" cannot substitute for effectively targeted program activities; the best information engagement effort is successful programming that meets the needs of the local populace.
- Intervention activities should—
  - Respond to priority issues of the local populace.
  - Focus effort on critical crosscutting activities.
  - Establish anticorruption measures early in the stability operation.
  - Identify and support key actors early to set the conditions for subsequent collaboration.
- Intervention activities should not—
  - Mistake "good deeds" for effective action.
  - Initiate projects not designed as program activities.
  - Attempt to impose "Western" standards.
  - Focus on quantity over quality.

SUMMARY

D-63. The TCAPF has been successfully implemented in practice to identify, prioritize, and target the causes of instability in a measurable and immediately accessible manner. Since it maximizes the use of assets in the field and gauges the effectiveness of activities in time and space, it is an important tool for conducting successful stability operations.

Appendix E

Humanitarian Response Principles

BACKGROUND

E-1. Even in those situations where military forces are not directly involved, a focused and integrated humanitarian response is essential to reestablishing a stable environment that fosters a lasting peace to support broader national and international interests. Providing humanitarian aid and assistance is primarily the responsibility of specialized civilian, national, international, governmental, and nongovernmental organizations and agencies. Nevertheless, military forces are often called upon to support humanitarian response activities either as part of a broader campaign, such as Operation Iraqi Freedom, or a specific humanitarian assistance or disaster relief operation. These activities consist of stability tasks and generally fall under the primary stability task, *restore essential services*. This appendix outlines the guiding principles used by the international community to frame humanitarian response activities.

E-2. Generally, the host nation or affected country coordinates humanitarian response. However, if the host nation or affected country is unable to do so, the United Nations often leads the international community response on its behalf. The principles that guide the military contribution to that response are fundamental to success in full spectrum operations. These principles reflect the collective experience of a diverse group of actors in a wide range of interventions conducted over decades across the world. They help to shape the humanitarian component of stability operations.

E-3. United Nations General Assembly Resolution 46/182 governs the humanitarian response efforts of the international community. It articulates the principal tenets for providing humanitarian assistance— humanity, neutrality, and impartiality—while promulgating the guiding principles that frame all humanitarian response activities. These guiding principles are drawn from four primary, albeit separate, sources:

- InterAction and the Department of Defense.
- International Red Cross and Red Crescent Movement.

- Oslo Guidelines.
- Interagency Standing Committee.

INTERACTION AND THE DEPARTMENT OF DEFENSE

E-4. InterAction is the largest coalition of U.S.-based nongovernmental organizations focused on the world's poorest and most vulnerable people. Collectively, its members work in every developing country. Members meet people halfway in expanding opportunities and support gender equality in education, health care, agriculture, small business, and other areas.

RECOMMENDED GUIDELINES

E-5. The following guidelines facilitate interaction between American forces and nongovernmental humanitarian agencies (NGHAs). This latter group engages in humanitarian relief efforts in hostile or potentially hostile environments. Simply, these guidelines recognize that military forces and NGHAs often occupy the same space, compete for the same resources, and will likely do so again. When they share an operational area, both should strive to follow these guidelines; they recognize that extreme circumstances or operational necessity may require deviation. When aid organizations deviate from established guidelines, they must make every effort to explain their reasoning.

E-6. Military forces use the following guidelines consistent with protection, mission accomplishment, and operational requirements:

- When conducting relief activities, military personnel wear uniforms or other distinctive clothing to avoid being mistaken for NGHA representatives. These personnel do not display NGHA logos on any clothing, vehicles, or equipment. This does not preclude the appropriate use of symbols recognized under the law of war, such as a red cross. U.S. forces may use the red cross on military clothing, vehicles, and equipment when appropriate.
- Military personnel visits to NGHA sites are by prior arrangement.
- NGHA views on the bearing of arms within NGHA sites are respected.
- NGHAs have the option of meeting with military personnel outside military installations for information exchanges.

- Military forces do not describe NGHAs as "force multipliers" or "partners" of the military, or in any fashion that could compromise their independence or their goal to be perceived by the population as independent.

- Military personnel and units avoid interfering with NGHA relief efforts directed toward segments of the civilian population that the military may regard as unfriendly.

- Military personnel and units respect the desire of NGHAs not to serve as implementing partners for the military in conducting relief activities. However, individual nongovernmental organizations may seek to cooperate with the military. In this case, such arrangements will be carried out while avoiding compromise of the security, safety, and independence of the NGHA community at large, NGHA representatives, or public perceptions of their independence.

E-7. NGHAs should observe the following guidelines:

- NGHA personnel do not wear military-style clothing. NGHA personnel can wear protective gear, such as helmets and protective vests, provided that such items are distinguishable in color or appearance from military-issue items.

- Only NGHA liaison personnel—and not other NGHA staff— may travel in military vehicles.

- NGHAs do not co-locate facilities with facilities inhabited by military personnel.

- NGHAs use their own logos on clothing, vehicles, and buildings when security conditions permit.

- Except for liaison arrangements, NGHAs limit activities at military bases and with military personnel that might compromise their independence.

- NGHAs may, as a last resort, request military protection for convoys delivering humanitarian assistance, take advantage of essential logistic support available only from the military, or accept evacuation assistance for medical treatment or for evacuating a hostile environment. Providing such military support to NGHAs is not obligatory but rests solely within the discretion of the military forces. Often it will be provided on a reimbursable basis in accordance with applicable U.S. law.

- NGHA personnel visits to military facilities or sites are by prior arrangement.

E-8. The third recommended guideline deals with forms of coordination. Military forces and NGHA staff coordinate to minimize the risk of confusion between military and NGHA roles in hostile or potentially hostile environments; they are subject to protection, mission accomplishment, and operations security requirements. They follow these guidelines:

- NGHA liaison officers participate in unclassified security briefings conducted by the military forces.

- Military forces share unclassified information with the NGHA liaison officer concerning security conditions, operational sites, location of mines and unexploded explosive ordnance, humanitarian activities, and population movements.

- NGHA staff arranges liaisons with military commands prior to and during military operations to deconflict military and relief activities. Such liaison includes protecting humanitarian installations and personnel. It also includes informing military personnel of humanitarian relief objectives, modalities of operation, and the extent of prospective or ongoing civilian humanitarian relief efforts.

- Military forces assist NGHAs for humanitarian relief activities when civilian providers are unavailable or unable to do so. Often, such assistance is provided on a reimbursable basis in accordance with applicable U.S. law.

RECOMMENDED PROCESSES

E-9. The dialog between NGHAs and military forces during contingency planning follows certain procedures. These procedures apply to Department of Defense relief operations in a hostile or potentially hostile environment:

- NGHAs engaged in humanitarian relief send a small number of liaison officers to the geographic combatant command for discussions with the contingency planners responsible for designing relief operations.

- NGHAs engaged in humanitarian relief assign a small number of liaison officers to the geographic combatant command. For example, one liaison officer was stationed at U.S. Central Command for six of the first twelve months of the war in Afghanistan, and one was in Kuwait City before U.S. forces entered Iraq in 2003.

- The relevant military planners, including but not limited to the civil affairs representatives of the geographic combatant command, meet with humanitarian relief NGHA liaison officers at a mutually agreed location.

E-10. NGHAs and military forces follow certain procedures to access assessments of humanitarian needs. Military and NGHA representatives—

- Access NGHA and military assessments directly from a Department of Defense or other United States Government (USG) Web site.
- Access NGHA and military assessments through a nongovernmental organization serving in a coordination role and identifying a common Web site.
- Access NGHA and military assessments through a United Nations' Web site.

E-11. Certain procedures exist for NGHA liaison relationships with combatant commands engaged in planning for military operations in hostile or potentially hostile environments. The NGHA community provides the following:

- One NGHA liaison officer physically located outside the military headquarters; if feasible, the officer is near it to facilitate daily contact.
- One NGHA liaison officer with appropriate access to senior-level officers within the geographic combatant commander's headquarters and who meets with them as necessary and feasible.
- Two-way information flow. The NGHA liaison officer provides such details as NGHA capabilities, infrastructure, plans, and concerns. Military forces provide details concerning minefields, unexploded explosive ordnance, other hazards to NGHAs, access to medical facilities, and evacuation plans.
- Military personnel with the opportunity to brief NGHAs, to the extent appropriate, on USG goals and policies, monitoring principles, and applicable laws and rules of engagement. Conversely, the International Committee of the Red Cross (ICRC) will typically brief military commanders on the role and capabilities of the International Red Cross and Red Crescent Movement. The NGHA liaison officer has the opportunity to brief military commanders on—
  - NGHA objectives.
  - Codes of conduct for the International Red Cross and Red Crescent Movement and the nongovernmental organizations.
  - The Interagency Standing Committee guidelines.
  - Country-specific guidelines based on the Interagency Standing Committee guidelines.

- If desired, Sphere Project Minimum Standards.
- The NGHA liaison officer could continue as a liaison to the combatant command headquarters even after a civil-military operations center (CMOC) or similar mechanism is established in country. Once this occurs, liaison officers of an individual NGHA can begin coordination in country through the CMOC for civil-military liaison.

E-12. Possible organizations can serve as a bridge between NGHAs and military forces in the field. (In situations in which no actor exists to serve as a bridge, a U.S. CMOC can serve as a temporary liaison between NGHAs and military forces.) These organizations can include the U.S. Agency for International Development's Office of Military Affairs, Department of State's Office of the Coordinator for Reconstruction and Stabilization, and the United Nation's humanitarian coordinator. The following are recommended procedures:

- If the U.S. Agency for International Development or the Department of State's Office of the Coordinator for Reconstruction and Stabilization agrees to serve a liaison, it should be prepared to work with NGHAs in addition to USG implementing partners.
- The United Nations' humanitarian coordinators or representatives can act as liaisons because they normally would be responsible for working with all NGHAs and maintaining contact with the host-nation government or a successor regime. An exception to this practice is the International Red Cross and Red Crescent Movement, which provides this function independently.

INTERNATIONAL RED CROSS AND RED CRESCENT MOVEMENT

E-13. The International Red Cross and Red Crescent Movement encompasses two institutions and nearly 200 national societies. The two institutions are the ICRC and the International Federation of Red Cross and Red Crescent Societies. The ICRC is an impartial, neutral, and independent organization. Established in 1863, its exclusively humanitarian mission aims to protect the lives and dignity of victims of war and internal violence and to provide them with assistance. It directs and coordinates the international relief activities conducted by the International Red Cross and Red Crescent Movement in conflicts. It also endeavors to prevent suffering by promoting and strengthening laws pertaining to human rights and universal humanitarian principles.

FUNDAMENTAL PRINCIPLES OF THE RED CROSS

E-14. The seven fundamental principles bond together the national Red Cross and Red Crescent Societies, the ICRC, and the International Federation of the Red Cross and Red Crescent Societies. The principles ensure the continuity of the International Red Cross and Red Crescent Movement and its humanitarian work. These principles are—

- Humanity.
- Impartiality.
- Neutrality.
- Independence.
- Voluntary service.
- Unity.
- Universality.

Humanity

E-15. The International Red Cross and Red Crescent Movement was developed to bring unbiased assistance to the wounded on the battlefield. It aims to prevent and alleviate human suffering wherever found. It aims to protect life and health and to ensure respect for the human being. It promotes mutual understanding, friendship, cooperation, and lasting peace among all people.

Impartiality

E-16. The second principle makes no discrimination as to nationality, race, religious beliefs, class, or political opinions. It tries to relieve the suffering of individuals—guided solely by their needs—and to give priority to the most urgent cases of distress.

Neutrality

E-17. Neutrality is the third fundamental principle of the International Red Cross and Red Crescent Movement. To continue to enjoy the confidence of all, the Movement may not take sides in hostilities. It may not engage at any time in controversies of a political, racial, religious, or ideological nature.

Independence

E-18. The fourth fundamental principle is independence. The national societies are auxiliaries in the humanitarian services of their governments and subject to the laws of their respective countries. As such, the societies must always maintain their autonomy. Such independence enables the societies to act in accordance with the principles of the Movement at all times.

Voluntary Service

E-19. Voluntary service is the fifth fundamental principle of the International Red Cross and Red Crescent Movement. It is a voluntary relief movement. It is not prompted in any manner by a desire for gain.

Unity

E-20. The sixth principle is unity. There can be only one Red Cross or one Red Crescent Society in any one country. It must be open to all. It must carry on its humanitarian work throughout its territory.

Universality

E-21. The seventh fundamental principle is universality. Universality ensures that all societies have equal status in the Movement. It also ensures that all societies share equal responsibilities and duties in helping each other. The Movement is worldwide.

CODE OF CONDUCT

E-22. In the summer of 1994, the code of conduct for the International Red Cross and Red Crescent Movement and nongovernmental organizations in disaster relief was developed. (See table E-1 on page E-9.) Eight of the world's largest disaster response agencies agreed on this code. It represents the body of international standards for disaster response. Before then, no accepted body of professional standards existed to guide their work. Today, the international community uses it to monitor its own standards of relief delivery and to encourage other agencies to set similar standards.

Table E-1. The International Red Cross and Red Crescent Movement and Nongovernmental Organization Code of Conduct in Disaster Relief

- The humanitarian imperative comes first.
- Aid is given regardless of the race, creed, or nationality of the recipients and without adverse distinction of any kind. Aid priorities are calculated based on need alone.
- Aid will not be used to further a particular political or religious standpoint.
- We shall endeavor not to act as instruments of government foreign policy.
- We shall respect culture and custom.
- We shall attempt to build disaster response on local capacities.
- Ways shall be found to involve program beneficiaries in the management of relief aid.
- Relief aid must strive to reduce future vulnerabilities to disaster as well as meeting basic needs.
- We hold ourselves accountable to both those we seek to assist and those from whom we accept resources.
- In our information, publicity, and advertising activities, we shall recognize disaster victims as dignified human beings, not hopeless objects.

E-23. Like most professional codes, the code of conduct is voluntary. It applies to any nongovernmental organization, national or international, regardless of size. It provides ten "points of principle" that all nongovernmental organizations should adhere to in their disaster response work. The code of conduct also describes the relationships that these groups should seek with donor organizations, host-nation governments, and the United Nations. The code is self-policing; no one nongovernmental organization is going to force another to act in a certain way. There is, as yet, no international association for disaster-response nongovernmental organizations that possesses any authority to sanction its members.

The Humanitarian Imperative Comes First

E-24. The right to receive humanitarian assistance, and to offer it, is a fundamental humanitarian principle that all citizens of all countries should have. As part of the international community, the International Red Cross and Red Crescent Movement recognizes its obligation to provide humanitarian assistance wherever needed. Hence, to provide humanitarian assistance, organizations need unimpeded access to affected populations. The International Red Cross and Red Crescent Movement's motivation to respond to disaster is to alleviate human suffering. It strives to help those least able to withstand the stress caused by disaster. Giving humanitarian aid is not a partisan or political act and should not be viewed as such.

Aid Is Given Regardless of Race, Creed, or Nationality

E-25. Aid priorities are calculated on need alone. Wherever possible, the International Red Cross and Red Crescent Movement provides relief aid after thoroughly assessing the situation. It assesses the needs of the disaster victims and the local capacities already in place to meet those needs. In all of its programs, the Movement provides aid in proportion to the need. Human suffering must be alleviated whenever it is found; life is as precious in one area as another. The Movement recognizes the crucial role women play in disaster-prone communities. It tries to support, not diminish, their role with its aid programs. Implementing such a universal, impartial, and independent policy is effective only when relief organizations have access to resources and all disaster victims. Only then can they provide equal relief.

Aid Will Not Be Used to Further Certain Standpoints

E-26. Humanitarian aid will be given according to the need of individuals, families, and communities. The International Red Cross and Red Crescent Movement affirms that assistance does not depend on the recipients to adhere to political or religious opinions. The Movement does not tie the promise, delivery, or distribution of assistance to the embracing or acceptance of a particular political or religious creed.

Agents of Aid Shall Not Act as Instruments of Government Foreign Policy

E-27. NGHAs act independently from governments. They form their own policies and implementation strategies. They do not seek to implement the policy of any government unless it coincides with their own independent policy. They never knowingly or through negligence allow themselves to be used to gather information. Information could be politically, military, or economically sensitive to governments or other bodies that may serve purposes other than those that are strictly humanitarian. NGHAs do not act as instruments of foreign policy of donor organizations. They use the assistance received to respond to needs. This assistance is not driven by the need to use surpluses or by the donor's political interest. Agents of aid value and promote the voluntary giving of labor and finances by individuals to support their work. To protect independence, agents of aid avoid depending on a single funding source.

Agents of Aid Shall Respect Culture and Custom

E-28. The International Red Cross and Red Crescent Movement tries to respect the culture, structures, and customs of the communities and countries in which the members work.

Agents of Aid Shall Attempt to Build Disaster Response on Local Capacities

E-29. All people and communities—even in disaster—possess capacities as well as vulnerabilities. Where possible, the International Red Cross and Red Crescent Movement strengthens these capacities by employing local staff, purchasing local materials, and trading with local companies. Where possible, these agents of aid work through local nongovernmental organizations providing humanitarian assistance as partners in planning and implementation; they cooperate with local governments where appropriate. The International Red Cross and Red Crescent Movement places a high priority on properly coordinating emergency responses. Coordination is best accomplished within the countries concerned by those most directly involved in the relief operations. Such efforts should include representatives of the relevant United Nations bodies and of the International Red Cross and Red Crescent Movement.

Involve Program Beneficiaries in Managing Relief Aid

E-30. Disaster response assistance should never be forced on those needing assistance. Effective relief and lasting rehabilitation can best be achieved when the intended beneficiaries help to design, manage, and implement the assistance program. The International Red Cross and Red Crescent Movement strives to achieve full community participation in relief and rehabilitation programs.

Aid Must Strive to Reduce Future Vulnerabilities and Meet Basic Needs

E-31. All relief actions affect the prospects for long-term development, either positively or negatively. Recognizing this, the agents of aid strive to implement relief programs that actively reduce the beneficiaries' vulnerability to future disasters and help create sustainable lifestyles. These agents pay particular attention to environmental concerns when designing and managing relief programs. The International Red Cross and Red Crescent Movement tries to minimize the negative impact of humanitarian assistance. The Movement tries to prevent the beneficiary from depending upon external aid for a long time.

Agents of Aid Hold Themselves Accountable

E-32. The International Red Cross and Red Crescent Movement often acts as an institutional link between those who wish to assist and those who need assistance during disasters. The Movement therefore holds itself accountable to both constituencies. All dealings with donors and beneficiaries are open and transparent. The agents of aid report on activities, both from a financial perspective and the perspective of effectiveness. They recognize they must appropriately monitor aid distributions and regularly assess the impact of disaster assistance. The International Red Cross and Red Crescent Movement openly reports on the impact of its work and the factors limiting or enhancing that impact. Relief programs are based on high standards of professionalism and expertise to minimize the wasting of valuable resources.

Agents of Aid Recognize Disaster Victims as Dignified Humans

E-33. Respect for the disaster victim as an equal partner in action should never be lost. In public information, the Movement portrays an objective image of the disaster situation. This image highlights the capacities and aspirations of disaster victims, not just their vulnerabilities and fears. While working with the media to enhance public response, the Movement prohibits external or internal demands for publicity to take precedence over the principle of maximizing overall relief assistance. These agents of aid avoid competing with other disaster response agencies for media coverage. In some situations, coverage may hinder the service provided to the beneficiaries or the security. Humanitarian response applies to men and women—both genders are to be helped equally. Bringing a gender perspective illuminates how gender inequalities, roles, responsibilities, and identities shape and influence vulnerabilities and capacities in a crisis. Men and women (individually and collectively) experience war, floods, earthquakes, and dislocation differently; they can have different priorities, responsibilities, and protection needs. They also can mobilize or draw on different resources to protect themselves, feed their families, or become leaders. Understanding gender inequalities, relations, and identities helps agents of aid understand how a crisis affects communities and how communities can best respond.

OSLO GUIDELINES

E-34. The Oslo Guidelines were completed in 1994. They were the result of a collaborative effort of over 180 delegates from 45 nations and 25 organizations. These delegates drafted the Oslo Guidelines to establish a framework. This framework aims to formalize and improve the effectiveness and efficiency when using United Nations military and civil defense assets for international disaster relief operations.

HUMANITY

E-35. Human suffering must be addressed wherever it is found. Relief groups pay particular attention to the most vulnerable populations, such as children, women, and the elderly. The dignity and rights of all victims are respected and protected.

NEUTRALITY

E-36. Agents of aid provide humanitarian assistance without engaging in hostilities or taking sides in controversies of a political, religious, or ideological nature.

IMPARTIALITY

E-37. Agents of aid provide humanitarian assistance without discriminating in regards to ethnic origin, gender, nationality, political opinions, race, or religion. Relief of the suffering is guided solely by needs; priority is given to the most urgent cases of distress.

SOVEREIGNTY

E-38. The United Nations provides humanitarian assistance with full respect for the sovereignty of states. Agents of aid fully respect the sovereignty, territorial integrity, and national unity of states in accordance with the Charter of the United Nations. In this context, humanitarian assistance is provided with the consent of the affected country and in principle because of an appeal by the affected country.

MILITARY AND CIVIL DEFENSE ASSETS

E-39. As a matter of principle, the military and civil defense assets of forces will not be used to support United Nations humanitarian activities under certain conditions; the forces are perceived as belligerents or units are actively engaged in combat in the affected country or region. Military and civil defense assets should be seen as a tool complementing existing relief efforts by providing specific support to specific requirements.

INTERAGENCY STANDING COMMITTEE

E-40. The Interagency Standing Committee was established in June 1992 in response to United Nations General Assembly Resolution 46/182 on the strengthening of humanitarian assistance. It is the primary mechanism for interagency coordination of humanitarian assistance. It is a unique forum involving the key United Nations and non-United Nations humanitarian partners. All humanitarian action, including civil-military coordination for humanitarian purposes in complex emergencies, must be conducted in accordance with the overarching principles of humanity, neutrality, and impartiality. This section outlines these principles and concepts to follow when planning or undertaking civil-military coordination.

HUMANITY, NEUTRALITY, AND IMPARTIALITY

E-41. Any civil-military coordination must serve the prime humanitarian principle of humanity; human suffering must be addressed wherever it is found. In determining whether and to what extent humanitarian agencies should coordinate with military forces, one must consider the potential consequences or perceptions of too close an affiliation with the military. These affiliations might jeopardize the humanitarian principles of neutrality and impartiality.

E-42. The concept of nonallegiance is central to the principle of neutrality in humanitarian action; likewise, the idea of nondiscrimination is crucial to the principle of impartiality. However, humanitarian assistance means providing protection and assistance to populations in need. Pragmatically, it might include civil-military coordination. Even so, agents of aid must find the right balance between a pragmatic and a principled response so that coordination with the military would not compromise humanitarian imperatives.

HUMANITARIAN ACCESS TO VULNERABLE POPULATIONS

E-43. Humanitarian agencies must have access to all vulnerable populations in all areas of the emergency. They also must be able to negotiate such access with all parties to the conflict. Particular care must be taken to ensure the sustainability of access. Coordination with the military facilitates, secures, and sustains—not hinders—humanitarian access.

PERCEPTION OF HUMANITARIAN ACTION

E-44. Delivering humanitarian assistance to all populations in need must be neutral and impartial. It must come without political or military conditions. Humanitarian staff must avoid taking sides in disputes or political positions. Such bias will harm the credibility and independence of humanitarian efforts in general. Any civil-military coordination must avoid jeopardizing the longstanding local network and trust that humanitarian agencies created and maintained.

NEEDS-BASED ASSISTANCE FREE OF DISCRIMINATION

E-45. Humanitarian assistance is provided based on needs of those affected, taking into account the local capacity already in place to meet those needs. The independent assessment and humanitarian assistance are given without adverse discrimination of any kind. Assistance is given regardless of race, ethnicity, gender, religion, social status, nationality, or political affiliation of the recipients. All populations in need receive aid equitably.

CIVILIAN-MILITARY DISTINCTION IN HUMANITARIAN ACTION

E-46. At all times, agents of aid clearly distinguish between combatants and noncombatants. They identify those actively engaged in hostilities as well as civilians and others who do not or no longer directly participate in the armed conflict. The latter group may include the sick, wounded, prisoners of war, and demobilized ex-combatants. The law of armed conflict protects noncombatants by providing immunity from attack. Thus, humanitarian workers must never present themselves or their work as part of a military operation, and military personnel must refrain from presenting themselves as civilian humanitarian workers.

OPERATIONAL INDEPENDENCE OF HUMANITARIAN ACTION

E-47. In any civil-military coordination, humanitarian actors take the lead role in undertaking and directing humanitarian activities. The agents preserve independence of humanitarian action and decisionmaking both at the operational and policy levels. Humanitarian organizations do not implement tasks on behalf of the military nor represent or implement their policies. Basic requisites must not be impeded. These requisites can include freedom of movement for humanitarian staff, freedom to complete independent assessments, freedom to select staff, freedom to identify beneficiaries of assistance based on their needs, or free flow of communications between humanitarian agencies as well as with the media.

SECURITY OF HUMANITARIAN PERSONNEL

E-48. Any perception that humanitarian actors are affiliated with the military could impact negatively on the security of humanitarian staff and their ability to access vulnerable populations. However, relief workers must identify the most expeditious, effective, and secure approach to ensure the delivery of vital assistance to vulnerable target populations. They balance this approach against the primary concern for ensuring staff safety. The decision to seek military-based security for humanitarian workers should be viewed as a last resort option when other staff security mechanisms are unavailable, inadequate, or inappropriate.

DO NO HARM

E-49. Considerations on civil-military coordination must be guided by a commitment to "do no harm." Humanitarian agencies must ensure at the policy and operational levels that any potential civil-military coordination will not contribute to further the conflict nor harm or endanger the beneficiaries of humanitarian assistance.

RESPECT FOR INTERNATIONAL LEGAL INSTRUMENTS

E-50. Both relief workers and military forces must respect laws pertaining to human rights as well as other international norms and regulations, including instruments for human rights.

RESPECT FOR CULTURE AND CUSTOM

E-51. Agents of aid maintain respect and sensitivities for the culture, structures, and customs of the communities and countries. Where possible and to the extent feasible, they find ways to involve the intended beneficiaries of humanitarian assistance and local personnel in the design, management, and implementation of assistance, including in civil-military coordination.

CONSENT OF PARTIES TO THE CONFLICT

E-52. The risk of compromising humanitarian operations by cooperating with the military might be reduced if all parties to the conflict recognize, agree, or acknowledge in advance that humanitarian activities might necessitate civil-military coordination in certain exceptional circumstances. Negotiating such acceptance entails contacts with all levels in the chain of command.

OPTION OF LAST RESORT

E-53. Use of military assets, armed escorts, joint humanitarian-military operations, and any other actions involving visible interaction with the military must be the option of last resort. Such actions may occur only when no comparable civilian alternative exists and only the use of military support can meet a critical humanitarian need.

AVOID RELIANCE ON THE MILITARY

E-54. Humanitarian agencies must avoid depending on resources or support provided solely by the military. Any resources or support provided by the military should be, at its onset, clearly limited in time and scale. Often resources provided by the military are transitory in nature. When higher priority military missions emerge, such support may be recalled at short notice and without any substitute support.

This page intentionally left blank.

Appendix F

Provincial Reconstruction Teams

For the post-September 11 period, the chief issue for global politics will not be how to cut back on stateness but how to build it up. For individual societies and for the global community, the withering away of the state is not a prelude to utopia but to disaster. A critical issue facing poor countries...is their inadequate level of institutional development. They do not need extensive states, but they do need strong and effective ones within the limited scope of necessary state functions.

Francis Fukuyama
State-Building: Governance and World Order in the 21st Century[3]

PRINCIPLES OF PROVINCIAL RECONSTRUCTION TEAMS

F-1. A provincial reconstruction team (PRT) is an interim civil-military organization designed to operate in an area with unstable or limited security. The PRT leverages all the instruments of national power—diplomatic, informational, military, and economic—to improve stability. However, the efforts of the PRT alone will not stabilize an area; the combined military and civil efforts are required to reduce conflict while developing the local institutions to take the lead in national governance, the provision of basic services, fostering economic development, and enforcement of rule of law.

F-2. The development community uses specific principles for reconstruction and development. (See appendix C.) These enduring principles represent years of practical application and understanding of the cultural and socioeconomic elements of developing nations. Understanding these principles enables development officials to incorporate techniques and procedures effectively to improve economic and social conditions for the

[3] © 2004 by Francis Fukuyama. Reproduced with permission of Cornell University Press.

local populace. By applying the principles of reconstruction and development, the development community significantly improves the probability of success. Timely emphasis on the principles increases the opportunity for success and provides the flexibility to adapt to the changing conditions. This community assumes risk in projects and programs by failing to adhere to the principles.

F-3.   A PRT does not conduct military operations or directly assist host-nation military forces. The PRT helps the central ministries distribute funds to respective provincial representatives for implementing projects. This assistance encompasses more than a distribution of funds; it includes mentoring, management, and accountability.

F-4.   PRTs aim to develop the infrastructure necessary for the local populace to succeed in a post-conflict environment. A PRT is an integral part of the long-term strategy to transition the functions of security, governance, and economics to the host-nation. This team serves as a combat multiplier for commanders engaged in governance and economic activity, as well as other lines of effort. The PRT also serves as a force multiplier for United States Government development agencies engaged across the stability sectors. A PRT assists local communities with reconciliation while strengthening the host-nation government and speeding the transition to self-reliance. To accomplish this mission, the PRT concentrates on three essential functions: governance, security, and reconstruction.

GOVERNANCE

F-5.   Within an operational area, a PRT focuses on improving the provincial government's ability to provide effective governance and essential services. Strengthening the provincial government is important given the decentralization of authority common to a post-conflict environment. For example, under Saddam Hussein's regime In Iraq, provincial officials received detailed directions from Baghdad. Under the current structure, provincial officials take initiatives without direct guidance from Baghdad.

F-6.   The United States Agency for International Development (USAID) contracts a three-person team of civilian specialists to provide training and technical assistance programs. These programs aim to improve the efficiency of provincial governments. They do this by providing policy analysis, training, and technical assistance to national ministries, their provincial representatives, provincial governors, and provincial councils. The team of civilian specialists works directly with provincial officials to increase competence and efficiency. For example, they help provincial council members conduct meetings, develop budgets, and oversee provincial government activities. The team also encourages transparency and popular participation by working with citizens and community organizations, hosting conferences, and promoting public forums.

F-7. The USAID team contains members with expertise in local government, financial management, and municipal planning. Up to 70 percent of the contracted staff members come from regional countries and include local professionals. Additional contracted experts are on call from regional offices. The USAID requires contract advisors that speak the host-nation language and possess extensive professional experience. USAID-trained instructors present training programs based on professionally developed modules in the host-nation language. The training and technical assistance programs emphasize practical application with focus areas in computers, planning, public administration, and provision of public services.

SECURITY

F-8. The absence of security impacts the effectiveness of PRT operations and efforts to develop effective local governments. Provincial governors and other senior officials may be intimidated, threatened, and assassinated in limited or unsecured areas. Provincial councils may potentially reduce or eliminate regular meetings if security deteriorates. Additionally, provincial-level ministry representatives could become reluctant to attend work because of security concerns. PRT personnel and local officials may lose the ability to meet openly or visit provincial government centers and military installations in limited security environments. During security alerts, PRT civilian personnel may be restricted to base, preventing interaction with host-nation counterparts. Unstable security situations limit PRT personnel from promoting economic development by counseling local officials, encouraging local leaders and business owners, and motivating outside investors.

F-9. Moving PRT personnel with military escorts contributes to the overall security presence. However, the PRT does not conduct military operations nor does it assist host-nation military forces. The only security role assigned to a PRT is protection; military forces provide vehicles and an advisor to escort PRT personnel to meetings with local officials. Military personnel assigned to escort civilian PRT members receive training in protecting civilian PRT personnel under an agreement with the Department of State. The training is designed to reinforce understanding of escort responsibilities and to avoid endangering PRT civilian personnel. Military forces escorting PRT personnel should not combine this responsibility with other missions. The problem of providing PRT civilian personnel with security is compounded by competing protection priorities.

Such priorities often prevent dedicated security teams in most situations limiting security teams to available personnel.

RECONSTRUCTION

F-10. The USAID representative of the PRT is responsible for developing the PRT economic development work plan including its assistance projects. The PRT emphasizes the construction of infrastructure, including schools, clinics, community centers, and government buildings. The PRT also focuses on developing human capacity through training and advisory programs.

F-11. A PRT, such as those operating in Afghanistan and Iraq, receives $10 million in U.S. military Commanders' Emergency Response Program funding in addition to project funds from USAID programs. Funds and financing for microcredit projects from the Commanders' Emergency Response Program are necessary to build host-nation capacity and strengthen the legitimacy of the governance. U.S. funds and other sources of outside funding are vital; however, host-nation governments should budget for the long-term financing of most projects. The PRT exists to encourage central ministries in distributing funds to provincial representatives. These funds are for project implementation, including accountability and management of funds.

F-12. Provincial reconstruction development committees (PRDCs) prioritize provincial development projects and ensure the necessary funding for economic progress. The PRDC was developed before the creation of the current PRT structure. The PRDC contains a USAID representative, a civil affairs advisor, one or more PRT members, and host-nation officials. A PRDC develops a list of potential projects after consulting with the national ministries, provincial authorities, and local citizens. It aims to coordinate projects with both national and provincial development plans. The PRDC examines possible funding sources to determine how project funding will be provided.

F-13. The PRT provincial program manager (a Department of State employee) works with the PRDC to review projects and determine compliance with project funding guidelines. The PRT engineer reviews construction projects to determine their technical feasibility. The list of projects is presented in a public forum to the provincial council for approval following PRDC deliberations. The list is presented to the host-nation coordination team. This team circulates the project list for final review and funding priority. A PRT has limited involvement in project implementation following project selection.

STRUCTURE OF PROVINCIAL RECONSTRUCTION TEAMS

F-14. The PRT structure is modular in nature with a core structure tailored to the respective operational area. A typical PRT contains the following personnel: six Department of State personnel; three senior military officers and staff; twenty Army civil affairs advisors; one Department of Agriculture representative; one Department of Justice representative; three international contractors; two USAID representatives; and a military or contract security force (size depends on local conditions). The size and composition of a PRT varies based on operational area maturity, local circumstances, and U.S. agency capacity. (See figure F-1.)

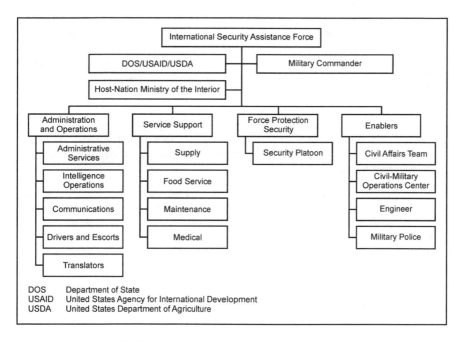

Figure F-1. Example of provincial reconstruction team organization

F-15. The PRT structure normally has sixty to ninety personnel. A PRT is intended to have the following complement of personnel:

- PRT team leader.
- Deputy team leader.
- Multinational force liaison officer.
- Rule of law coordinator.

- Provincial action officer.
- Public diplomacy officer.
- Agricultural advisor.
- Engineer.
- Development officer.
- Governance team.
- Civil affairs team.
- Bilingual bicultural advisor.

F-16. PRT civilian personnel normally serve twelve months, while civil affairs and other advisors may serve from six to nine months. Changes in personnel often result in changes in PRT objectives and programs. Ensuring continuity between redeploying personnel and new arrivals maintains project priorities and prevents unnecessary program termination and restart that expend time and resources and deprive the local populace. Department of Defense support of PRTs is contingent upon approval of a formal request for forces initiated by Department of State.

STAFF FUNCTIONS

F-17. PRT operations differ depending on location, personnel, environment, and circumstances. PRT personnel perform specific tasks to support reconstruction and stabilization.

F-18. The team leader is a senior U.S. foreign service officer. This leader represents the Department of State and chairs the executive steering committee responsible for establishing priorities and coordinating activities. The team leader is a civilian and does not command PRT military personnel, who remain subordinate to the commander of multinational forces. This leader meets with the provincial governor, the provincial council, mayors, tribal elders, and religious figures and is the primary contact with the host-nation coordination team and American embassy officials. The team leader builds relationships with host-nation institutions and monitors logistic and administrative arrangement.

F-19. The deputy team leader is typically an Army lieutenant colonel who serves as the PRT chief of staff and executive officer. This officer manages daily operations, coordinates schedules, and liaises with the forward operating base commander on sustainment, transportation, and security. The deputy team leader is the senior representative of the commander of multinational forces. This leader approves security for PRT convoys and off-site operations.

F-20. The multinational force liaison officer is a senior military officer responsible for coordinating PRT activities with the division and forward operating base commander. These activities include intelligence, route security, communications, and emergency response in case of attacks on convoys. The liaison officer tracks PRT movements and coordinates with other military units in the operational area.

F-21. The rule of law coordinator is a Department of Justice official responsible for monitoring and reporting the local government judicial system activities. The coordinator leads the rule of law team consisting of civil affairs and local government personnel. This coordinator visits judicial, police, and corrections officials and reports local conditions to the American embassy. The rule of law coordinator advises the embassy on response measures to local government problems. This coordinator also provides advice and limited training to local government officials. The program emphasizes improvement of court administration, case management, protection of judicial personnel, training of judges, and promotion of legal education. Rule of law coordinators meet with corrections officials to monitor and report on prison conditions and the treatment of prisoners. However, in Iraq, the rule of law officer works for the Multi-National Security Transition Command–Iraq. The officer manages training and assistance for police, courts, and prisons without reference to a PRT.

F-22. The provincial action officer is a Department of State foreign service representative and primary reporting officer. This officer meets with local authorities and reports daily to American embassy officials on PRT activities, weekly summaries, analysis of local political and economic developments, and meetings with local officials and private citizens. The provincial action officer assists others in the PRT with promoting local governance. Political and economic reporting by the PRT Department of State officers provides firsthand information on conditions outside of forward operating base.

F-23. The public diplomacy officer is a Department of State foreign service officer. This officer is responsible for press relations, public affairs programming, and public outreach through meetings between the PRT and local officials. The public diplomacy officer also escorts visitors to the PRT and its operational area.

F-24. The agricultural advisor is a representative of the Department of Agriculture. The agricultural advisor works with provincial authorities to develop agricultural assistance programs and promote agriculture-related industries. Agricultural advisors are volunteer representatives recruited from each agency of the Department of Agriculture to serve one-year tours. The Department of Agriculture tries to match its personnel specialties to the specific needs of each PRT.

F-25. The engineer is a representative of the U.S. Army Corps of Engineers. The engineer trains and advises host-nation engineers working on provincial development projects. The engineer assists the PRT with project assessments, designing scope-of-work statements for contracts with local companies, site supervision, and project management. The engineer advises the team leader on reconstruction projects and development activities in the province.

F-26. The development officer is a USAID representative. The development officer coordinates USAID assistance and training programs and works with provincial authorities to promote economic and infrastructure development. This officer coordinates development-related activities within the PRT and supervises locally hired USAID staff.

F-27. The governance team is under a USAID contract. A contracted organization provides a three-person team that offers training and technical advice to members of provincial councils and provincial administrators. These small teams aim to improve the operation, efficiency, and effectiveness of provincial governments. The team provides hands-on training in the provision of public services, finance, accounting, and personnel management. Contracted personnel take guidance from the USAID representative but function under a national contract administered from the American embassy. The contracted organization maintains offices (nodes) that can provide additional specialists on request in major cities.

F-28. The civil affairs team represents the largest component of the PRT with Army civil affairs advisors performing tasks across each area of PRT operations. Civil affairs advisors are mostly military reserve personnel on temporary duty; they represent a broad range of civilian occupations. The PRT makes special efforts to use these personnel in areas where their civilian specialties apply. For example, a civil affairs reservist who is a police officer in civilian life is normally assigned to the PRT rule of law team.

F-29. The bilingual bicultural advisor is typically a host-nation expatriate with U.S. or coalition citizenship under contract to the Department of Defense. This advisor serves as a primary contact with provincial government officials and local citizens. The bilingual bicultural advisor advises other PRT members on local culture, politics, and social issues. Advisors must possess a college degree and speak both English and the indigenous language of the operational area.

OPERATIONS

F-30. A PRT resides at a forward operating base and operates within a brigade combat team's operational area. A PRT relies on the maneuver unit capabilities for security, transport, and sustainment. The brigade combat team provides available military assets to the PRT under an agreement between the American embassy and the multination force. The military assets and personnel enable convoy movements for PRT personnel.

F-31. Security operations are not a Department of State capability. Normally, military forces take the lead while operating in the current post-conflict environment characterized by continuing violence. For example, in Iraq, the military directs operations and the PRT is embedded within a brigade combat team's operational area. The PRT maintains its primary functions—governance, security, and reconstruction—as a Department of State competency. In Afghanistan, military officers lead a PRT. The Department of State and other civilian agencies have an essential role in the operation of the PRT, but military leadership provides unity of command.

F-32. The PRT must possess a clear concept of operations, objectives, and guidelines following a period of experimentation. This effort must include a delineation of civil-military command authority within a PRT, including the supervision of contractors. These measures should also be coordinated with coalition partners so they are consistent with the operational concepts that govern the PRT.

F-33. Priority assignments and specialized training produce better teams than volunteers and on-the-job learning. A PRT often operates in stressful, uncertain, and dangerous environments. PRT assignments require officers with the proper rank and experience. This applies to USAID and other civilian agencies. Employing retirees, junior officers, or civil affairs advisors as substitutes for civilian experts limits competence and reduces effectiveness. Contractors are not designed to permanently replace Federal representatives, despite their training or level of expertise. A PRT requires Federal employees with an understanding of Federal agency function and knowledge of requirements necessary to influence and deliver project results. Junior officers bring energy and enthusiasm but may not have the same impact as veteran government employees, especially in the areas of languages and social and cultural expertise.

SUMMARY

F-34. A PRT is an essential part of a long-term strategy to transition the functions of security, governance, and economics to provincial governments. It is a potential combat multiplier for maneuver commanders performing governance and economics functions and providing expertise to programs designed to strengthen infrastructure and the institutions of local governments. The PRT leverages the principles of reconstruction and development to build host-nation capacity while speeding the transition of security, justice, and economic development to the control of the host nation.

Appendix G

Summary of Changes

SUMMARY OF MAJOR CHANGES

G-1. This appendix summarizes the major doctrinal changes made by this field manual.

CHAPTER 1 – THE STRATEGIC CONTEXT

G-2. Chapter 1 makes the following changes:

- Introduces the comprehensive approach to stability operations that combines the integration achieved through unified action and whole of government engagement to forge **unity of effort.** Prescribes the term **whole of government approach** as an approach that integrates the collaborative efforts of the departments and agencies of the United States Government to achieve unity of effort toward a shared goal. Prescribes the term **comprehensive approach** as an approach that integrates the cooperative efforts of the departments and agencies of the United States Government, intergovernmental and nongovernmental organizations, multinational partners, and private sector entities to achieve unity of effort toward a shared goal.

- Prescribes the term **conflict transformation** as the overarching term for unified action to change the conditions of a fragile state to those of enduring peace and stability.

- Prescribes the term **capacity building** as the overarching term for the process that aims to build host-nation capacity in stability operations.

- Prescribes the term **rule of law** as the principle that ensures accountability to laws that are publically promulgated, equally enforced, and independently adjudicated.

- Prescribes the term **fragile state** to encompass broad spectrum of recovering, failing, and failed states. Describes a fragile state as either **a vulnerable state** or **a crisis state**.

- Prescribes the term **reconstruction** as the process of rebuilding degraded, damaged or destroyed political, socioeconomic, or physical infrastructure of a country.
- Prescribes the term **stabilization** as the process by which underlying tensions that might lead to resurgence in violence or a breakdown in law and order are managed and reduced.

CHAPTER 2 – STABILITY IN FULL SPECTRUM OPERATIONS

G-3. Chapter 2 makes the following changes:

- Prescribes the term **governance** to account for the rules, processes, and behavior by which interests are articulated, resources are managed, and power is exercised in a society.
- Introduces the **failed states spectrum** to understand engagement and intervention activities in terms of the progress toward stabilizing the operational environment.
- Introduces the **stability operations framework** to link Army stability operations with joint and interagency approaches. This framework uses the failed states spectrum to describe the operational environment and the essential stability task matrix phases to delineate intervention activities.
- Describes how full spectrum operations support unified action and integrated information engagement in stability operations.

CHAPTER 3 – ESSENTIAL STABILITY TASKS

G-4. Chapter 3 makes the following changes:

- Addresses **essential stability tasks** in terms of those always performed by military forces, those military forces must be prepared to perform, and those best performed by civilians with the appropriate level of expertise. This discussion further defines these terms according to their likely execution horizon according to the Office of the Coordinator for Reconstruction and Stabilization essential task matrix.
- Establishes stability-focused core and directed mission-essential task lists for corps-, division-, and brigade-level organizations.

CHAPTER 4 – PLANNING FOR STABILITY OPERATIONS

G-5. Chapter 4 makes the following changes:

- Describes how **leader and Soldier engagement** helps to develop understanding.

- Expands on the discussion of **stability mechanisms** from capstone doctrine and describes how those mechanisms are combined with **defeat mechanisms** to produce a decisive effect in the operational environment.

- Describes how **lines of effort** are used at different echelons to focus the constructive capabilities of the force to achieve the broad objectives and conditions established for a stability operation.

- Introduces a discussion of **transitions** that is expanded upon to include the opportunity and risk associated with transitions among military forces, civilian agencies and organizations, and the host nation.

CHAPTER 5 – TRANSITIONAL MILITARY AUTHORITY

G-6. Chapter 5 makes the following changes:

- Describes how **transitional military authority** provides the basic civil functions of the host-nation government when the host nation no longer is capable of providing those functions.

- Introduces doctrine for transitional military authority that provides the principles and fundamentals necessary for military commanders to provide government capability in the absence of a host-nation government.

- Provides guidelines for transitional military authority to ensure such authority is provided according to The Hague and Geneva Conventions.

CHAPTER 6 – SECURITY SECTOR REFORM

G-7. Chapter 6 makes the following changes:

- Prescribes the term **security sector reform** as the overarching definition for efforts to establish or reform the individuals and institutions that provide for the safety and security of the host nation and its people.

- Introduces the security sector reform as a fundamental component of stability operations that combines subordinate tasks from the primary stability tasks. It includes guiding principles and foundations for security sector reform that help to coordinate the efforts of the wide array of actors involved.

- Prescribes the term **security force assistance** to encompass efforts to organize, train, equip, rebuild, and advise host-nation security forces.

- Introduces **disarmament, demobilization, and reintegration** as a necessary precursor to security sector reform.
- Prescribes the terms **disarmament** for the collection, documentation, control, and disposal of small arms, ammunition, explosives, and light and heavy weapons of former combatants, belligerents, and the local populace; and **reintegration** as the process through which former combatants and belligerents acquire civilian status and gain sustainable employment and income. Uses the joint term **demobilization** to further describe the formal and controlled discharge of active combatants from armed forces or other armed groups.

APPENDIX A – INTERAGENCY, INTERGOVERNMENTAL, AND NONGOVERNMENTAL ORGANIZATIONS IN STABILITY OPERATIONS

G-8. Appendix A describes the roles and responsibilities of the various agencies and organizations involved in most stability operations. It also addresses the critical role of civil affairs forces in providing liaison and coordination among these groups.

APPENDIX B – INTERAGENCY MANAGEMENT SYSTEM

G-9. Appendix B provides an overview of the Interagency Management System, an interagency initiative that will ensure other government agencies will possess the expeditionary and campaign capabilities necessary to provide initial response and sustained support to reconstruction and stabilization operations.

APPENDIX C – USAID PRINCIPLES FOR RECONSTRUCTION AND DEVELOPMENT

G-10. Appendix C describes the fundamental principles for reconstruction and development used by the United States Agency for International Development.

APPENDIX D – INTERAGENCY CONFLICT ASSESSMENT OVERVIEW

G-11. Appendix D describes the conflict assessment frameworks in wide use by the other departments and agencies of the United States Government.

APPENDIX E – HUMANITARIAN RESPONSE PRINCIPLES

G-12. Appendix E outlines the humanitarian response principles adopted and observed by most nongovernmental organizations. These principles inform military understanding with respect to these organizations and help to establish a cooperative environment when conducting operations in areas where such organizations are already present.

APPENDIX F – PROVINCIAL RECONSTRUCTION TEAMS

G-13. Appendix F provides an overview of provincial reconstruction teams and describes how their efforts can support and complement the broader efforts of the military force.

TERMS AND DEFINITIONS

G-14. Table G-1 lists new Army terms for which FM 3-07 is the proponent field manual.

Table G-1. New Army terms

capacity building	reintegration
comprehensive approach	rule of law
conflict transformation	security force assistance
crisis state	security sector reform
disarmament	stabilization
fragile state	transitional military authority
governance	vulnerable state
reconstruction	whole of government approach

This page intentionally left blank.

Source Notes

These are the sources used, quoted, or paraphrased in this publication. They are listed by page number.

vi "[Stability operations encompass] various…": JP 3-0, *Joint Operations* (Washington, DC: Department of Defense, 17 September 2006, incorporating Change 1, 13 February 2008), GL-25.

vi "Stability operations are a core …": DODD 3000.05, *Military Support for Stability, Security, Transition, and Reconstruction (SSTR) Operations* (Washington, DC: Department of Defense, 28 November 2005), 2 (hereafter cited as DODD 3000.05).

1-1 "It is needless to say that …": Butler, Colonel Sir William F., *Charles George Gordon* (New York: MacMillian and Company, 1889), 84–85.

2-1 "Repeating an Afghanistan or an …": Gates, Robert M. (Secretary of Defense), "U.S. Global Leadership Campaign" as speech given on 15 July 2008 at the U.S. Global Leadership Campaign (Washington, DC), http://www.defenselink.mil/speeches/speech.aspx?speechid=1262 (accessed 4 September 2008).

3-1 "Many stability operations tasks …": DODD 3000.05, 2.

4-1 "A plan, like a tree,…": Hart, Captain Sir Basil Liddell, *Thoughts on War* (London: Faber and Faber Limited, 1944), 246.

5-1 "Because of the ideological …": Coles, Harry L. and Albert K. Weinberg, *Civil Affairs: Soldiers Become Governors* (Washington, DC: U.S. Government Printing Office, 1992), vii.

6-1 "Establishing security involves …": Stephenson, James, *Losing the Golden Hour: An Insider's View of Iraq's Reconstruction* (Washington, DC: Potomac Books, Incorporated, 2007), 21.

B-1   "Weak and failed states ...": Herbst, John E., "Stabilization and Reconstruction Operations: Learning from the Provincial Reconstruction Team (PRT) Experience," in a *Statement Before House Armed Services Subcommittee on Oversight and Investigations* on 30 October 2007 (Washington, DC), http://www.state.gov/s/crs/rls/rm/94379.htm (accessed 4 September 2008).

C-1   "The development community and ...": Natsios, Andrew S., "The Nine Principles of Reconstruction and Development," *Parameters*, Autumn 2005: 19.

F-1   "For the post-September 11 period, ...": Fukuyama, Francis, *State-Building: Governance and World Order in the 21st Century* (Ithaca, New York: Cornell University Press, 2004), 120.

Glossary

The glossary lists acronyms and terms with Army, multi-Service, or joint definitions, and other selected terms. Where Army and joint definitions are different, (Army) follows the term. Terms for which FM 3-07 is the proponent (authority) manual are marked with an asterisk (*). The proponent manual for other terms is listed in parentheses after the definition.

SECTION I – ACRONYMS AND ABBREVIATIONS

CA	civil affairs
CBRN	chemical, biological, radiological, and nuclear
CIA	Central Intelligence Agency
CMETL	core mission-essential task list
CMOC	civil-military operations center
CRC	Civilian Response Corps
CRSG	country reconstruction and stabilization group
DDR	disarmament, demobilization, and reintegration
DMETL	directed mission-essential task list
DOD	Department of Defense
DODD	Department of Defense directive
DOS	Department of State
FM	field manual
ICAF	interagency conflict assessment framework
ICRC	International Committee of the Red Cross
IMS	Interagency Management System
IPC	integration planning cell
JP	joint publication
NATO	North Atlantic Treaty Organization

NDI	National Democratic Institute
NGHA	nongovernmental humanitarian agency
NGO	nongovernmental organization
NSC	National Security Council
NSPD	national security Presidential directive
OCHA	Office for the Coordination of Humanitarian Affairs
PAO	public affairs officer
PRDC	provincial reconstruction development committee
PRT	provincial reconstruction team
RSO	regional security officer
RTI	Research Triangle Institute
SAO	security assistance organization
S/CRS	Department of State, Office of the Coordinator for Reconstruction and Stabilization
SFA	security force assistance
SSR	security sector reform
SWEAT-MSO	sewage, water, electricity, academics, trash, medical, safety, and other considerations
TCAPF	tactical conflict assessment and planning framework
UN	United Nations
UNDPKO	United Nations Department for Peacekeeping Operations
UNSG	United Nations Secretary General
U.S.	United States
USAID	United States Agency for International Development
USG	United States Government

SECTION II – TERMS

adversary

(joint) A party acknowledged as potentially hostile to a friendly party and against which the use of force may be envisaged. (JP 3-0)

alliance

(joint) The relationship that results from a formal agreement (for example, a treaty) between two or more nations for broad, long-term objectives that further the common interests of the members. (JP 3-0)

area of operations

(joint) An operational area defined by the joint force commander for land and maritime forces. Areas of operation do not typically encompass the entire operational area of the joint force commander, but should be large enough for component commanders to accomplish their missions and protect their forces. (JP 3-0)

assessment

(joint) 1. A continuous process that measures the overall effectiveness of employing joint force capabilities during military operations. 2. Determination of the progress toward accomplishing a task, creating an effect, or achieving an objective. 3. Analysis of the security, effectiveness, and potential of an existing or planned intelligence activity. 4. Judgment of the motives, qualifications, and characteristics of present or prospective employees or "agents. (JP 3-0) (Army) The continuous monitoring and evaluation of the current situation and progress of an operation. (FM 3-0)

branch

(joint) 1. A subdivision of any organization. 2. A geographically separate unit of an activity, which performs all or part of the primary functions of the parent activity on a smaller scale. Unlike an annex, a branch is not merely an overflow addition. 3. An arm or service of the Army. 4. The contingency options built into the base plan. A branch is used for changing the mission, orientation, or direction of movement of a force to aid success of the operation based on anticipated events, opportunities, or disruptions caused by enemy actions and reactions. (JP 5-0)

campaign

(joint) A series of related major operations aimed at achieving strategic and operational objectives within a given time and space. (JP 5-0)

*capacity building

The process of creating an environment that fosters host-nation institutional development, community participation, human resources development, and strengthening managerial systems.

civil affairs operations

(joint) Those military operations conducted by civil affairs forces that (1) enhance the relationship between military forces and civil authorities in localities where military forces are present; (2) require coordination with other interagency organizations, intergovernmental organizations, nongovernmental organizations, indigenous populations and institutions, and the private sector; and (3) involve application of functional specialty skills that normally are the responsibility of civil government to enhance the conduct of civil-military operations. (JP 3-57)

coalition

(joint) An ad hoc arrangement between two or more nations for common action. (JP 5-0)

combat power

(joint) The total means of destructive and/or disruptive force which a military unit/formation can apply against the opponent at a given time. (JP 4-0) (Army) The total means of destructive and/or disruptive force which a military unit/formation can apply against the opponent at a given time. Army forces generate combat power by converting fighting potential into effective action. Combat power includes a unit's constructive and information capabilities as well as its disruptive and destructive force. (FM 3-0)

command

(joint) The authority that a commander in the armed forces lawfully exercises over subordinates by virtue of rank or assignment. Command includes the authority and responsibility for effectively using available resources and for planning the employment of, organizing, directing, coordinating, and controlling military forces for the accomplishment of assigned missions. It also includes responsibility for health, welfare, morale, and discipline of assigned personnel. 2. An order given by a commander; that is, the will of the commander expressed for the purpose of bringing about a particular action. 3. A unit or units, an organization, or an area under the command of one individual. (JP 1)

command and control

(joint) The exercise of authority and direction by a properly designated commander over assigned and attached forces in the accomplishment of a mission. Command and control functions are performed through an arrangement of personnel, equipment, communications, facilities, and procedures employed by a commander in planning, directing, coordinating, and controlling forces and operations in the accomplishment of the mission. (JP 1) (Army) The exercise of authority and direction by a properly designated commander over assigned and attached forces in the accomplishment of a mission. Commanders perform command and control functions through a command and control system. (FM 6-0)

commander's intent

(joint) A concise expression of the purpose of the operation and the desired end state. It may also include the commander's assessment of the adversary commander's intent and an assessment of where and how much risk is acceptable during the operation. (JP 3-0) (Army) A clear, concise statement of what the force must do and the conditions the force must establish with respect to the enemy, terrain, and civil considerations that represent the desired end state. (FM 3-0)

commander's visualization

The mental process of developing situational understanding, determining a desired end state, and envisioning the broad sequence of events by which the force will achieve that end state. (FM 3-0)

compel

To use, or threaten to use, lethal force to establish control and dominance, effect behavioral change, or enforce compliance with mandates, agreements, or civil authority. (FM 3-0)

*comprehensive approach

An approach that integrates the cooperative efforts of the departments and agencies of the United States Government, intergovernmental and nongovernmental organizations, multinational partners, and private sector entities to achieve unity of effort toward a shared goal.

concept of operations

(joint) A verbal or graphic statement that clearly and concisely expresses what the joint force commander intends to accomplish and how it will be done using available resources. The concept is designed to give an overall picture of the operation. (JP 5-0) (Army) A statement that directs the manner in which subordinate units cooperate to accomplish the mission and establishes the sequence of actions the force will use to achieve the end state. It is normally expressed in terms of decisive, shaping, and sustaining operations. (FM 3-0)

conduct

To perform the activities of the operations process: planning, preparing, executing, and continuously assessing. (FM 6-0)

*conflict transformation

The process of reducing the means and motivations for violent conflict while developing more viable, peaceful alternatives for the competitive pursuit of political and socioeconomic aspirations.

control

(joint) 1. Authority that may be less than full command exercised by a commander over part of the activities of subordinate or other organizations. 2. In mapping, charting, and photogrammetry, a collective term for a system of marks or objects on the Earth or on a map or a photograph, whose positions or elevations (or both) have been or will be determined. 3. Physical or psychological pressures exerted with the intent to assure that an agent or group will respond as directed. 4. An indicator governing the distribution and use of documents, information, or material. Such indicators are the subject of intelligence community agreement and are specifically defined in appropriate regulations. (JP 1-02) (Army) 1. In the context of command and control, the regulation of forces and warfighting functions to accomplish the mission in accordance with the commander's intent. (FM 3-0) 2. A tactical mission task that requires the commander to maintain physical influence over a specified area to prevent its use by an enemy. (FM 3-90) 3. An action taken to eliminate a hazard or reduce its risk. (FM 5-19) 4. In the context of stability mechanisms, to impose civil order. (FM 3-0)

country team

The senior, in-country, U.S. coordinating and supervising body, headed by the chief of the U.S. diplomatic mission, and composed of the senior member of each represented U.S. department or agency, as desired by the chief of the U.S. diplomatic mission. (JP 3-07.4)

*crisis state

A nation in which the central government does not exert effective control over its own territory.

decisive operation

The operation that directly accomplishes the mission. It determines the outcome of a major operation, battle, or engagement. The decisive operation is the focal point around which commanders design the entire operation. (FM 3-0)

decisive point

(joint) A geographic place, specific key event, critical factor, or function that, when acted upon, allows commanders to gain a marked advantage over an adversary or contribute materially to achieving success. (JP 3-0) [Note: In this context, adversary also refers to enemies.]

defeat mechanism

The method through which friendly forces accomplish their mission against enemy opposition. (FM 3-0)

defensive operations

Combat operations conducted to defeat an enemy attack, gain time, economize forces, and develop conditions favorable for offensive or stability operations. (FM 3-0)

demobilization

(joint) The process of transitioning a conflict or wartime military establishment and defense-based civilian economy to a peacetime configuration while maintaining national security and economic vitality. (JP 4-05)

depth

(Army) The extension of operations in time, space, and resources. (FM 3-0)

destroy

1. In the context of defeat mechaisms, to apply lethal combat power on an enemy capability so that it can no longer perform any function and cannot be restored to a usable condition without being entirely rebuilt. (FM 3-0) 2. A tactical mission task that physically renders an enemy force combat-ineffective until it is reconstituted. (FM 3-90)

*disarmament

(Army) The collection, documentation, control, and disposal of small arms, ammunition, explosives, and light and heavy weapons of former combatants, belligerents, and the local populace.

disintegrate

To disrupt the enemy's command and control system, degrading the ability to conduct operations while leading to a rapid collapse of enemy capabilities or the will to fight. (FM 3-0)

dislocate

To employ forces to obtain significant positional advantage, rendering the enemy's dispositions less valuable, perhaps even irrelevant. (FM 3-0)

end state

(joint) The set of required conditions that defines achievement of the commander's objectives. (JP 3-0)

enemy

A party identified as hostile against which the use of force is authorized. (FM 3-0)

engagement

(joint) 1. In air defense, an attack with guns or air-to-air missiles by an interceptor aircraft, or the launch of an air defense missile by air defense artillery and the missile's subsequent travel to intercept. 2. A tactical conflict, usually between opposing, lower echelon maneuver forces. (JP 1-02)

execution

Putting a plan into action by applying combat power to accomplish the mission and using situational understanding to assess progress and make execution and adjustment decisions. (FM 3-0)

force tailoring

The process of determining the right mix of forces and the sequence of their deployment in support of a joint force commander. (FM 3-0)

*fragile state

A country that suffers from institutional weaknesses serious enough to threaten the stability of the central government.

*governance

The state's ability to serve the citizens through the rules, processes, and behavior by which interests are articulated, resources are managed, and power is exercised in a society, including the representative participatory decisionmaking processes typically guaranteed under inclusive, constitutional authority.

influence

In the context of stability mechanisms, to alter the opinions and attitudes of a civilian population through information engagement, presence, and conduct. (FM 3-0)

information engagement

The integrated employment of public affairs to inform U.S. and friendly audiences; psychological operations, combat camera, U.S. Government strategic communication and defense support to public diplomacy, and other means necessary to influence foreign audiences; and, leader and Soldier engagements to support both efforts. (FM 3-0)

infrastructure reconnaissance

A multidiscipline variant of reconnaissance to collect technical information on various categories of the public systems, services, and facilities of a country or region. This task may take the form of either an assessment or a survey and develops the situational understanding of the local capability to support the infrastructure requirements of the local populace and/or military operations within a specific area. (FM 3-34.170)

insurgency

An organized movement aimed at the overthrow of a constituted government through use of subversion and armed conflict. (JP 3-05)

intelligence

(joint) The product resulting from the collection, processing, integration, evaluation, analysis, and interpretation of available information concerning foreign nations, hostile or potentially hostile forces or elements, or areas of actual or potential operations. The term is also applied to the activity which results in the product and to the organizations engaged in such activity. (JP 2-0)

interagency

(joint) United States Government agencies and departments, including the Department of Defense. (JP 3-08)

interagency coordination

(joint) Within the context of Department of Defense involvement, the coordination that occurs between elements of Department of Defense and engaged U.S. Government agencies for the purpose of achieving an objective. (JP 3-0)

intergovernmental organization

(joint) An organization created by a formal agreement (e.g., a treaty) between two or more governments. It may be established on a global, regional, or functional basis for wide-ranging or narrowly defined purposes. Formed to protect and promote national interests shared by member states. Examples include the United Nations, North Atlantic Treaty Organization, and the African Union. (JP 3-08)

isolate

In the context of defeat mechanisms, to deny an enemy or adversary access to capabilities that enable the exercise of coercion, influence, potential advantage, and freedom of action. (FM 3-0)

knowledge management

The art of creating, organizing, applying, and transferring knowledge to facilitate situational understanding and decision-making. Knowledge management supports improving organizational learning, innovation, and performance. Knowledge management processes ensure that knowledge products and services are relevant, accurate, timely, and useable to commanders and decision makers. (FM 3-0)

leadership

The process of influencing people by providing purpose, direction, and motivation, while operating to accomplish the mission and improving the organization. (FM 6-22)

maneuver

(joint) 1. A movement to place ships, aircraft, or land forces in a position of advantage over the enemy. 2. A tactical exercise carried out at sea, in the air, on the ground, or on a map in imitation of war. 3. The operation of a ship, aircraft, or vehicle, to cause it to perform desired movements. 4. Employment of forces in the operational area through movement in combination with fires to achieve a position of advantage in respect to the enemy in order to accomplish the mission. (JP 3-0)

measure of effectiveness

(joint) A criterion used to assess changes in system behavior, capability, or operational environment that is tied to measuring the attainment of an end state, achievement of an objective, or creation of an effect. (JP 3-0)

measure of performance

(joint) A criterion used to assess friendly actions that is tied to measuring task accomplishment. (JP 3-0)

military engagement

(joint) Routine contact and interaction between individuals or elements of the Armed Forces of the United States and those of another nation's armed forces, or foreign and domestic civilian authorities or agencies to build trust and confidence, share information, coordinate mutual activities, and maintain influence. (JP 3-0)

mission

(joint) The task, together with the purpose, that clearly indicates the action to be taken and the reason therefore. 2. In common usage, especially when applied to lower military units, a duty assigned to an individual or unit; a task. 3. The dispatching of one or more aircraft to accomplish one particular task. (JP 1-02)

multinational operations

(joint) A collective term to describe military actions conducted by forces of two or more nations, usually undertaken within the structure of a coalition or alliance. (JP 3-16)

neutral

(joint) In combat and combat support operations, an identity applied to a track whose characteristics, behavior, origin, or nationality indicate that it is neither supporting nor opposing friendly forces. (JP 1-02) (Army) A party identified as neither supporting nor opposing friendly or enemy forces. (FM 3-0)

noncombatant evacuation operations

(joint) Operations directed by the Department of State or other appropriate authority, in conjunction with the Department of Defense, whereby noncombatants are evacuated from foreign countries when their lives are endangered by war, civil unrest, or natural disaster to safe havens or to the United States. (JP 3-0)

nongovernmental organization

(joint) A private, self-governing, not-for-profit organization dedicated to alleviating human suffering; and/or promoting education, health care, economic development, environmental protection, human rights, and conflict resolution; and/or encouraging the establishment of democratic institutions and civil society. (JP 3-08)

offensive operations

Combat operations conducted to defeat and destroy enemy forces and seize terrain, resources, and population centers. They impose the commander's will on the enemy. (FM 3-0)

operational approach

The manner in which a commander contends with a center of gravity. (FM 3-0)

operational area

(joint) An overarching term encompassing more descriptive terms for geographic areas in which military operations are conducted. Operational areas include, but are not limited to, such descriptors as area of responsibility, theater of war, theater of operations, joint operations area, amphibious objective area, joint special operations area, and area of operations. (JP 3-0)

operational environment

(joint) A composite of the conditions, circumstances, and influences that affect the employment of capabilities and bear on the decisions of the commander. (JP 3-0)

operational theme

The character of the dominant major operation being conducted at any time within a land force commander's area of operations. (FM 3-0)

operations process

The major command and control activities performed during operations: planning, preparing, executing, and continuously assessing the operation. The commander drives the operations process. (FM 3-0)

peacekeeping

(joint) Military operations undertaken with the consent of all major parties to a dispute, designed to monitor and facilitate implementation of an agreement (cease fire, truce, or other such agreement) and support diplomatic efforts to reach a long-term political settlement. (JP 3-07.3)

peace operations

(joint) A broad term that encompasses multiagency and multinational crisis response and limited contingency operations inviving all instruments of national power with military missions to contain conflict, redress the peace, and shape the environment to support reconciliation and rebuilding and facilitate the transition to legitimate governance. Peace operations include peacekeeping, peace enforcement, peacemaking, peace building, and conflict prevention efforts. (JP 3-07.3)

peacetime military engagement

All military activities that involve other nations and are intended to shape the security environment in peacetime. It includes programs and exercises that the United States military conducts with other nations to shape the international environment, improve mutual understanding, and improve interoperability with treaty partners or potential coalition partners. Peacetime military engagement activities are designed to support a combatant commander's objectives within the theater security cooperation plan. (FM 3-0)

phase

(joint) In joint operation planning, a definitive stage of an operation or campaign during which a large portion of the forces and capabilities are involved in similar or mutually supporting activities for a common purpose. (JP 5-0) (Army) A planning and execution tool used to divide an operation in duration or activity. A change in phase usually involves a change of mission, task organization, or rules of engagement. Phasing helps in planning and controlling and may be indicated by time, distance, terrain, or an event. (FM 3-0)

plan

A design for a future or anticipated operation. (FM 5-0)

planning

The process by which commanders (and the staff, if available) translate the commander's visualization into a specific course of action for preparation and execution, focusing on the expected results. (FM 3-0)

preparation

Activities performed by units to improve their ability to execute an operation. Preparation includes, but is not limited to, plan refinement; rehearsals; intelligence, surveillance, and reconnaissance; coordination; inspections; and movement. (FM 3-0)

protection

(joint) 1. Preservation of the effectiveness and survivability of mission-related military and nonmilitary personnel, equipment, facilities, information, and infrastructure deployed or located within or outside the boundaries of a given operational area. 2. Measures that are taken to keep nuclear, biological, and chemical hazards from having an adverse effect on personnel, equipment, or critical assets and facilities. Protection consists of five groups of activities: hardening of positions; protecting personnel; assuming mission-oriented protective posture; using physical defense measures; and reacting to attack. 3. In space usage, active and passive defensive measures to ensure that United States and friendly space systems perform as designed by seeking to overcome an adversary's attempts to negate them and to minimize damage if negation is attempted. (JP 3-0)

*reconstruction

The process of rebuilding degraded, damaged, or destroyed political, socioeconomic, and physical infrastructure of a country or territory to create the foundation for long-term development.

refugee

(joint) A person who, by reason of real or imagined danger, has left their home country or country of their nationality and is unwilling or unable to return. (JP 3-07.6)

*reintegration

The process through which former combatants, belligerents, and dislocated civilians receive amnesty, reenter civil society, gain sustainable employment, and become contributing members of the local populace.

*rule of law

A principle under which all persons, institutions, and entities, public and private, including the state itself, are accountable to laws that are publicly promulgated, equally enforced, and independently adjudicated, and that are consistent with international human rights principles.

rules of engagement

(joint) Directives issued by competent military authority that delineate the circumstances and limitations under which United States forces will initiate and/or continue combat engagement with other forces encountered. (JP 1-02)

*security force assistance

The unified action to generate, employ, and sustain local, host-nation, or regional security forces in support of a legitimate authority.

*security sector reform

The set of policies, plans, programs, and activities that a government undertakes to improve the way it provides safety, security, and justice.

sequel

(joint) In a campaign, a major operation that follows the current major operation. In a single major operation, a sequel is the next phase. Plans for a sequel are based on the possible outcomes (success, stalemate, or defeat) associated with the current operation. (JP 5-0)

stability mechanism

The primary method through which friendly forces affect civilians in order to attain conditions that support establishing a lasting, stable peace. (FM 3-0)

stability operations

(joint) An overarching term encompassing various military missions, tasks, and activities conducted outside the United States in coordination with other instruments of national power to maintain or reestablish a safe and secure environment, provide essential governmental services, emergency infrastructure reconstruction, and humanitarian relief. (JP 3-0)

*stabilization

The process by which underlying tensions that might lead to resurgence in violence and a breakdown in law and order are managed and reduced, while efforts are made to support preconditions for successful long-term development.

support

(joint) The action of a force that aids, protects, complements, or sustains another force in accordance with a directive requiring such action. 2. A unit that helps another unit in battle. 3. An element of a command that assists, protects, or supplies other forces in combat. (JP 1) (Army) In the context of stability mechanisms, to establish, reinforce, or set the conditions necessary for the other instruments of national power to function effectively. (FM 3-0)

synchronization

(joint) 1. The arrangement of military actions in time, space, and purpose to produce maximum relative combat power at a decisive place and time. 2. In the intelligence context, application of intelligence sources and methods in concert with the operation plan to ensure intelligence requirements are answered in time to influence the decisions they support. (JP 2-0)

system

(joint) A functionally, physically, and/or behaviorally related group of regularly interacting or interdependent elements; that group of elements forming a unified whole. (JP 3-0)

task-organizing

(Army) The act of designing an operating force, support staff, or logistic package of specific size and composition to meet a unique task or mission. Characteristics to examine when task-organizing the force include, but are not limited to: training, experience, equipage, sustainability, operating environment, enemy threat, and mobility. For Army forces, it includes allocating available assets to subordinate commanders and establishing their command and support relationships. (FM 3-0)

*transitional military authority

A temporary military government exercising the functions of civil administration in the absence of a legitimate civil authority.

unified action

(joint) The synchronization, coordination, and/or integration of the activities of governmental and nongovernmental entities with military operations to achieve unity of effort. (JP 1)

unity of effort

(joint) The coordination and cooperation toward common objectives, even if the participants are not necessarily part of the same command or organization—the product of successful unified action. (JP 1)

*vulnerable state

A nation either unable or unwilling to provide adequate security and essential services to significant portions of the population.

*whole of government approach

An approach that integrates the collaborative efforts of the departments and agencies of the United States Government to achieve unity of effort toward a shared goal.

References

Field manuals and selected joint publications are listed by new number followed by old number.

REQUIRED PUBLICATIONS

These documents must be available to intended users of this publication.

FM 1-02 (101-5-1). *Operational Terms and Graphics*. 21 September 2004.

JP 1-02. *Department of Defense Dictionary of Military and Associated Terms*. 12 April 2001. (As amended through 30 May 2008.)

RELATED PUBLICATIONS

These documents contain relevant supplemental information.

JOINT AND DEPARTMENT OF DEFENSE PUBLICATIONS

Most joint publications are available online at http://www.dtic.mil/doctrine/jpcapstonepubs.htm.

Department of State publication. *Post-Conflict Reconstruction Essential Tasks*. April 2005. http://www.state.gov/documents/organization/53464.pdf (accessed 4 September 2008).

DODD 3000.05. *Military Support for Stability, Security, Transition, and Reconstruction (SSTR) Operations*. 28 November 2005.

DODD 5105.65. *Defense Security Cooperation Agency (DSCA)*. 31 October 2000. (Incorporating Change 1, 23 September 2003.).

DODD 5132.3. *DOD Policy and Responsibilities Relating to Security Assistance*. 10 March 1981. (Incorporating Change 1, 16 November 1994).

JP 1. *Doctrine for the Armed Forces of the United States*. 14 May 2007.

JP 2-0. *Joint Intelligence.* 22 June 2007.

JP 3-0. *Joint Operations.* 17 September 2006. (Incorporating Change 1, 13 February 2008.)

JP 3-05. *Doctrine for Joint Special Operations.* 17 December 2003.

JP 3-07.3. *Peace Operations.* 17 October 2007.

JP 3-07.4. *Joint Counterdrug Operations.* 13 June 2007.

JP 3-08. *Interagency, Intergovernmental Organization, and Nongovernmental Organization Coordination During Joint Operations* (2 volumes). 17 March 2006.

JP 3-16. *Multinational Operations.* 7 March 2007.

JP 3-57. *Civil-Military Operations.* 8 July 2008.

JP 4-05. *Joint Mobilization Planning.* 11 January 2006.

JP 5-0. *Joint Operation Planning.* 26 December 2006.

ARMY PUBLICATIONS

Most Army doctrinal publications are available online at http://www.army.mil/usapa/doctrine/Active_FM.html. Army regulations are produced only in electronic media. Most are available online at: http://www.army.mil/usapa/epubs/index.html.

AR 27-20. *Claims.* 8 February 2008.

FM 3-0. *Operations.* 27 February 2008.

FM 3-05.40 (41-10). *Civil Affairs Operations.* 29 September 2006.

FM 3-13 (100-6). *Information Operations: Doctrine, Tactics, Techniques, and Procedures.* 28 November 2003.

FM 3-24. *Counterinsurgency.* 15 December 2006.

FM 3-34.170 (5-170). *Engineer Reconnaissance.* 25 March 2008.

FM 3-34.210 (20-32). *Explosive Hazards Operations.* 27 March 2007.

FM 5-0 (101-5). *Army Planning and Orders Production.* 20 January 2005.

FM 6-0. *Mission Command: Command and Control of Army Forces.* 11 August 2003.

FM 6-01.1. *Knowledge Management Section.* 29 August 2008.

FM 7-0 (25-100). *Training the Force.* 22 October 2002.

FM 27-10. *The Law of Land Warfare.* 18 July 1956. (Incorporating Change 1, 15 July 1976.)

FM 46-1. *Public Affairs Operations.* 30 May 1997.

OTHER PUBLICATIONS

Agricultural Trade Development and Assistance Act of 1954. Title 7. United States Code, Section 1691.

Arms Export Control Act of 1976. Title 22. United States Code, Section 2751.

Executive Order 10206. http://www.archives.gov/federal-register/codification/executive-order/10206.html (accessed 4 September 2008).

Executive Order 12333. http://www.defenselink.mil/atsdio/documents/eo1233.html (accessed 4 September 2008).

Foreign Assistance Act of 1961. Title 22. United States Code, Section 2151.

John Warner National Defense Authorization Act for Fiscal Year 2007. Title 10. United States Code, Section 598.

Lessons-Learned: Disarmament, Demobilization, and Reintegration (DDR) in Reconstruction and Stabilization Operations—A Guide for United States Government Planners. April 2006. http://www.crs.state.gov/index.cfm?fuseaction=public.display&id=3b94dac3-e9be-48e0-8fc4-6b95a68c89e2 (accessed 4 September 2008).

Manual for Military Commissions. http://www.defense.gov/pubs/pdfs/MMC%20Executive%20Summary.pdf (accessed 4 September 2008).

National Defense Authorization Act for Fiscal Year 2006. Title 10. United States Code, Section 1207.

National Defense Strategy. June 2008. http://www.defenselink.mil/pubs/2008NationalDefenseStrategy.pdf (accessed 4 September 2008).

The National Military Strategy of the United States of America. 2004. http://www.defenselink.mil/news/Mar2005/d20050318nms.pdf (accessed 4 September 2008).

National Security Act of 1947. Title 50. United States Code.

National Security Action Memorandum 182. *Counterinsurgency Doctrine.*

National Security Decision Memorandum 3. *The Direction, Coordination, and Supervision of Interdepartmental Activities Overseas.*

National Security Presidential Directive 1. *Organization of the National Security Council System.*

National Security Presidential Directive 44 (NSPD-44). *Management of Interagency Efforts Concerning Reconstruction and Stabilization.*

The National Security Strategy of the United States of America. March 2006. http://www.whitehouse.gov/nsc/nss/2006/ (accessed 4 September 2008).

National Strategy for Combating Terrorism. September 2006. http://www.whitehouse.gov/nsc/nsct/2006/ (accessed 4 September 2008).

National Strategy for Homeland Security. October 2007. http://www.dhs.gov/xlibrary/assets/nat_strat_homelandsecu rity_2007.pdf (accessed 4 September 2008).

National Strategy to Combat Weapons of Mass Destruction. December 2002. http://www.whitehouse.gov/news/releases/2002/12/WMDSt rategy.pdf (accessed 4 September 2008).

Presidential Decision Directive 56. *Managing Complex Contingency Operations.*

The Principles and Guidelines on Children Associated with Armed Forces or Armed Groups. http://www.unicef.org/emerg/files/ParisPrinciples310107En glish.pdf (accessed 4 September 2008).

Reconstruction Acts of 1867. http://www.tsl.state.tx.us/ref/abouttx/secession/reconstructio n.html (accessed 4 September 2008).

Rogers Act. Title 22. United States Code, Section 3901.

Royal Proclamation of 1763. http://www.ushistory.org/declaration/related/proc63.htm (accessed 4 September 2008).

Treaty of Paris. 3 September 1783. http://www.ourdocuments.gov/doc.php?flash=true&doc=6 &page=transcript (accessed 4 September 2008).

United Nations General Assembly Resolution 46/182. *Strengthening of the Coordination of Humanitarian Emergency Assistance of the United Nations.* http://www.reliefweb.int/ocha_ol/about/resol/resol_e.html (accessed 4 September 2008).

United Nations Participation Act of 1945. Title 22. United States Code, Section 287.

War Powers Resolution. Title 50. United States Code, Section 1541.

WEB SITES

Office of the Coordinator for Reconstruction and Stabilization Web site. http://www.state.gov/s/crs/ (accessed 4 September 2008).

United Nations Department of Public Information Nongovernmental Organization Web site. http://www.un.org/dpi/ngosection/dpingo-directory.asp (accessed 4 September 2008).

SOURCES USED

These sources are quoted or paraphrased in this publication.

Butler, William F. *Charles George Gordon*. New York: MacMillan and Company, 1889.

Coles, Harry L. and Albert K. Weinberg. *Civil Affairs: Soldiers Become Governors*. Washington, DC: U.S. Government Printing Office, 1992. http://www.history.army.mil/books/wwii/civaff/index.htm (accessed 4 September 2008).

Fukuyama, Francis. *State-Building: Governance and World Order in the 21st Century*. Ithaca, NY: Cornell University Press, 2004.

Gates, Robert M. Remarks by Secretary Gates at United States Global Leadership Campaign Tribute Dinner. 15 July 2008. http://www.defenselink.mil/speeches/speech.aspx?speechid=1262 (accessed 4 September 2008).

Hart, Liddell. *Thoughts on War*. London: Faber and Faber Ltd., 1944.

Herbst, John E. "Stabilization and Reconstruction Operations: Learning from the Provincial Reconstruction Team (PRT) Experience." A *Statement Before House Armed Services Subcommittee on Oversight and Investigations*. 30 October 2007. http://www.state.gov/s/crs/rls/rm/94379.htm (accessed 4 September 2008).

Natsios, Andrew S. "The Nine Principles of Reconstruction and Development." *Parameters*. Autumn 2005: 4–20.

The Ordinance for the Regulation of Indian Affairs. 1786.

The [Organisation for Economic Co-operation and Development Development Assistance Committee] Handbook on Security System Reform (SSR): Supporting Security and Justice. Paris: OECD, 2007.

Stephenson, James. *Losing the Golden Hour: An Insider's View of Iraq's Reconstruction.* Washington, DC: Potomac Books, Incorporated, 2007.

Index

Entries are by paragraph number unless specified otherwise.

FM 3-07
6 October 2008

By order of the Secretary of the Army:

GEORGE W. CASEY, JR.
General, United States Army
Chief of Staff

Official:

JOYCE E. MORROW
Administrative Assistant to the
Secretary of the Army

DISTRIBUTION:
Active Army, Army National Guard, and U.S. Army Reserve: To be distributed in accordance with initial distribution number 115882, requirements for FM 3-07.

PIN: 080499-000